Pitman Publishing
128 Long Acre, London WC2E 9AN

A Division of Pearson Professional Limited

First published in 1992
Reprinted 1995,1996

© Longman Group UK Ltd, 1992

British Library Cataloguing in Publication Data
A CIP catalogue record for this book is available from the British Library.

ISBN 0 7121 1193 X

Typeset by FDS Ltd, Penarth
Printed and bound in Singapore

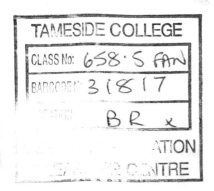

Logistics Management

P. Fawcett
FCIT, MBIM, Cert. Ed.

R.E. McLeish
BSc (Econ), MILDM, MCIT

I.D. Ogden
FCIT, MILDM

THE M & E HANDBOOK SERIES

Contents

Preface

The principal aim of this book is to familiarise readers with the main elements of logistics and distribution management. This discipline has grown significantly in the last decade or so, and its relative importance in both manufacturing and service industries is demonstrated by the scope of its employment and activities, as well as the fact that it has boasted, for some years, its own professional association, the Institute of Logistics and Distribution Management.

Logistics Management will be found useful by students involved on ILDM professional courses (both the Diploma and Certificate in Logistics Management) and as essential supplementary/ background reading for Paper 24 of the Chartered Institute of Transport's Qualifying Examinations — Logistics and Distribution Management. Students on BTEC National and Higher National Certificates and Diplomas in Business Studies with a Distribution Option, and studying for first degrees in Business Studies in Colleges, Polytechnics and Universities will find the book a useful introduction to what is now one of the main business disciplines.

Like all of the new M&E Handbook series, the book is highly structured in order to meet the learning objectives of the appropriate professional examining bodies. It will also help students on competence-based courses directly related to the distribution industry, on which they are assessed with reference to performance criteria accredited by the National Council for Vocational Qualifications.

The book is also a useful guide to managers who wish to better acquaint themselves with the significance of logistics within the general business field and to both supervisors and managers in logistics and distribution who wish to gain a broader view of their own discipline.

After a general introductory chapter covering the concept of integrated logistics, the book divides into sections devoted to logistics policies and planning, management of the logistics function, human resource management, the economics and finance of logistics, and logistics in a European Context. The roles of modern techniques, such as dynamic channel strategies, 'Just-in-Time' delivery, MRP and Distribution Resource Planning are described, as are the more traditional disciplines of forecasting, inventory control, warehousing and order processing. The usefulness of Information Technology is emphasised throughout. The authors hope that this approach will assist students and business managers to relate the many and varied aspects of the 'logistics mix' to each other, and to appreciate the interaction between them.

The authors are grateful to Pitman Publishing, who have encouraged and supported them throughout, and to Frances, Anne and Kath, their wives, for their forbearance during the extended writing period when they became temporary 'logistics widows'.

1

Introduction to logistics management

Advances in business and industry over the last 10–15 years have been considerable. Driven by developments in business philosophies such as marketing, in national and international trade, in technology, and not least the need for survival in an increasingly competitive and demanding world, business strategies and methods of operating have changed — and continue to do so — at an increasing rate.

Nowhere have these changes been more graphically outlined than in the area of business logistics. Levels of competition and customer expectations have engendered an industry-wide search for overall quality, higher levels of customer service and greater cost-effectiveness. Integrated logistics management has been identified as the key to success in achieving these vital goals.

Significance of logistics

1. Definition and scope

But what is logistics, and where does it fit into the average company's structure and operations? The *Concise Oxford Dictionary* defines it as 'the movement, storage and supply of troops and equipment'; *Chambers' Dictionary* likewise sets its definition in a military context. Having previously modelled its basic management style and structure along army lines, industry has again slightly adapted another military term to include the management of commercial supplies.

In manufacturing industry, the traditional sequence of a company's activities was purchasing and supply of materials and components, production or processing, and dispatch or transport of finished products or commodities to customers, sales outlets and end-users. This sequence remains largely unaltered, but advances in business management thinking have established the need for a more coordinated approach.

It is some time now since Peter Drucker described physical distribution management as 'the last great frontier of cost reduction'. On the basis that production had been automated to achieve economies of scale and that the business world was fast adopting the total marketing concept rather than the narrower, product-led sales-oriented approach, it seemed only logical that a closer appraisal of physical distribution, its role, costs and management, would produce worthwhile commercial gains.

But, as with many an innovative approach to business, once started, the momentum of transforming previously separate transport and storage, materials handling and stock control functions into a single, integrated management discipline carried on. Not only were substantial cost reductions possible through implementing total distribution management techniques, but improved operational performance and service standards were also achieved. Further consolidation of the management of physical commodity movement was therefore seen as the way forward.

Thus, amalgamation of physical distribution management and materials management created the concept of total business logistics, and references to managing the chain of distribution soon became what most companies now recognise as supply chain management. For any company, the supply chain begins at the point of planning both production activities and acquisition of materials, and ends with the monitoring of customer service in terms of delivery and product quality.

Business logistics management therefore currently encompasses not only the management of transport, warehousing, packaging and materials handling for distribution, but also of order processing, inventory management and certain elements of both purchasing and production. Wherever an activity exists for the control of supply, movement and storage of products and materials, it is now considered to be part of the total supply chain — and thus the responsibility of logistics management.

2. Implications of marketing

Ballou provides a more comprehensive definition of the concept:

> Business logistics deals with all movement and storage activities that facilitate product flow, from the point of raw material acquisition to the point of final consumption, as well as the information flows that set the product in motion, for the purpose of providing adequate levels of customer service at a reasonable cost.

If interpreted in this way, logistics management is a business strategy, the focal point of which is customer service. Notwithstanding the appropriateness or otherwise of such words as 'adequate' and 'reasonable', there is a close resemblance to the marketing concept, where the customer or end-user is the centre, heart or focus of a business or organisation's activities, namely its raison d'être.

Yet another well-worn cliché is: 'Distribution adds cost, not value.' Contrary to this statement, effective logistics and particularly physical distribution management create time and place utility, in ensuring that the right goods and commodities are in the right place at the right time — and at competitive cost. In other words, they represent the 'place' element of the marketing 'mix', achieving high levels of product availability in the market-place in order to maximise sales opportunities and build sustained business. With such high expectations among consumers of goods and services and industrial customers alike, similar levels of service are becoming the norm. In order to survive and grow, firms must now compete on grounds of quality and service. In achieving these aims, effective logistics management can play a major role.

3. Logistics strategy

The basic aim of a broad-brush logistics strategy is to achieve the highest possible levels of customer service at the lowest possible cost. This might seem rather simplistic and utopian, but framed more precisely, it should help to achieve corporate objectives — which, in turn, should be largely customer-related.

Such a strategy will normally consist of four main elements:

(a) Manufacturing locations
(b) Transport methods
(c) Stockholding policies
(d) Management systems.

Effective planning and control of these elements is crucial to good supply chain management. But such management must be sufficiently flexible to detect the need for and implement changes in what are essentially areas of long-term business planning. Continuous appraisal of markets, competitors and a company's own performance must be part of the strategy, so that the optimum balance can be achieved between these elements — often by trading off a distinct disadvantage in one area against a greater overall benefit in another.

The total distribution concept

4. Definition
In the light of Peter Drucker's comments and some of the commercial developments mentioned earlier, the varied but complementary activities along the physical distribution chain were drawn together by industry management. Physical distribution consists of five main elements:

(a) Packaging
(b) Materials handling
(c) Storage and warehousing
(d) Transport
(e) Data processing and communications.

The aim of the *total distribution concept* was to plan, organise and manage these elements — at least some of which had traditionally formed part of different business functions and departments — in a coordinated fashion, to achieve greater overall benefits.

It was recognised that certain relationships existed between these elements, with the result that monitoring interaction between them could assist in achieving a more effective total management strategy. Not only was this process related to the operational level, but also to the level of financial performance.

The need for more efficient distribution operations was sharpened by managers' awareness of cost reduction opportunities.

5. Costs and profit leverage

Costs of physical distribution can amount to as much as 20 per cent of sales revenue. Hence, any reduction in distribution costs, preferably without any corresponding reduction in service levels, will reduce total costs, make the company more competitive, and increase profits.

As an example of profit leverage, let us say a large national company sets a profit margin on sales revenue of 10 per cent. A reduction in its costs of physical distribution of £100,000 will have the same effect as if its turnover had increased by £1,000,000. This kind of result is often easier to achieve through effective distribution management, as the activity remains within the company and is thus more easily controllable.

6. Trade-offs

Awareness of the benefits of trade-offs is essential to the business manager. If a company increases its advertising and promotions budget, it would be logical for its management to expect an increase in the sales of its products. The firm has increased its cost in one area, hopefully to gain a greater advantage in another, in terms of increased sales revenue and profit. If this principle is applied in a physical distribution context and, for example, the number of depots in a distribution network is increased, three things will happen:

(a) there will be higher transport costs, moving bulk loads to more depots;
(b) stock-holding costs will be higher as product ranges will have to be held at a greater number of locations;
(c) delivery costs will be lower, as each depot will be that much closer to the customers it serves.

Thus the increased costs of a more comprehensive network may be traded off against consequent lower costs of final deliveries from the greater number of distribution centres, giving overall improved performance. This would be a good example of the total distribution concept in practice.

There are, however, two kinds of trade-off:

(a) Direct trade-offs — where additional expenditure on one element brings a proportionally greater saving in the cost of another element. If a cost or trade-off model is constructed, or a graph drawn, a point can be identified at which total costs can be optimised. This information can then be used as a guide to decision making.

(b) Indirect trade-offs — where greater expenditure on one element brings either no savings at all, or a less than proportionate saving in other elements' costs. However, sales revenue increases more than the increase in total distribution costs.

Exploiting the benefits and opportunities of the total distribution concept and its associated trade-off principles has thus provided a platform for physical distribution management to adopt a higher profile within companies and industries.

Integrated logistics

7.   Supply chain management

Having generated the momentum and proved the success of coordinated distribution management, planning and implementing even more fully-integrated materials and commodity movement was a logical development. Materials-management activities, involving the planning and management of raw materials and components purchasing, appropriate inventory policies and management techniques — as well as their physical movement — were 'bolted on' to the front end of the distribution chain.

This created a longer 'supply chain', with a more broadly-based, but integrated management, thus creating opportunities for companies to control more effectively one of the major resources crucial to their continued survival and success. All physical materials and inventory could, through total business logistics, be controlled in a coordinated manner throughout the organisation and its operations.

8.   Information technology

None of these improvements in the management of materials

and product flows could have taken place without substantial improvement and innovation in the field of data processing and information management. Increasing use of computer systems and appropriate programs have assisted distribution and logistics managers to increase the speed and accuracy with which many operational tasks can be accomplished. For example, automatic data capture now simplifies and accelerates many goods receiving, sorting and dispatch operations. Furthermore, speed of response and quality of operation have been much improved through fast, direct transmission of information between suppliers, manufacturers and their customers. Ballou, in his definition of business logistics, refers to the importance of informations flows in triggering physical movement of products and materials. Such flows of information must be timely and accurate for companies to become and remain competitive — whether they are used for operational purposes or as part of performance reporting mechanisms. Electronic data interchange (EDI) is now being used and developed in many organisations in order to meet these objectives, as information and communications technology continue to play a major role in the development of state-of-the-art logistics management.

Progress test 1

1. What is logistics management? (1)

2. List its main elements or subfunctions, with a brief description. (3)

3. How close is the connection between logistics and marketing, and why? (2)

4. 'Distribution adds cost, not value.' State whether this is true or false, and give your reasons. (2)

5. What do you understand by the total distribution concept? (4)

6. As distribution costs account for a significant proportion of the selling price of a product, what, typically, would this proportion be?   **(5)**

7. Explain what is meant by 'profit leverage'.   **(6)**

8. Trade-offs occur within the industrial logistics management function. What exactly is a 'trade-off'?   **(7)**

9. Give an example of (*a*) a direct trade-off, and (*b*) an indirect trade-off.   **(8)**

2
Customer service

1. Introduction

Logistics and distribution activities are synonymous with the 'place' element of the marketing mix — the need to have the right product available in the right place at the right time and the right cost, in order to maximise sales opportunities. In many companies, this is seen as the prime objective of logistics management. Effective operation and management of a supply chain necessitates planning and coordination of multiple movements, so that goods and materials are conveniently available at a particular point in time and space. But is this always for the direct benefit of the customer, purchaser or end-user of that product? Often the user is an internal customer within the same organisation, who also has a role in ensuring product availability further along the chain.

Logistics and customer service

2. Respective roles

Logistics and distribution, similar to transport generally, is all about bridging the time and space gap between suppliers of goods and materials and those who demand them. In an ideal world, if resources were infinite and money no object, then very high levels of demand satisfaction could be achieved without commensurate levels of management control. But in business, both resources and money are limited, and the planned, coordinated approach mentioned above is the only way to achieve appreciable levels of customer satisfaction.

Although marketing and distribution are very closely linked, they can be seen as having two distinctly different but complementary roles. Marketing can be seen as 'demand creation', whereas distribution's major role is 'demand satisfaction'. The truth of this statement is evident when one analyses the validity of a well-known comment on distribution as a service which 'Distinctly adds cost, not value'. It is precisely that time and place value, which efficient logistics and distribution management adds to materials, products and commodities both disproves the previously quoted statement and satisfies customer demand created by marketing efforts.

Such demand satisfaction could loosely be termed customer service, but there are various levels, and customers' interpretations of its meaning also vary between sectors of industry and even between different segments within the same market.

3.   Definitions
Customer service has been variously described as:

(a) 'The quality of performance of a distribution system.'
(b) 'Dimensions of order cycle and fulfilment, which enhance sales.'
(c) 'Matching the pace of supply with that of demand.'
(d) 'Delivered satisfaction' — in terms of the product bought, and the way in which it is enhanced by the time, place and manner of distribution.

No matter which definition is seen as best fitting a given company and its market, this important factor in marketing and distribution must be analysed in more detail to arrive at the correct model to suit a given situation.

4.   Commercial elements
Customer service is said to relate to one of three stages in the commercial exchange process:

(a) *Pre-transaction* — customer service policy statements, e.g. order size constraints, methods of ordering.
(b) *Transaction* — stock availability, order cycle time, order preparation and delivery.

(c) *Post-transaction* — after-sales service, warranty, complaints procedure.

Although each element in the customer service equation will relate to one of these stages, it is the identification of the most important in a given commercial situation which is crucial to a successful customer service policy. Firmly establishing which combination of these factors will create the required degree of satisfaction — and planning and organising their implementation in managing the supply chain — will create the added value, and justify the position of logistics and distribution management as a prime business function.

5. Practical considerations

The most important criteria for customer service are set out below, along with brief additional comments:

(a) The elapsed time between the placement of an order by a customer, and the delivery of goods ordered to the customer's place of business. Order cycle or lead time, which this represents, is a very important factor — it reflects the ability of a supplier to react promptly to demand.

(b) The minimum order size or assortment limits which a supplier will accept from its customers. Constraints on order sizes and mixes are often a feature of modern distribution, and can be seen as reducing the flexibility of the service offered to the market.

(c) The percentage of items in a supplier's warehouse which might be found to be out of stock at any given point in time. Stock availability is another prime factor in customer service. Order completeness negates the possibility of part-orders to follow, with the consequent delay in satisfying end-user demand.

(d) The proportion of customers' orders filled accurately. The consequences of failure in this area are similar to those of **(c)** above, but might also be construed as a measure of the overall efficiency of the supplier organisation.

(e) The percentage of customers or their orders served (or delivered) within a certain time period from the receipt of the order at the supplier's warehouse, a further indication of the degree of success achieved in meeting targeted order cycle times.

(f) The proportion of goods which arrive at a customer's place of business in saleable condition. Here the emphasis is on product quality on reaching the buyer. With increasing expectations in this area, a high success rate is necessary to maximise sales and minimise returns.

(g) The ease and flexibility with which a customer can place an order. An often neglected aspect of the place element of the marketing mix is product or service accessibility. How convenient does the supplier make it for prospective buyers to purchase?

6. Ranking of service criteria

Examining the components of customer service from another viewpoint, and perhaps a useful exercise in checking which emerge as the key issues, the list in Table 2.1 is a ranking of relevant factors as perceived by a selection of head-office buyers in a market research programme.

Table 2.1 Customer service — buyers' 'top twelve' variables

VARIABLE	RANK
Product availability	1
Promotional activity	2
Representation	3
Order status	4
Distribution: direct or via depot	5
Delivery time	6
Pricing	7
Merchandising	8
Product positioning	9
Invoice accuracy	10
New product introductions	11
Advertising	12

The significance and validity of such a ranking will of course vary from company to company, depending on their market priorities. The variables included in Table 2.1, and their order, may well produce some surprises, and some are more widely marketing-based than specifically related to aspects of logistics and distribution.

Though product availability comes what many buyers would consider to be a natural first choice, order cycle or delivery time is relatively poorly placed at number six. In addition, there is no reference in the ranking to order completeness or accuracy, unless the former is covered by item number one. A cursory examination of the ranking will also highlight the absence of any requirement regarding product quality.

7. Alternative customer choices

The broader significance of customer service can perhaps be illustrated by taking two examples. First of all, consider non-availability of a consumer item at a particular retail outlet. Prospective buyers of that item have three options:

(a) possible substitution within the same product range;
(b) substitution from another product range;
(c) not make the purchase.

Any of these options could mean loss of business to the supplier of the required item, or perhaps loss of business to the distributor or retailer — it is not always possible to determine whose organisation is at fault. Depending on whether or not this non-availability were an isolated example, any loss of business might be temporary. If customers' demands were not being met on something approaching a regular basis, any loss of business due to unacceptable customer service might be permanent.

A second example might be non-availability of a specific component or material at a given point in an assembly or manufacturing process. Here again, three options are open to the manufacturer:

(a) press the supplier or internal department for urgent delivery;
(b) find an alternative supplier;
(c) shut down production and/or change over to another product.

The first alternative (a), if successful, would redress the situation fairly quickly, but still incur the costs of any unproductive time. The danger for the supplier or supplying department would be that production would consider — and might implement — contingency plans regarding further supply, depending on any future recurrence.

If the second course of action (b) were taken, it would have similar repercussions concerning costs, and perhaps a more detrimental effect on business with the original supplier. Substantial costs would be incurred should the manufacturer need to resort to alternative (c) with a commensurate high level of risk to the supplier's business. In all three situations, however, it is likely there may be some repercussions along the supply chain, with the likelihood of interrupted supply to the commodity end-user. This serves to illustrate that 'internal' customer service is of equal importance to 'external' customers in the market-place.

Customer service vs. costs

8. An important relationship

Notwithstanding the importance of customer service level as a marketing and distribution variable, some form of trade-off against the costs of providing that service must be determined. Numerous cost elements can be identified when total customer service costs are analysed, but some are more significant than others, and usually relate to the most important factors of customer service itself. Here, we shall consider three main service cost issues:

(a) Stock availability
(b) Order cycle time
(c) Delivery frequency.

9. Stock availability

Investment in inventory to provide required levels of stock and product availability is one of the most costly items. Such costs, in reality, are of course not limited only to investment in the stock itself, but include costs of increased storage, handling, transport and insurance — in short, the total costs incurred in servicing the higher levels of inventory needed.

10. Order cycle time

Chapter 4 on network strategy shows how models can be created to calculate the optimum number of stock locations from the viewpoint of transport costs. Even though stockholding costs increase as the depot network increases, the nature of the transport cost curve will still produce a dip in the total distribution cost curve when transport and stockholding costs are added together. Thus a cost-based optimum number of depots can be calculated and, where cost is the dominant criterion, such a solution would be acceptable. In many cases, companies might well choose to go beyond this optimum network, incurring increased costs, the reason being that a larger number of depots will provide higher levels of customer service, as each stock location will be closer to its market area, and order cycle times will be shorter.

11. Delivery frequency

In recent years, the trend has been for companies to hold less stock and require suppliers to deliver smaller quantities more frequently. As a consequence, distributing companies have had to look carefully at the transport cost implications of keeping their customers happy. There is an inverse relationship between drop size and unit transport cost, and provided proportionately higher unit transport costs can be passed on to the customer to support this kind of delivery pattern, there is little problem. But this is rarely the case, and to reach a compromise, many manufacturers and distributors have introduced minimum order quantities for direct delivery — a fact which some customers might see as a reduction in service level.

In establishing customer service needs, a manufacturing or distributing company must ascertain whether or not the required levels of service can be justified in financial terms.

12. Customer account profitability

When suppliers to the grocery trade addressed this issue several years ago, many found themselves beset by the same three problems:

(a) upward-spiralling service level expectations;
(b) corresponding increases in distribution costs;
(c) pressure from grocery multiples to maintain, if not increase, discounts.

Accordingly, senior managers and accountants in many supplier firms began a thorough analysis of doing business on such terms. How could they provide improved levels of service in terms of more frequent deliveries of smaller orders, incurring higher distribution costs in the process, while the grocery and supermarket chains were negotiating substantial trade discounts? Inevitably, such a business analysis included a close examination of their marketing policy and distribution practice, and resulted in the concept of *customer account profitability* (CAP).

The main principle of CAP was that companies should undertake a thorough and highly detailed analysis of their customer base. Each individual element of cost incurred through servicing a particular customer, one specific kind of customer or outlet, or maybe even a given range of products, should be identified, listed and totalled. This total servicing cost should then be set against total contribution from the relevant source, showing the profitability or otherwise of that segment of business.

CAP has, by now, developed beyond the food and drinks industry. A chemicals distributor found on similar examination of its customers that it could cease trading with a surprising percentage of them — and increase its profitability. Simply enough, the accounts they dispensed with were costing them too much money to service direct, and were in reality loss-makers.

The cost of the customer can be a high one. Both corporate management and distribution specialists must ensure that each account, market segment or range of line items attracts a revenue and contribution to overheads and profit which will justify the costs incurred in servicing their distribution.

13. Performance indicators

As with all measures of business performance, it is important that actual customer service should be monitored. In order to manage and control this vital area, measures should be readily quantifiable so that actual results can be easily compared with targeted performance.

Current practice in the industry has been developed by interpreting the percentage of customer demand actually satisfied as the service level achieved. The calculation of these percentages usually relates to one of the main customer service variables, most often order response times or order completeness, for example:

(a) percentage of orders completely satisfied (over time);
(b) percentage of lines delivered per order;

(c) percentage of units delivered per order;

(d) percentage of orders delivered within order cycle time.

Other examples might relate to order accuracy or delivered product quality (percentage of returns, complaints, refusals, etc.), and in many companies service level percentages are now often in the 90s.

Performance targets must be realistic and achievable, and will initially be based on performance to date. But, as previously mentioned, in devising them, account should be taken of both customers' service perceptions and, where possible, competitors' performance — although the latter may be difficult to assess accurately.

In consideration of customers' service perceptions, one important point which should not be overlooked is that: 'Assessment of the impact of service on market share and profits' and 'establishment of realistic, competitive and economical service goals' can be linked. Increased levels of customer service attract costs at an increasing rate, thus a 2 per cent improvement in customer service, say from 95 per cent, will cost correspondingly more than a 2 per cent increase from 85 per cent. The question of whether the costs of such increases are recovered through revenue and profit has already been examined. What is finally at issue here is whether the customer will see such a small improvement — albeit at considerable cost to the supplier — as significant and sufficiently worthwhile to enhance the supplier's status in the customer's eyes.

Progress test 2

1. In what ways is logistics and distribution management synonymous with the place element of the marketing mix? **(1)**

2. Marketing and distribution can have two distinct roles. What are they? **(2)**

3. How would *you* define customer service? **(3)**

4. Customer service can be broken down into three commercial phases. What are they? **(4)**

5. Describe in your own words the significance of:

    (a) product availability;
    (b) delivery reliability.   **(5, 6)**

6. Is product quality a function of customer service? Give your reasons.   **(6)**

7. Briefly outline the concept of customer account profitability. **(12)**

3

Channel strategy

In the early stages of distribution planning and marketing policy development, one of the foremost issues to be resolved is the method of product distribution, or *distribution channel*, which will be used. From a marketing viewpoint, the distribution channel will be an important component of the 'place' element of the marketing 'mix'. It will become an integral part of the process of getting the right product to the right place at the right time. The means chosen will determine the extent to which commodities are conveniently available to potential buyers.

Distribution channels

1. Definition

Seen from a logistics management standpoint, a channel of distribution is a route taken by a commodity between the point of its production and the point of its sale and/or consumption. Here, the concept is somewhat more tangible, as it deals literally with the physical movement of goods.

2. Aspects of distribution channels

There are two aspects to any distribution channel — a commercial one, and a physical one. The former is linked more closely to marketing, the latter to logistics and distribution management.

The commercial mechanism in any distribution channel relates to the number of transactions or stages a product goes through between manufacturer and consumer. Channel length will depend on the type of product, and its traditional or developed trade structure. Each transaction or stage will involve transfer of the product to an intermediary, both physically and in terms of ownership. Commodity price will also increase at each stage, as intermediaries, add their profit percentage for making items available closer to the market-place. Such channels of distribution can be very short, for example mail-order of a variety of consumer goods available direct from manufacturers. They can also involve two or more intermediaries, as when fast moving consumer goods (FMCG) are transferred from manufacturer to wholesaler to retailer to the consumer. In commerce and industry as a whole, various permutations exist, involving use of agents and distributors, wholesalers and retailers, before goods reach the end-user. These stages or links in the channel process are sometimes referred to as *echelons*, where each intermediary is seen as occupying their own level in the chain. Some examples are given in Fig. 3.1.

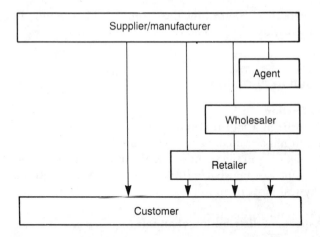

Fig. 3.1 *Examples of some typical distribution channels.*

The physical aspect concerns the number of movement stages a range of products will go through in being transferred from manufacturer to the final customer. Here, the consideration is simply how many people are involved in the distribution chain, and the fact that ownership changes or price increases is not important. What is important, however, is the make-up of the distribution chain, i.e. the kind of organisations it comprises.

3.   Make-up of the distribution chain
The two main options available are:

(a) Use of a company's own storage and distribution facilities — whether the company is a supplier, manufacturer distributor or retailer.
(b) Use of a third-party distribution service — usually some kind of transport and distribution specialist.

Channels and their networks

Having established that there are different channels which can be used, a closer look at some of the more common examples will indicate the choices that are available to companies. As mentioned above, the channel used in a specific instance will often depend on the market or market segment in which a given product is being promoted and distributed. It is also worth noting that a 'retailer' in this sense is not always a retail shop or store selling direct to the public — it may be an agent or distributor or merchant, whose end-user or customer is a small business or company.

4.   Manufacturer direct to retailer
This is one of the shortest channels, and is used mostly where full-load consignments need to be moved from factories to the largest of retail outlets. It is a relatively uncommon channel, as most manufacturers need to hold a minimum amount of stock on which they can draw to fulfil orders. An everyday example might be bread deliveries from bakeries to shops and supermarkets. Local and regional companies would deliver direct from their bakery, and national brand leaders would ensure effective distribution by using regional production points.

5.   Manufacturer–own warehouse–retailer
Manufacturers which need to hold stock often do so at factory or other sites nearby. Wherever such stock is held, provided it is

under the manufacturer's control, this is the channel which will often be used to move the goods to retailers. It has, however, been superseded by other methods of distribution, but the extent to which this has happened depends on the product and area of industry concerned. Such diverse items as ceramic sanitary ware and biscuits are distributed via this channel. In FMCG markets, direct distribution to retail outlets from factory warehouses is again normally reserved for servicing larger outlets with consignments of corresponding size.

Note that these first two examples of distribution channels relate only to the stages of physical movement, and do not involve intermediaries.

6. Manufacturer–wholesale warehouse–retailer

This is a traditional, well-established distribution channel which has been affected considerably by recent developments in logistics and distribution policies and practices. These changes have been most prominent in the grocery business, where wholesaling organisations have become heavily involved in physical distribution as well as retaining their role as 'middlemen' in the trade. Typically, stages of movement are combined with the commercial transactions referred to earlier. As well as the grocery trade, other areas of business in which this classic channel is used are confectionery, toys and building materials. A slight variation on this route exists where the wholesaling point is a cash-and-carry warehouse. In this instance, the retailers purchase their requirements and take them away in their own vehicles.

7. Manufacturer–retailer's warehouse–outlets

This is another channel favoured to a great extent by the FMCG retail chains. It is often referred to as 'central warehousing', as suppliers deliver to retailers' strategically placed warehouses in bulk, and the retailer, or his chosen distribution contractor, delivers mixed-product loads to the various outlet locations. Using such a method gives retail companies a high degree of control over product and stock availability through stock management and monitoring supplier deliveries, but there are heavy costs incurred. Frequent examples occur in grocery, toiletries and cosmetics distribution, as well as a variety of consumer durables.

8. Manufacturer–third-party distributor–retailer

For the most part, there is little difference between this channel of distribution and that described in **7**. In this case, however, a distribution contractor has taken on the stockholding and secondary distribution role previously undertaken by the retail company itself. Similar trades employ this method of distribution as in **7**, particularly where retail-led distribution has moved over substantially to some kind of third-party service. And it is here that the distinction becomes blurred, as there can be various permutations of ownership and management of buildings, stock, employment of staff and even control systems in either of these channels. In some cases, all facilities are owned by or the responsibility of the distribution contractor; in others the distribution centre building and stock belong to the retailer, and the contractor's management, staff and vehicles run the operation from it. These are but two examples of the variety of circumstances in which third-party contractors will provide a specialist and often dedicated distribution service to large retail organisations.

9. Use of distribution channels

These are the most commonly used types of distribution channel. Others do exist, but in more specialised areas of business. It should be remembered that, although a company may use one particular channel for a major proportion of its lines, it will use others for the remainder of its full range. A firm's perspective on the question of distribution channels will also differ, depending on whether it is a manufacturer/supplier or retailer. Nonetheless, numerous channel networks will be developed to service goods and material flows into the market-place, differentiated mainly by the number and type of intermediaries who make up each individual channel.

Aims of channel selection

10. General

As part of the logistics and distribution planning process, channel selection will play an important role. Add to this its significance in respect of a company's marketing effort, and this role is even further enhanced. All the more reason, then, why the channel selection process should be analysed in a certain amount of detail, before any costly and/or commercially damaging decisions are made.

Channel selection has several aims:

(a) maximisation of sales opportunities;
(b) achieving high levels of product availability;
(c) achieving high levels of customer service;
(d) minimising costs;
(e) gaining timely, accurate market intelligence;
(f) ensuring smooth integration of both commercial and physical aspects of the distribution chain, e.g. order size requirements, unit-load characteristics, etc.

These are discussed in more detail below.

11. Maximisation of sales opportunities

Part of the definition of marketing is the satisfaction of customers' and consumers' demands profitably, through the sale of products, commodities and services. Each sale made will, presumably, bring in its individual element of profit, and the more sales that can be made, the greater the profit. Additionally, the place element of the marketing mix requires that the right product should be available — or exposed for sale — in the right place at the right time. This behoves the seller to identify the most appropriate times and places for each of his products — and subsequently an efficient distribution channel to get them there whenever they are needed, in order to make the most of sales opportunities.

12. Achieving high levels of product availability

At first glance, this objective may seem rather too similar to that in **11** — and they are very closely related. But here the emphasis is on two particular aspects of the same issue — the suitability of sales outlets, and increasing customer expectations.

Identification and selection of the most suitable types of sales outlet is merely an extension of the market segmentation process, in which different types of customer or consumer represent discrete sectors of a larger market and their needs are met in ways, times and places most suited to each sector. Such segmentation therefore impinges on logistics and distribution planning inasmuch as the nature of point-of-sale establishments will, to a certain extent, determine the channels of distribution used to service them.

Customer expectations of product availability have increased in recent years, not only in FMCG and consumer durables markets, but in others also. This trend has been fed by increased product and commodity choices in many markets, and by the sharpening of competition.

With so many alternatives available to customers and consumers, manufacturers and distributors must carefully select their outlets and channels of distribution in line with their targeted markets.

13. Achieving high levels of customer service

The significance of customer service as a marketing and distribution variable has already been established in a previous chapter. Its importance in channel selection lies mainly in the extent to which both suppliers or manufacturers and distributors or retailers will agree on the levels of service to be achieved and maintained.

Availability of line items from stock, and frequency or reliability of delivery, will feature prominently here, but in many markets nowadays, product quality, presentation, packaging and accuracy of order fill are often of equal importance. Added to these is the number of returns and complaints, and the convenience and promptness of refund procedures — and most other aspects of after-sales service. The chosen distribution channel must be able to communicate and deal effectively with all of these eventualities.

14. Minimising costs

Price is a major element of marketing. Cost reduction and control is one of the main grounds upon which present-day logistics and distribution management has been founded. It is therefore impossible that such an important variable would not have a bearing on channel selection. As a general rule, the shorter the distribution channel, the lower the proportion of an item's price which is allocated to distribution costs — and vice versa in respect of longer channels.

Although each transit point and/or transaction along a

distribution channel will incur additional costs, each channel should be selected and managed in such a way as to reduce unnecessary costs.

15. Feeding back information

Channels of outward communication and distribution are also useful for the gathering and reporting of information relevant to activities within and beyond the channel itself. As goods and materials flow outwards along their respective channels of distribution, so information on that flow and trends and developments in various market segments can be fed back up the channel to assist the logistics manager. Organisations comprising channel structures can serve as important sources of data on logistics and distribution performance and market intelligence.

Data on sales, customer service levels and the impact of inventory management policies, in addition to the monitoring of costs, are examples of management information available through channel structures. Not only will information technology be instrumental in capturing and arranging such management information, but computer software is now available to enable simulation or modelling techniques to be applied to channel selection, to assist decision-making on such issues as choice of transport and levels of stock and customer service.

16. Ensuring smooth integration

Last, but certainly not least among these aims, is securing integration and coordination of commercial and physical aspects of channel operations. In achieving this objective, it will be necessary to examine some of the more detailed operational issues involved in the interface between echelons in the channel, such as agreement on types of unit-load, materials handling methods and delivery requirements. These examples relate to the purely physical aspects of channel operation, whereas attention to matters such as order-size constraints and order-processing methods would help in coordinating the commercial facet.

Although channel selection will in most cases be a strategic decision, attention to detail at the operational level is necessary to ensure as smooth as possible a flow of goods and materials through the system. Similar to feedback of information, achievement of this aim ought to be a two-way process, seen from both suppliers' and receivers' viewpoints.

Major factors in channel selection ·

17. General
All of these objectives may not be relevant to every channel situation, and to the extent that they are of significance, that significance will vary in each case. This degree of importance will in turn differ according to certain other factors which are basic to any logistics and distribution strategy, and more particularly to the evaluation and selection of a channel structure. These factors are:

(a) Product
(b) Market
(c) Competition
(d) Channel
(e) Company.

These factors are discussed further below.

18. Product
The physical nature of the product not only determines the means of its transport and storage, but may also place constraints on channel selection. For example, product value may be a consideration, whether from a security viewpoint, or that of the ease with which profit margins may cover marketing and distribution costs. Specialist or time-sensitive goods may often require channel structures which can deal effectively with their unique features — whether the items in question be newspapers, ice-cream or hanging garments.

Product complexity or technology may dictate use of a channel where companies or their sales agents can explain or demonstrate the product in detail. Examples of this might perhaps be quality audio-visual equipment or motor cars.

19. Market
This factor is closely allied to product availability, but focuses on the physical characteristics of a given market segment. Is the market large and geographically dispersed or relatively small and

concentrated? Distribution of mail and parcels, or of products used by the chemical industry would exhibit markedly different characteristics in this sense, which would be reflected in the distribution channels chosen for each. In more dispersed markets, such channels are likely to be longer with perhaps more echelons, therefore incurring higher distribution costs.

20. Competition

The commercial wisdom of channelling one's products along the same or similar routes to those of competitors must be carefully analysed. Exclusivity of outlets may enhance product uniqueness. On the other hand, such a policy might result in under-exposure of the item to prospective buyers. Careful analysis of the competitive situation — particularly with regard to product differentiation and market segmentation — is needed in order to establish the extent to which a particular good can successfully be exposed to both competitor's wares and customer expectations in terms of choice, quality and value for money.

21. Channel

Does the channel itself serve the required purpose? In many trades and industries, there are established channel structures and practices. It is important to ascertain whether or not these traditional avenues continue to meet marketing and distribution requirements, with regard to such variables as sales potential and order size.

22. Company

Despite all the foregoing, one factor which cannot be overlooked is that of the company itself and its resources. These are often governed by company size, although this factor itself is capable of various interpretations — geographic spread, turnover, market share, etc. Generally speaking, larger firms will have sufficient resources to be substantially involved in channel selection and structures — often operating echelons themselves. Smaller businesses, however, will be less able to create such a network or presence, and must rely on agents and intermediaries to form their channels of distribution to the market-place. The obvious danger here is that the levels of service provided may not be as high as the manufacturers or suppliers would like their customers to enjoy. Speciality model products are an example of this, where many small firms are in the hands of agents or wholesalers, whose stocking and customer service levels often do not meet retailers' and customers' needs.

Choosing the optimum channel strategy

23. Structured approach

Devising the most appropriate channel structure is, as demonstrated by the foregoing points, an essential part of any logistics or marketing plan or distribution operation. As in many other areas of business management, it is necessary to take a structured approach in order to arrive at the channel solution best suited to the appropriate product or range.

This approach could be described in a sequence of steps:

(a) Recognising the significance of distribution channels.
(b) Deciding on the aims and objectives of the distribution function.
(c) Identifying the possible alternatives in terms of channel networks.
(d) Analysing alternative channel structures.
(e) Choosing the optimum structure.
(f) Selecting and engaging channel members.

24. Review of channel selection

Like many areas of business and logistics management, channel strategy should be reviewed on a frequent if not continuous basis. As consumer and industrial markets change over time, logistics and distribution management must become aware of such changes, planning and adapting their strategy and operations as necessary — including their channel networks.

Some larger distribution organisations have already adopted such an approach, termed *dynamic channel strategy*. Under this regime, centrally controlled orders can be switched from one depot or distribution centre to another in order to optimise workload and operating costs. In doing so, depot or agent delivery areas change from day to day depending on total system demand, matching the latter with supply of available product and distribution resources at the warehouses and depots concerned.

The concept is further explained in Chapter 4 on network strategy, but is only effective where manufacturers or distributors have a substantial degree of involvement in or control over their channels of distribution.

Information technology, more specifically electronic data interchange, has enabled the development of such techniques, and no doubt the capability to mould a network's workload to maximise resource utilisation and minimise cost is an extremely useful one which other companies will wish to investigate. Foremost in importance, however, is the extent to which the chosen channel helps a company to achieve its planned cost, customer service and profit objectives.

Progress test 3

1. How would you define the term 'channel of distribution'? **(1)**

2. There are two aspects to any distribution channel. What are they? **(2)**

3. What are the two broad options open to a company regarding channels of distribution? **(3)**

4. What is an echelon? **(3)**

5. Explain what happens along the distribution channel apart from actual physical movement of goods and commodities. **(4–9)**

6. List and explain three important aims of channel selection. **(10–16)**

7. In what ways do the following affect channel strategy:

    (a) product?
    (b) market?
    (c) competition? **(18–20)**

4

Network strategy

Storage is one of the elements of logistics planning, and in Chapter 6 the ways in which the type and number of storage facilities affect all the other functions included under the distribution umbrella will be demonstrated.

Depots

Depots are extremely important aspects of any logistics system. As already seen in the previous chapter, most channel strategies rely on some intermediate break-bulk and storage facility between producer and retailer/consumer. Depots are not only a large capital investment in their own right, they also relate to other elements in the 'distribution mix' to create significant 'trade-off' opportunities.

1. The need for depots

There are a number of good reasons for holding inventory. Chief amongst them are that:

(a) it may be necessary to carry out production in long runs to reduce unit production costs and stabilise production;

(b) it may be that because of seasonal demand fluctuations production has to be carried out in advance (the fireworks industry is an extreme example of this!);

(c) it may be attractive, because of the economies of employing bulk transport from ports or factories, or on account of environmental considerations, to break bulk at depots and use smaller vehicles for high street deliveries;

(d) it may be possible to make savings in material handling and movement by 'unitising' the product (e.g. using containers, pallets and standard size packaging);

(e) it may be a requirement of some customers, such as supermarkets, that orders are delivered assembled, say on pallets or in cages;

(f) it may be prudent to invest in stock likely to be in short supply in the future in order to exploit the market opportunities this gives;

(g) it may be sensible to build up stocks in advance of a major product promotion (e.g. a TV advertising campaign).

2.   The function of depots

Any of the points given in 1 can justify the use of warehouse or depot facilities which can provide:

(a)   a storage point where safety stocks can be held;
(b)   a transhipment point along the supply chain;
(c)   a break-bulk and order assembly facility.

In many industries production and supply cannot be instantaneous, but demand usually is! Often this instantaneous demand can only be met adequately by the storage of goods near to the market-place. Even given improved techniques of demand forecasting it is often impossible to match the rate of production to the forecast demand.

Depots can also be perceived as an 'insurance' against interruptions of a distributor's own, or his supplier's, production facilities. These can be caused by such eventualities as breakdown or employees taking industrial action.

As intermediate points in the supply chain they can help to absorb the effects of long economic production runs and of procuring 'economic order quantities'. (This point is dealt with fully in Chapter 6 on inventory management.)

Finally, a depot strategically placed to serve a discrete marketing area can often be used as the focus for a marketing effort in that area or to trial launch a new product before making it nationally available.

3.   The number of depots

Decisions relating to the most cost effective number, size and location of depots are dependent upon:

(a) existing and likely future demands on the company;

(b) internal and external factors which might provide opportunities or constraints relevant to distribution;

(c) possible alternative distribution policies.

Such decisions interact with a wide range of planning and operational decisions in distribution. These wider decisions tend to fall into three categories, as discussed below.

4. Strategic, tactical and operational decisions

Strategic decisions, which are reviewed every three to five years, will include such factors as warehouse technology and the number, size and location of existing depots.

Tactical decisions are usually reviewed annually, and possibly include such factors as transport methods, vehicle fleet mix and methods of vehicle procurement, company delivery policies, customer satisfaction levels and inventory level aimed for.

Operational decisions, which are reviewed many times a year, can include factors such as daily routeing of vehicles and load planning, staffing overtime levels and depot replenishment requests.

Some of these decisions are very complicated, involving trading off costs between variables, and some of these costs are very hard to quantify.

Cost behaviour

5. Regression analysis of depot costs

The behaviour of certain costs which vary in relation to the number of depots is quite fundamental to the making of decisions about depot provisions. There is, for example, a linear, or straight line, relationship between total depot costs (the sum of all the costs associated with each and every depot) and their throughput (or total amount of goods which they handle).

One method, known as *regression analysis,* is very useful in studying the pattern of depot costs. Thus, in Fig. 4.1 it would be reasonable to expect that a depot of throughput X would have annual costs of approximately £Y p.a. (If the different costs (on

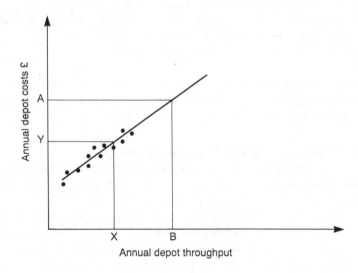

Fig. 4.1 *Regression analysis.*

the vertical axis of a graph) associated with different throughputs (shown on the horizontal axis) are plotted on the graph then the sloping line, or line of best fit, between the point plotted is known as the *regression line*. It represents a straight proportional relationship between the dependent variable (depot costs) and the other, independent variable, (throughput).) However, it is not good practice to extrapolate a regression curve to conclude, for example, that throughput B will cost £A p.a., since the 'line of best fit' of cost v. throughput may be different over different ranges of the independent variable.

6. Fixed and variable depot costs

It is instructive to compare the costs of single and multiple depot provision.

Depot costs can be divided into two types, *fixed costs* which do not vary with throughput (for example, the business rate payable

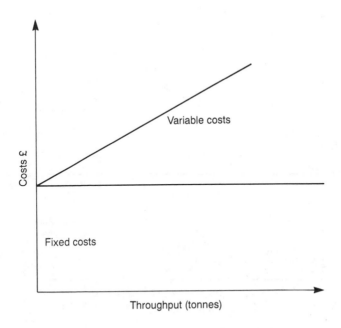

Fig. 4.2 *Fixed and variable costs — single depot.*

on the buildings and the overheads associated with managing it), and *variable costs* which are directly proportional to throughput (for example, the costs associated with the depot delivery fleet). Thus the cost curve for a single depot would look like Fig. 4.2.

However, if we graph the cost curves for different numbers of depots as in Fig. 4.3 then the graph looks, at first sight, quite different to that in Fig. 4.1. This is because the fixed costs are not constant but increase in proportion to the number of depots (despite each individual depot's fixed costs being constant in the short run).

However, the total variable costs are related, as already described, to the total throughput of the system, whether this is channelled through a single depot or a multiplicity of depots. In the main these variable costs reflect the total size of the delivery fleet.

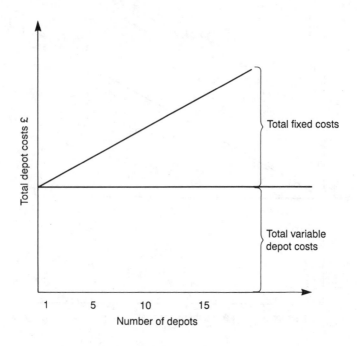

Fig. 4.3 *Fixed and variable costs — multiple depots.*

7. The behaviour of fixed and variable costs

The behaviour of fixed and variable costs is important when considering the decisions which have to be taken when the level of throughput has to change. If a system is expanding then what is important is the incremental cost of that expansion, which may or may not involve additional fixed costs (e.g. extra depots), but will certainly, in the long run, involve an increase in variable costs.

If the service has to contract then it is important to be able to identify the avoidable costs, or those which it will no longer be necessary to incur. If, for example, there is only one depot then the only avoidable cost would be the cost of the vehicles and drivers no longer required, but if there are a number of depots, then closure of one rather than contraction spread over them all might be one option.

The identification of short-term avoidable costs is also a

means, known as *marginal costing*, often used to price a change in the level of a distribution service.

8. **The relationship between depot costs and total transport costs**

Traditionally, transport costs can be divided into:

(a) *Trunking costs* (factory/warehouse to depot);
(b) *Delivery costs* (depot to customers).

Quite simply — and predictably — trunking costs increase with the number of depots, but delivery costs decrease.

So, as can be seen from the graph in Fig. 4.4 which shows these costs and the composite total cost curve, there is a trade-off between these two cost elements. A specific number of depots (*x*) will produce a minimum total transport cost. This relationship is often described as the classic industrial logistic management 'trade-off'.

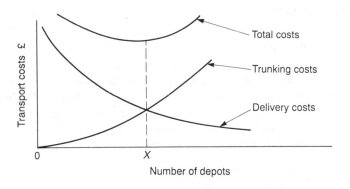

Fig. 4.4 *Relationship between depot costs and total transport costs.*

9. **Depot costs in relation to total distribution costs**

Of course it is useless to take warehousing or transport costs in isolation when deciding the number and location of depots. It is necessary to be able to observe the behaviour of the total of all distribution costs. When warehouse costs and transport costs are put on the same graph and summed to give a total distribution cost, as in Fig. 4.5, it can easily be seen that there is a theoretical optimum number of depots.

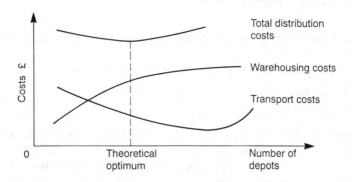

Fig. 4.5 *Relationship between depot costs and total distribution costs.*

Depot strategy

10. Basic decisions

Not every distribution company or organisation, when considering its depot needs, starts with a clean sheet. Often the organisation inherits a legacy of existing depot provisions which may or may not, totally or in part, satisfy its requirements.

The basic decisions which have to be made relate to the number, size and location of depots. Specifically:

(a) Is a depot strategy demanded, or can all customers be supplied most efficiently and economically 'ex works'?
(b) Is a single 'hub' or are multiple regional depots the optimum solution?
(c) What is the optimum depot size, and what is the optimum size of delivery area?
(d) Where should these depot(s) be located?

11. Internal and external factors to be considered

A thorough analysis of the decision requires consideration of a large number of factors, some of which are, from the company's point of view, 'internal' factors in that they can influence these by their marketing, production and transport policies, whereas others are 'external' factors, outside their control. Amongst the latter are factors such as the level of competition faced and various economic factors affecting both the product market and the labour market.

Current and likely future demands on the system can be analysed in terms of sales volume, the nature of sales (large or small outlets, or a mixture of both) and customer service requirements, and an attempt can be made to determine the network of facilities, including depots, best suited to meeting these requirements.

It may be useful to consider policies in the context of discrete 'drop sizes'. An example might be:

Less than 100 kg
100–500 kg
Over 500 kg

The resulting resources and costs involved in operating these facilities and their associated transport operations (including any capital costs) must also be computed and taken into account.

Other considerations include:

(a) *Customer service requirements*, expressed as delivery frequencies, must be considered.

(b) *Geographical features* too must be taken into account. Information should be assembled about major barriers and hazards, such as river estuaries, mountain roads, congested routes, motorway links, etc. In this way the costs associated with the transport links required can be evaluated.

(c) Consideration must of course be given not only to existing *facility locations* but also to possible future sites. Possible locations, e.g. major towns, major transport route 'crossroads', should be listed at this stage.

(d) *Cost information* for current operations and possible future operations should be estimated. For example, if a move to fully automate the warehousing facilities is contemplated, either on an existing site or on new sites, the cost relationships implied in this should be estimated. Information about current *transport costs* and the costs of possible future transport methods should be assembled.

12. Information required

Much of the decision-making process involves collection of information. The information which you will require depends very much on your own situation but in general it will comprise:

(a) existing and future demands;
(b) geographical factors;
(c) existing and potential operational locations;
(d) demographic factors and the local labour market in the location of any planned depot;
(e) cost relationships for current and possible future operations;
(f) both internal and external constraints and limitations.

There will, for example, be constraints within which the person with the depot planning function has to work. These might typically include the capacity of handling equipment associated with both current and planned depots, factories and transport operations, which might be inadequate at busy times or following a growth in activity and have to be upgraded.

13. Assumptions and trade-offs

Assumptions may have to be made about some of the following matters before determining the number, location and size of depot:

(a) inventory policies;
(b) the level of warehouse technology employed;
(c) delivery policies to be adopted and their likely costs;
(d) the nature and cost of trunking operations.

Even within the depot strategy decision, 'trade-offs' occur. For example, easier availability of labour in a new town or Urban Development Corporation site may have to be traded off against cheaper 'greenfield' land in an out-of-town location where there could be possible labour shortages.

Optimisation

14. General

Ultimately the answer to the depot strategy decision must provide:

(a) the optimum number of depots;
(b) the optimum location of depots;
(c) the optimum capacity of depots.

These three outcomes are not independent of each other, but are interdependent. Thus size is affected by number and location, and so on. Additionally, there will be 'trade-offs' between all three!

15. Depot strategy algorithm

Many decisions can be arrived at by taking a series of steps, which can often be described as a sort of recipe or algorithm. Sometimes, as in the algorithm suggested below, it is necessary to repeat some of the steps several times in order to refine a solution. Such algorithms, sometimes described as iterative, are said to loop, as they return to the same point more than once.

A suggested algorithm for addressing the depot strategy decision is as follows:

(a) Select locations for a specified number of depots.
(b) Allocate flows through each depot site.
(c) Allocate the transport flows involved in servicing these.
(d) Cost the depot and transport flows.
(e) Interpret the resulting operating and marketing implications in the light of company policies.
(f) *If necessary re-select locations and repeat the above steps.*

16. Optimum number of depots

Reference has already been made to the classic industrial logistics trade-off graphs (Figs. 4.4 and 4.5). These give a theoretical optimum least-cost solution, but in practice the choice will also be influenced by operating and marketing considerations. However, the graphs will generally be close to the optimum.

17. Optimum location of depots

Whilst in theory there are an infinite number of sites, in practice there is a 'feasible set' of solutions, since only certain locations would be suitable or indeed available. The actual site chosen will be a compromise arrived at for any number of different reasons, including the availability of land and finance. The factors listed below should certainly be taken into consideration:

(a) availability of labour locally;
(b) accessibility to vehicles using the depot;
(c) the value of land in the area;
(d) availability of land bearing in mind current needs and the possibility of later expansion being needed;
(e) proximity to customers.

It is possible to construct mathematical models to simulate some or all of the costs and benefits of the above constraints. In recent years there has been a great increase in the use of computers for such modelling and an ever increasing number of packages is becoming available. These, and depot siting models such as the gravity model, are discussed in much greater detail in Chapter 9 dealing with the uses of information technology in logistics and distribution management.

18. Optimum allocations/size

We can allocate customers to depots in a number of ways. Our allocation decision can be based on:

(a) what is the nearest depot or factory;
(b) what gives the cheapest total costs;
(c) what are the customers' requirements;
(d) what is the current allocation!

The assignment of customers to depots obviously affects the size of the depot, but other factors, such as physical constraints on land at the site chosen can also have an effect on this final parameter.

The assignment problem, and how customers' orders can be most efficiently allocated to depots, is more fully described in Chapter 8. In some cases, the use of 'dynamic channel strategy' software enables this decision to be taken on a daily basis.

In an ideal world we could plan a new distribution system starting with a clean sheet of paper. This kind of luxury is, however, only a dream for most depot/distribution managers!

Progress test 4

1. What are the most important reasons for establishing depots? **(1)**

2. Explain the function of depots and warehouses. **(2)**

3. How do costs (*a*) in case of a single depot, and (*b*) in the case of two or more depots, vary with throughput? **(6–7)**

4. Suggest which depot costs are 'marginal'. **(7)**

5. In what ways are depot costs and total distribution costs related? **(9)**

6. What are the most important considerations concerning the optimum:

    (a) number of depots;
    (b) location of depots
    (c) capacity of depots? **(16–18)**

5
Modal selection and transport systems

Although each major function of logistics and physical distribution is as important as the others in achieving the ideal 'mix', careful evaluation and selection of the appropriate transport element is crucial to the success of the whole activity.

Effective logistics and distribution management is based on efficient physical movement — in terms of time taken, energy and resources used, cost incurred and results obtained with regard to the desired level of commodity availability and condition. Hence, as in most other areas of this 'management of physical movement' activity, the method used must suit both the materials to be moved and the other components of the system as precisely as possible.

To carry out such an analysis, it is necessary first to look at each mode of transport, recognise the main characteristics, and then identify in what ways the benefits of these features can best be utilised to move products or commodities along the supply chain.

Road

1. **General**
   The main features of road transport include:

(a) Flexibility
(b) Versatility
(c) Economy
(d) Infrastructure.

These aspects are discussed in detail below.

2. Flexibility

Owing to its ability to operate door-to-door, road transport has the facility to move anything almost anywhere. Not only is it the most useful method of land transport in this sense, but its very nature makes it possible for other modes of transport to carry road vehicles as part of their payload, thereby rendering this basic flexibility not only applicable to domestic land transport, but also to international journeys.

The role of road-freight transport at the forefront of international surface transport and distribution has, of course, been much enhanced by the modification of short-sea ferries to accept goods vehicles as cargo. For more than 20 years, international hauliers and freight forwarders have been crossing international borders and using roll-on/roll-off (RO/RO) ferry services to bridge relatively narrow channels of sea between European and Eurasian land masses.

Whether vehicles travel accompanied by their drivers, or unaccompanied — such as loaded semi-trailers for delivery by forwarding agents' contractors from the port of destination — road-based international freight transport and distribution have, over time, become the standard method of movement for a large proportion of both export and import consignments in both the UK and EC, largely as a result of its intrinsic flexibility.

3. Versatility

Although road vehicles were originally of one or two basic types, vehicle technology has over the years produced all kinds of specialised bodies for a multitude of products and commodities, giving the basic road transport vehicle the capability to carry such diverse commodities as frozen foods, livestock, hanging garments and liquid industrial gases. Road transport distributors of foodstuffs have, for some time now, had the capability to carry frozen, chilled and ambient temperature goods all on the same vehicle at the same time for the same customer.

4. Economy

In comparison with other modes, road transport is competitively priced — particularly as a bought-in service from third-party operators. Owing to the fragmented and traditionally independent nature of the haulage and distribution industry, there has always been a high degree of competition, which has ensured that — on the basis of price alone — road operators have frequently had the sharper competitive edge.

5. Infrastructure

One of the main factors which has helped road transport gain this unique competitive position is the development and maintenance of a comprehensive, publicly-funded road network. This is not to say, of course, that the road haulier or distributor does not pay their proportion of track costs. If the question were posed to any operator in the sector, the answer would surely be that such a proportion had been grossly miscalculated — to the benefit of the Exchequer! Even so, this proportion is now in the process of being broadened, as government policies on environmental issues turn increasingly toward making the transport industry — and the road sector in particular — responsible for paying the full costs of the environmental impact of their activities.

6. Other factors

In addition to the above, road transport is the only means of transport which is — for most businesses — relatively easy to own and operate as part of the own-account sector. Combining these factors with that of the relative shortness of many journeys has meant that, over a period of time, road freight transport has become the dominant means of transport in many areas of logistics and distribution (*see* Fig. 5.1).

Typical examples are the FMCG and automotive industries, where the added advantage of consignments remaining on a transport vehicle from the place of origin to that of destination has improved performance not only in terms of cost, but also in terms of product availability and condition. Both primary distribution — trunking operations for movement of bulk quantities — and secondary distribution, in the form of multiple collections or deliveries, can be undertaken with equal ease by road, thereby bringing both the bulk and multi-consignment aspects of the operation conveniently within the sphere of the same transport medium.

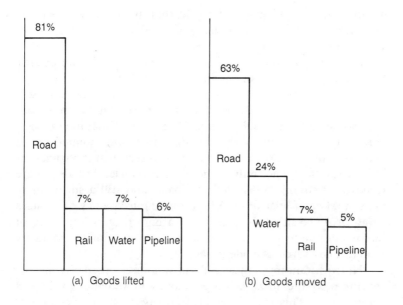

Fig. 5.1 *Transport and distribution of goods by mode.*

7. Factors against road transport

Despite its perceived advantages, however, road-based distribution has to a certain extent become a victim of its own success. Collection and delivery operations by road — largely in urban areas — continue to be hampered by mounting congestion in town and city centres, thereby increasing operating costs and perpetuating the environmentally unfriendly image of the lorry. Even trunking operations can frequently be delayed by motorway hold-ups, and HGVs may often be considered as one of the major threats to safe motorway travel.

Added to this is the vulnerability of road transport to weather conditions which, in the UK and Europe, can often be severe and sometimes unpredictable. Movement of goods may be delayed under these conditions, and this will often impact on customer service.

Increasingly complex legislation also continues to regulate road freight operators, and burdens them with more stringent controls. The net effect of such a trend will be continued increases in operating costs, matched by further pressure for realistic returns on investment through higher levels of vehicle utilisation and driver productivity.

In spite of improvements in vehicle and component technology, security is an ongoing source of concern and a target for much management attention. As the means of transport closest to the public at large, road distribution is at greatest risk from both the casual pilferer and organised groups. Carrying a high percentage of consumer merchandise, including bonded goods and easily disposable electrical items, this sector of the transport industry is subject not only to thefts from vehicles, but also to the removal of complete vehicles and loads, and still a surprisingly high number of hijackings. Add to this the frequency of vehicles being involved in road accidents — a high proportion being in motorway pile-ups — and the unseen costs of moving goods by road can be more easily identified.

Notwithstanding these disadvantages, road transport continues as the most favoured means of moving goods and commodities. This applies equally to many inward movements of raw materials for manufacturing or processing industries, as it does to outward movements of individually smaller consignments of finished goods or components. Provided a road vehicle can physically accommodate the product in convenient and cost-effective quantities, both types of transport can be dealt with by a road-based operation.

Rail

8. General
Rail transport may be said to possess four main advantages:

(a) Capacity
(b) Speed
(c) Safety and security
(d) Reduced delays in bad weather.

These will be discussed in detail below.

9. Capacity
As a means of transport, rail's main advantage is its high

carrying capacity in terms of both volume and deadweight. This has been increasingly exploited over the years by use of measures advocated in the Beeching Committee's *Reshaping of British Railways* report. Since then, rail vehicle sizes and designs have changed almost beyond recognition to accommodate weights and quantities substantially in excess of those carried 30 years ago. The introduction of liner trains and block train services was the beginning of an irreversible trend towards using the railway's strength to exploit markets which it is best equipped to serve. Despite such developments, rail traffic has fallen consistently over the last 20-plus years (*see* Fig. 5.2).

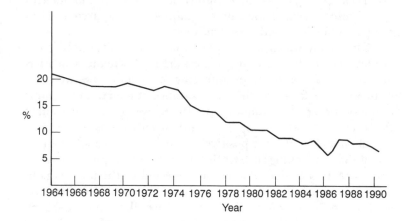

Fig. 5.2 *Percentage of all freight traffic moved by rail in the UK (1964–1990).*

Such bulk transport by rail is best undertaken by moving single commodities in trainloads. Freightliner — the container-operating arm of BR Railfreight Distribution — operates fixed-formation trains in excess of 1,000 tonnes on scheduled services between main UK centres and ports. In the aftermath of sectorisation, BR Railfreight was divided into subsectors to deal with discrete market segments, each of which now operates block trains consisting of one particular commodity — either aggregates, petroleum products, chemicals or one of several other groups of homogeneous materials handled in huge quantities each day by that particular rail subsector.

10. Speed

As a perceived advantage of rail transport, speed has a somewhat limited value. Some railfreight services now regularly travel at speeds in excess of 75 mph on main lines, and often during evenings or overnight, thus achieving what would normally be very competitive point-to-point times. When delivery and collection times to and from rail terminals are added, however, along with consignment handling times, total elapsed journey times often become much less attractive. Nonetheless, where distances are longer — and certainly in excess of 200 kilometres — and minimum intermediate transhipment is required, rail can compete effectively with road transport.

One factor which has a positive effect on this aspect is the availability or otherwise of private sidings. A scheme which has existed for some time, encouraging companies to invest in rail-connected facilities with the assistance of government grants under Section 8 of the Railways Act 1974, gives assistance towards the costs of company sidings or private-owner wagons. Such grants are obtainable only if a positive environmental benefit can be established in sending such traffic flows by rail as opposed to road transport. It is evident that certain selected traffic flows benefit from use of private sidings in conjunction with high-speed rail transit. For the most part, these traffics are bulk commodities such as raw materials for production and processing, but finished goods in very substantial quantities would benefit from this treatment too.

11. Safety and security

As sole system user, railways are in a good position to exploit two particular factors of advantage to system users — safety and security. Although rail accidents do occur — sometimes more frequently than desirable — those involving freight trains seem to be noticeably fewer than those with passengers. Use of rail transport therefore, particularly containerised traffic, can influence the level of claims, damages and even goods-in-transit (GIT) insurance premiums as part of the transport cost equation. Levels of customer service, in terms of delivery reliability, would benefit from using a system with such a highly structured operational control mechanism as is used by the railways — particularly now that British Rail have their own containerised consignment tracking system in the form of a 'container operations processing system' (COPS) for individual consignment trains.

Similar comments apply to security. Although not entirely free from theft and pilferage, rail-based consignments are by the physical nature of the rail infrastructure at less risk than the equivalent consignment moving by road. Although many kinds of load now transported by rail are not valuable to most would-be thieves, a good deal of general merchandise traffic still travels by freight train — in particular, import/export traffic. Fortunately, a high percentage of this is containerised, which itself is an aid to greater security, whilst the unit-load is on the rail system. Put onto a road vehicle for collection/delivery, it then becomes correspondingly more vulnerable.

12. Reduced delays
In contrast to its road-based competitors, rail transport is rarely adversely affected by weather conditions — unless high winds, heavy snow or ice bring down electric catenary wires and freeze points. Generally speaking, rail transport is not a victim of congestion in its own system. This could prove a distinct advantage in the attempts by rail to better its competitive position as a means of logistics transport for the 1990s, particularly when one considers this advantage in the context of international journeys, where road-based transport is often vulnerable to more severe continental weather conditions.

13. Factors against rail transport
The major disadvantage of rail transport is its basic inflexibility. Its unfavourable comparison with road transport's door-to-door capability means it is not seriously considered as a viable alternative in many cases. A certain degree of integration has been achieved in the form of cooperation with road hauliers and distribution contractors, with trunk movements undertaken by rail and localised collection/delivery by road-based operators. Current examples of this are the BR Freightliner container transport operation, and the erstwhile Speedlink operation for wagon-load traffic. Otherwise, rail retains its role primarily as a

bulk transport medium involved largely in the earlier stages of the supply chain in the movement of raw materials, though it still retains a very small percentage of finished goods transport.

Air

14. General

As relative newcomers to the field of freight and logistics transport, many airlines and air transport operators have found their niche as carriers of general or specialist cargoes. In such a role, the most significant features of their operations are:

(a) Speed
(b) Comprehensive scheduled network
(c) Safety and security.

These aspects are discussed in detail below.

15. Speed

As a feature of air transport operations, speed is of varying significance, depending on whether it is the domestic or the international transport scene which is under consideration. Domestically, and within the constraints of short-haul European operations, airlines can achieve short point-to-point timings between airports. However, when time required for collection and delivery of consignments to and from air cargo terminals is brought into the equation — particularly as a percentage of total journey time — the benefit of such high-speed air transit can be considerably eroded. Exceptions in these circumstances are such time-sensitive items as mail and newspapers.

At long-haul international level, the non-flying portion of air freight transit time will account for a much smaller percentage of total journey time, and the benefit of fast journeys over comparatively longer distances will be maximised. Here, in the freight categories most suited to it, air transport has virtually no competition, as the commercial nature and value of consignments dictate the need for fast journey times.

As mentioned above, air cargo services are mostly used for time-sensitive products such as spring flowers, exotic fruits, high-fashion goods, urgently required components and spares and high-value items, where transport cost is often a noticeably lesser proportion of a consignment's commercial value. Once again, this commercial 'perishability' determines that, in order for the goods to be available in the right place at the right time, the fastest means of transport should be used, whether the ultimate object is to maximise sales or minimise cost.

16. Network

Today's far-reaching air networks connect most main centres of any consequence, both domestically and internationally. The best examples of how such networks have been developed into purpose-designed structures to best exploit both long- and short-haul services are the 'hub and spoke' systems which have been built up most notably in Europe and the USA. In these systems, carriers at both long-haul level between major national and international centres, and feeder level shuttling between lesser centres regionally or nationally, perform a vital role in creating and maintaining a high level of service to both passengers and freight users in the form of a comprehensive and cohesive network.

Moreover, the scheduled nature of services enables senders to plan cargo shipments and, where necessary, use alternative airline operators in getting their freight on the next available flight to a particular destination. Such scheduled, high-speed transport operations developed by air operators have been exploited in recent years by a growing number of specialist international air courier services, where rapid transit for important documents and parcels is the very essence of a high-value service — a further example of the ways in which air transport has filled a specialist niche in the transport and distribution market-place.

17. Safety and security

Despite their tendency to make news headlines, air accidents are few in comparison to the journeys made and distance flown. This is due largely to the strict regulatory regime imposed on aviation operations both in the UK and internationally, which of course makes air transport a safe, reliable environment for shippers of air cargo as well as passengers. In addition, much air freight is containerised, thereby increasing the degree of physical protection and security afforded both during handling operations and transport.

The often unitised or securely packaged nature of many air cargo shipments, combined with frequent calls for increased levels of airport security, provides a substantial deterrent — certainly against both the opportunist thief and more organised groups.

18. Factors against air transport

As with other modes, certain disadvantages exist in using air transport. These relate to cost, capacity limits, transport of dangerous goods and delays. These are discussed in detail below.

19. High cost

This aspect is considered the dominant factor here. As with passenger transport, air tends to be the most expensive method of cargo movement in comparison with others. Perhaps this is more a case of perception rather than an operating fact. There are, however, two mitigating factors in this issue — groupage operations and the implications for inventory levels.

As groupage operators — often freight forwarders — combine a number of smaller consignments to constitute a larger unit-load, a lower unit transport cost is achieved which then accrues to the shipper. Using this method can produce worthwhile savings in air-freight charges, depending on consignment size.

Notwithstanding the high cost of transporting goods by air, fast journey times — particularly over international or even intercontinental distances — may mean that stocks can be replenished that much faster. Consequently, inventory levels can realistically be kept much closer to a stock-out position and, in some cases, replenishment can be planned and organised to JIT standards.

20. Capacity limits

These restrict the use that can be made of air as a means of transport and constitute a further drawback. Consignment limits exist not only in terms of weight and volume, but also in the nature of the commodities which it is permissible and safe to carry on board commercial aircraft. Constraints on consignment weight and volume will, to a degree, be influenced by the extent of cargo-only operations among airlines. Dedicated cargo aircraft will, of course, be able to use their full fuselage capacity, whereas operators of passenger aircraft and 'combi' types will be limited largely to belly-hold cargo stowed below passenger decks, and therefore will be subject to tighter restrictions on size and volume, if not also on weight.

21. Dangerous goods

A high proportion of dangerous goods are restricted to using surface transport as a result of the risks to which crew and aircraft might be exposed in the event of an accident — to say nothing of the population at ground level.

22. Delays

Further ways in which air transport may be occasionally affected, relate to delays. There are three main categories — weather, other terminal delays and industrial action.

23. Poor weather conditions

Although not an entirely insurmountable problem, poor weather conditions — mainly in the form of low visibility — can and do adversely affect air transport operations. In many cases, even this is no longer a drawback, due to advanced aviation technology which has, for some time, been increasing the capability of certain aircraft to take off and land in CAT III weather conditions, i.e. in very low visibility. Nevertheless, bad weather at destination airports can mean diversions, with consequent loss of delivery time due to re-routeing and/or scheduling of road collection and delivery vehicles.

24. Other ground-based problems

These may have a number of causes, e.g. genuine operational delays, or some kind of industrial action (*see* **25** below). The former occurs where routine turn-round activities such as the fuelling and loading of aircraft take longer than scheduled, transfer flights are late in arriving or there is a wait for clearance from air traffic control. Delays of this kind are normally minimal but can sometimes have a cumulative effect, resulting in some flights being delayed for a matter of an hour or two. With most air-freight consignments, such an occurrence would not be critical, whereas with others a similar delay might not be acceptable.

25. Industrial action

This often affects airline operations, but to varying degrees. Often caused by a dispute involving handling staff, these incidents can carry on for days, or even longer, if effective industrial relations machinery cannot be brought into play to achieve at least a temporary solution. In these situations, air-freight customers must often use another airline, airport or perhaps even transfer to another mode of transport altogether in order to ensure goods get to their own customers as promised.

Maritime transport and inland waterways

26. General

In 1989, 58bn/tonne/km of logistics and distribution transport was undertaken by inland waterways and coastal shipping — 26 per cent of goods moved in the UK. Likewise, 298 million tonnes of import and export commodities were transported in and out of Britain by shipping operators in the same year.

Although water-based transport falls clearly into the two categories of maritime transport and inland waterways, both possess very similar characteristics:

(a) High carrying capacity
(b) Economy
(c) Versatility.

These aspects are discussed in detail below.

27. High carrying capacity

Such a factor will of course depend on vessel size and type, but comparatively speaking, water-borne transport has the capability to accommodate huge consignments in terms of deadweight, volume or, in many cases, both. It is therefore an ideal medium for the movement of raw materials, where such bulk transport is necessary — partly due to the international nature of many movements, but also as a result of their low intrinsic value. Tremendous quantities of basic commodities for manufacturing and process industries need to be fed into companies in order to maintain the momentum of their production and process activities which must keep going in order to remain economic and pass economies of scale on down the line. By bringing in raw materials at low cost, manufacturing and process operations can then add value to them, and create a product useful to the company's customers.

28. Economy

Both sea and inland water transport provide relatively low unit transport costs for many commodities by using economies of scale very similar to those mentioned in **26**. This does mean, however, that the best of such economies are in many cases achieved when vessels carry bulk commodities, or perhaps container cargoes. Again, as far as many raw materials and bulk commodities are concerned, their basic value is quite low and a very economic means of transport is required not only to cope with the weight and bulk which needs to be moved at any one time, but also to achieve a sufficiently low unit transport cost.

29. Versatility

In a similar way to the railways, water-borne transport and particularly shipping has in recent years become highly specialised in maximising its advantage to handle high capacity cargoes. This trend has produced supertankers, gas and other bulk carriers and four generations of cellular container vessels, to name but a few of the types which are now in use, alongside a substantial number of conventional cargo vessels which continue to operate world-wide. Both deep-sea and coastal shipping — as well as inland waterway transport in the form of barges and smaller cargo-carriers — can therefore effectively deal with consignments of varying types.

One of the best-exploited market niches, and a good example of versatility, is that occupied by short-haul sea ferries. In addition to the more specialised train ferries, these multi-purpose vessels have the capability to handle a variety of traffic from foot passengers to maximum capacity road freight vehicles. In fulfilling this role, they provide what still remains a vital link in the international logistics and distribution chain between the UK and mainland Europe in the form of a surface transport medium for the conveyance of road- and rail-based freight units across the Channel and the North Sea. What remains to be seen is the extent to which ferry operators can maintain this link and valuable business sector — and their competitive edge in terms of service levels — once the Channel Tunnel becomes an operational reality.

30. Liner services

Often operated by conference groups, liner services are another advantage of modern shipping. Fast, scheduled services follow established routes calling at specific main ports in a number of countries which each route is designed to service. Linking the major trading nations across the main oceans, or forming part of a round-the-world service, liner services offer a speedy, pre-planned timetable of departures from many UK ports to most deep-sea international destinations. The extent of competition generally in the shipping industry, and particularly in liner service operations, means that the level of service to the shipper in terms of frequency of sailings, ports of call and journey times is of a high order. Freight rates are also competitive, thereby ensuring that such cargoes as container traffic enjoy the benefit of quality services at relatively low unit transport costs.

31. Factors against maritime transport and inland waterways

Water-borne transport in general has a rather restricted role domestically, limited to bulk, low-value commodities of a non-urgent nature. Economies of scale are important here in order to achieve the required savings in total transport costs and materials handling time — where water-connected facilities using bulk handling methods are available. With average UK transport distances being so short, more urgent consignments would be moved by road or rail.

A wider international role, however, is undertaken by deep-sea shipping and RO/RO ferry operators, whose services attract a much wider variety of cargoes. Yet again, a major factor for bulk, general cargo and container shippers is the relatively small percentage of total transit time taken up by the loading and discharge of vessels.

Given the constraints already mentioned within which water-based transport methods can most effectively operate, such methods have two basic disadvantages — relatively long journey times due to low operating speeds, and exposure to the risks of weather and port delays.

Low travel speeds are an accepted part of most shipping operations. This, combined with its capability for high capacity, accounts largely for the heavy concentration of bulk, non-urgent commodities among shipping cargoes. The trade-off is in the low transport cost.

Weather delays will, of course, only constitute a risk factor where certain routes or geographic regions are concerned. Some ports may be inaccessible and waterways impassable at certain times of year, but the experienced operator will be aware of such problems and can recommend to the shipper suitable alternative routes or methods of transport.

Delays in or around ports seem to arise less frequently in the 1990s than they did in previous decades. Many delays, particularly in the UK, were as a result of industrial action of one kind or another. Although there is no guarantee that such things are now a practice of the past, competition for business in the ports and shipping industries world-wide is so fierce that many groups in both industries take a much more realistic attitude to the provision of service to their users.

Political incidents can sometimes prove problematic to shipping operators, but this is yet another area which many operators and shippers tend to deal with by means of good planning and management.

Pipelines and cables

32. General

Often overlooked, pipelines and cables should perhaps be considered as further modes of transport. Their use is, however, considerably restricted to those particular commodities which can be effectively and efficiently handled by such means, and is often further restricted in terms of maximum transit distances.

Despite this, pipelines are used not only to transport industrial gases from supplier centres to local firms, but also to bring ashore oil and natural gas from considerable distances out in the North Sea.

As a means of transport, pipelines account for more than 5 per cent of freight movement. This is not insignificant, but it is an indication of their limitations.

33. Important factors

(a) The *capital cost* involved in laying/construction is the major disadvantage of pipelines.

(b) *Operating costs* are likely to be relatively low, as only flow controls are required to move bulk quantities.

(c) *System integrity* is, however, a problem resulting from exposure to such hazards as the effects of weather on above- and below-ground networks, and deliberately malicious actions such as vandalism and terrorist activity.

Even so, pipelines and cables fill a vital niche in the transport and distribution area of logistics, in such industries as chemical, petro-chemical, gas, electricity, water and communications.

Factors determining modal selection

There are a number of these to be considered when evaluating a transport situation. The most important are as follows.

34. State

Is the product or commodity a solid, liquid or gas? This will often limit the choice of mode or vehicle on grounds of physical compatibility.

35. Mass

Weight, volume and dimensions are factors which will more precisely determine the size and capacity of transport vehicle required for a given consignment or commodity. Here again, limits may be imposed by purely physical constraints or legal requirements.

36. Urgency

Speed of delivery can often be critical. Transit times of more than one mode may need to be compared in order to decide which method or operator is likely to meet delivery deadlines. This factor is often otherwise known as *commercial perishability*.

37. Cost vs. value

The relationship between transport costs and commodity

value is crucial. It may be a direct comparison between them, or between transport costs and costs incurred as a result of a freight consignment not being there when required.

38. Market
    Geographic dispersion or concentration of a product or commodity market can have considerable relevance for modal selection. It can be highly significant in the choice of primary distribution transport —trunk-haul operations — and in the selection of a suitable means of secondary distribution.

Progress test 5

1. Why has road transport become the dominant form of logistics and distribution transport?   **(1–6)**

2. What are the strengths of rail transport for logistics managers?   **(8–12)**

3. Air transport incurs very high costs. Say why you agree or disagree.   **(19–20)**

4. Explain how (*a*) state, (*b*) perishability and (*c*) value can affect modal selection.   **(33, 36)**

Inventory management

Inventory management policy

In this chapter we look at how the management of inventory, one of the major components of the distributors mix, can contribute to more cost effective operation.

Manufacturers, distributors and retailers resort to holding inventories of raw materials, components, assemblies and subassemblies, work-in-progress and finished goods at different points in the supply chain because production and supply cannot be instantaneous, but demand usually is and often can only be met adequately by the storage of goods near the market-place.

1. The purpose of stockholding

One reason why stock is held is in order to 'de-couple' supply and demand. Stocks are held at a cost — the cost of warehouse and depot space, of staff who 'rotate' the stock, and the transport associated with its movement and positioning. However, inventory costs can be traded off against other elements of the distribution management mix, such as, for example, improved customer satisfaction levels. There are many reasons for holding inventory, some of which were given in 4:1. Any of these reasons can justify the use of warehouse or depot facilities which can provide:

(a) a storage point where safety stocks can be held;
(b) a transhipment point along the supply chain;
(c) a break bulk and order assembly facility.

Inventory management implies a stockholding strategy, embracing such considerations as inventory levels and replenishment policies. This will be influenced by market intelligence and forecasting, the latter being based on one or both of two systems. Either the forecast is entirely 'extrapolative', projecting into the future seasonally adjusted trends based on historic demand data, or it is 'causal' relying on the correct interpretation of external factors, (economic, social, demographic, technical, etc.). In reality forecasting is often a blend of these two systems.

2. Demand patterns

The pattern of demand for a product must be the starting point for any forecast of future demand. In some cases, this can provide quite accurate predictions — for example, demand may have been stable over a long period (e.g. the demand for light-bulbs), or there may be an underlying and easily discernible trend towards more or less consumption of the product (e.g. lager and wine sales are increasing at the expense of beer sales), or demand may be seasonal (as with Christmas goods, summer fashions or ice-cream).

However, factors such as the Single European Market (lager and wine sales), a very hot summer (beer and ice-cream) or increased use in the home of more sophisticated lighting (fluorescent or spot lights) can all have a causal effect on sales of the above products. Also, of course, one brewery's sales of beer can decline in the face of competition from another brewer, or from increased sales of a competitor's 'real ale' or perhaps from the introduction into the brewery's outlets (public houses) of 'guest beers'.

Thus demand for a particular manufacturer's product, or for products where there is strong competition in the market, can be quite random. In some instances, sudden 'rogue' demands may be manifest, for example, where a competitor is unable to meet his orders, or — again using the sale of beer as an illustration — a major sporting event is due to take place in the brewer's market area.

3. 'ABC analysis' or differential deployment

Because inventory will usually comprise slow- and fast-moving lines, management of the inventory is often based on a technique known as ABC analysis. This relies on the well-known

Pareto's law of distribution which states that approximately 20 per cent of the items in an inventory account for up to 80 per cent of turnover. These items, once identified, are classified as A products. Conversely, the majority of items which together account for the remaining 20 per cent of turnover are classified as B items. It is possible to refine the classifications to include A — fast, B — average and C — slow. A further refinement is to base the classification on either the volume, weight or value of the items.

4. Normal demand

It is a simple matter to calculate the average or mean demand for a product on a period basis — for example, a small brewery's mean weekly sales may be 100 barrels. However, unless demand is absolutely stable, there will be variations within this mean. In some weeks demand will exceed 100 barrels, in other weeks it will fall short.

This variation can be measured over a period of time. If the sum of the deviations from the mean is taken, this will, of course, by definition be zero.

5. The standard deviation

However, if each deviation from the mean described in **4** is squared (to remove negative values), the sum of the squares computed, the result divided by the number of observations and the square root of the quotient taken, this will give a measure of dispersion known as the *standard deviation*.

The calculation can be performed from an assumed mean, and many calculators contain a standard deviation function to assist the calculation. With large amounts of data, computer programs are available. The simple formula for the standard deviation is:

$$\sqrt{\frac{d}{n}}$$

where $d =$ the sum of the squares of the deviations from the mean
and $n =$ the number of deviations observed.

(For a comprehensive account of this technique see the M&E Handbook *Statistics*, 6th edn)

6. Use of the standard deviation

What is important about the standard deviation (s.d.) is that it can be used by statisticians to describe the normal curve of distribution (in this brewery case the distribution of weekly orders around a mean figure of 100 per week). If the deviations from the mean are evenly distributed around it, giving the bell-shaped normal curve of distribution (*see* Fig. 6.1), then we can say with some confidence that:

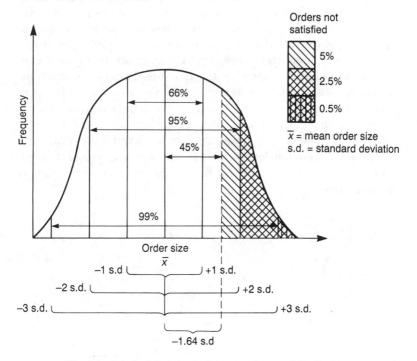

Fig. 6.1 *Standard deviation and the normal curve of distribution.*

(a) 66 per cent of all orders will fall within +/– 1 s.d. of the mean (i.e. between 100 + 1 s.d. and 100 – 1 s.d.);

(b) 95 per cent of all orders will fall within +/– 2 s.d. of the mean (i.e. between 100 + 2 s.d. and 100 – 2 s.d.);

(c) 99 per cent of all orders will fall within +/– 3 s.d. of the mean (i.e. between 100 + 3 s.d. and 100 – 3 s.d.).

Thus if the s.d. of the brewery's orders is 10 and the brewery carries stock of 100 barrels plus 2 s.d. (i.e. 120 barrels) then on 95 per cent of occasions the weekly orders received will not exceed 120 or be less than 80. Since they will do so on only 5 per cent of times, and half of these (i.e. 2.5 per cent of times) they will fall below 80 rather than above 120, the percentage probability of the brewery being out of stock will be 2.5 per cent. In other words, the brewery will be able to give a 97.5 per cent level of customer satisfaction, assuming customers order weekly.

It can be shown (*see* Figs. 6.1 and 6.2) that by holding a safety stock of mean demand + 1.64 s.d. of the mean, a producer can give 95 per cent customer satisfaction. It will never be possible to give 100 per cent satisfaction, as the size of the largest rogue order can never be predicted. However, a graph such as Fig. 6.2 can easily be constructed showing the relationship between levels of safety stock and customer service levels. From this it can be seen that at the 95 per cent service level large stock increases are needed to effect quite small increases in satisfaction, whilst small reductions in stock can produce correspondingly quite dramatic drops in satisfaction levels. This is why accurate calculation of safety stock levels is such an important element of inventory management.

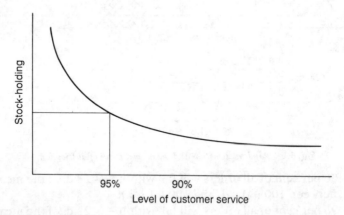

Fig. 6.2 *Relationship between stock-holding and customer service level.*

Forecasting

7. General

It is possible to make reasonable predictions of future sales based on historical data of past sales. These predictions may need to be adjusted in the light of experience to take account of external factors which might cause sales either to rise or fall. They may also need to be adjusted in order to strip out purely seasonal fluctuations so that any underlying trend line can be more clearly identified.

8. Moving averages

Probably the most simple method of forecasting is to construct a 'moving average' of sales based on historical data. Sales figures for a significant number of preceding sales periods (e.g. monthly sales) are listed in a column. The average of a number of the earliest month's figures is then computed and entered in the column to the right at the mid-point of the group of monthly sales figures chosen.

The calculation is then repeated for the same size group of monthly sales which includes the next following monthly sales figure but excludes the earliest figure. Thus, if initially the average of months 1–5 was selected, the next computation would be for months 2–6, then for months 3–7 and so on.

Care must be taken not to select too long a 'rolling' group of sales figures, as this will simply tend towards an average sales figure for, say, the year; similarly too short a 'rolling' period will fail to detect significant seasonal variations.

If necessary, where there are an even number of sales or demand figures, a moving average of the moving averages can be taken in order to arrive at a centred average.

9. Use of moving averages

Moving averages by their nature can only capture recent historical data, and can only be extrapolated forward for a short period. A crude trend line can be constructed by connecting on a graph of sales the mean monthly sales figure for early years with the mean monthly sales figure for the later years. These can be computed using moving averages rather as the draw table for the FA cup is devised. In this analogy, the two moving averages are the two semi-finalists!

It is also possible to 'weight' moving averages so that later or more recent demand or sales figures are given more weight in the calculations. This is done by multiplying each moving average in the group of data which generated the average by different weighting factors in such a way that the sum of the factors is zero. Thus, if the moving average for a four-month period is taken the weightings could be:

$$
\begin{array}{llll}
\text{Month 1} & \times & -1.5 & = & \text{w1} \\
\text{Month 2} & \times & -0.5 & = & \text{w2} \\
\text{Month 3} & \times & +0.5 & = & \text{w3} \\
\text{Month 4} & \times & +1.5 & = & \text{w4} \\
\end{array}
$$

$$\underline{W} \; = \; \text{weighted total}$$

and the formula: $$\dfrac{12 \times W}{n(n^2 - 1)}$$

where n = the number of periods used to compute W (4 in the example above), gives a value for the trend.

10. Exponential smoothing

A method of short-term forecasting which retains all historical data is exponential smoothing. This estimates demand for the following sales period by adding to or subtracting from a previous forecast a fraction of the difference between the actual demand for this period and the forecast for the same period:

Forecast = Previous forecast + s(Demand – Previous forecast)

This can be written:

$$F = f + s(d - f)$$

where F = Forecast
  f = forecast for previous period
  d = demand for previous period
  s = smoothing factor.

From the above:

$$
\begin{aligned}
F & = f + sd - sf \\
  & = f - sf + sd \\
  & = f(1 - s) + sd
\end{aligned}
$$

The choice of the smoothing factor s is initially arbitrary. It will lie between 0 and 1. If $s = 1$ then the forecast will simply equate to the previous period's demand (i.e. F = *d*), and if *s* = 0 then the new forecast will simply equate to the previous forecast (i.e. F = *f*).

Thus too high a smoothing factor will give too much weight to previous forecasts, too low a factor will give inordinate weight to past demand. After a number of forecasts have been made in this way it should be possible to calibrate the smoothing factor, that is identify if it is too high or too low and adjust it accordingly.

The formula can also be written:

$$f_{(n + 1)} = f_n(1 - s) + d_n s$$

where f_n = forecast for previous period *n*
  $f_{(n + 1)}$ = new forecast for next period *n* + 1
    d_n = demand (or sales) for previous period.

If $d_{(n + 1)}$ is known, it is then possible to compute $f_{(n + 2)}$ and so on.

Providing the sales and forecast are both known for the previous period and the value of the smoothing constant has been calculated, it is a simple matter to forecast sales for the following period. If the latest forecast is used as a proxy for demand and this process is repeated several times the difference between 'demand' and forecast $(d - f)$ becomes progressively less and is thus smoothed out — hence the name of this technique.

11. Long-term forecasting

A common approach is simply to graph historical sales figures and attempt to draw in a trend line by eye. A more accurate way is to use mathematical techniques to fit a line or curve to the existing data. The method of *least square regression analysis* does this in such a way that the sum of the squared (to eliminate minus quantities) deviations of the observed values from the line of best fit is minimised.

The generalised equation for a linear trend line is:

$$x = a + bd$$

where *d* is demand measured along the vertical or y-axis and *x* is the time scale in years, months or sales periods.

Whilst there are statistical formulae for calculating the coefficients *a* and *b*, there are also extremely good curve fitting software programs which will not only calculate these values, but also suggest other non-linear equations which might more precisely describe the long-term trends sought for forecasting purposes.

12. Seasonal adjustment

It is possible to isolate seasonality from the underlying trend lines — be they derived by exponential smoothing, moving averages or regression analysis — by calculating, and then applying, seasonal indices.

Thus if d = the demand in, say, the winter period, and m = the moving average for the same period, then the winter seasonal index will be:

$$I = \frac{100 \times d}{m}$$

Such indices if summed, say quarterly or monthly over a year, should equate to zero, and if not, any slight difference can easily be distributed between them. It is then a simple matter to 'de-seasonalise' the figures by multiplying $d \times I$ to arrive at a de-seasonalised trend.

Stock levels

13. General

The amount of stock carried at all locations, or at any one particular location along a supply chain, can drastically affect the costs — and hence the profitability — of manufacturers, third-party distribution agents (such as wholesalers or transport and warehousing contractors) and retailers. Although the saying 'Distribution adds costs not value' is not strictly correct in economic terms since a product in the market-place can be seen to have more value than at the factory gates, nevertheless it is true in so far as it is possible to make very significant savings by 'trading off' elements of the total distribution mix such as warehouse and delivery costs, or levels of stockholding and customer satisfaction levels.

14. The square root law

Total warehousing costs vary significantly with the number of depots employed. It has been calculated that the total inventory needed within a system is proportional to the square root of the number of locations at which the product is stocked. (This relationship is known as Maister's law.)

What does this 'law' tell us? Suppose we have nine warehouses and manage to reduce these to four. Our new stock level, as a proportion of the old level, would be:

$$\frac{\sqrt{4}}{\sqrt{9}} = \frac{2}{3}$$

i.e. a saving of one third of our stock.

15. Stockholding costs

Clearly the more stock that is held, the greater the holding costs will be. Stock has to be manufactured or purchased and thus represents cash tied up in the business, cash which could be put to more productive uses or invested to produce a dividend.

Stock also has to be accommodated, taking up warehouse floor space and possibly occupying racking or pallets. Warehouses have to be provided, staffed, heated (or, in the case of some temperature-controlled products, refrigerated), and the stock often has to be 'rotated' to ensure that it does not become out of date.

There are also inventory costs associated with stockholding, and where stock has to be repositioned within the distribution chain, there can be trunking costs.

It will be apparent from this that the highest stockholding costs are often associated with valuable or bulky items.

Clearly, stock tied up in the supply chain accounts for a significant part of total stockholding costs, and reducing the amount of stock so committed presents a major cost-saving opportunity. Such a strategy is helped today by the amount of 'real time' data currently accessible in modern distribution systems. Since it is information which makes goods flow, by making full use of information technology it is quite feasible to treat goods in transit as an integral part of current stockholding.

Thus the total of goods at the factory, goods in transit, and warehouse and depot stocks may be used as the basis of a reorder decision-making process based on demand forecasting. This method, known as *distribution requirements planning* (DRP), overcomes some of the limitations of traditional reorder point systems where restocking is carried out at each point in the distribution chain. This is especially so if DRP is combined with a system of *dynamic channel selection* (*see* 3:**24**, 6:**34**).

16. Distribution resource planning (DRP)

The basic principles of DRP are merely MRP principles applied to distribution inventories and transport. But its benefits go far beyond distribution into marketing, manufacturing, planning and finance.

DRP is largely a matching process, calculating distribution needs and assessing the matching pattern required at supply sources, thus creating a distribution-driven 'pull' system as opposed to a production-driven 'push' system. For each echelon in the distribution channel, DRP programs receive outputs (time-phased demand forecasts), and generate time-phased inputs (purchase or manufacturing orders). The planning horizons involved can often extend for 18 months, providing high-distance visibility for both inventory management and time-phased transport planning.

17. Stock acquisition

It is equally true to say that there are costs associated with the acquisition of stock. Transport is obviously one such cost. Another which is not always appreciated is the *opportunity cost* associated with bulk purchasing where suppliers are often prepared to offer significant discounts.

From the supplier's point of view, a bulk sale minimises unit transport costs (especially if the order exactly fills a delivery vehicle) and the transfer of the stock to his customer relieves him of some of his holding costs! The customer, however, must then weigh the discount he is offered against his increased holding costs.

18. Lead time

A critical factor in both the supplier's and customer's calculations will be the length of time taken to receive an order after it is placed. Many customers assess their suppliers on the time taken to satisfy their orders, as well as their reliability. Indeed these two factors are at the heart of the supplier/customer relationship. Past failures in this relationship are the most probable cause of the growth in retailer-led distribution systems.

The shorter the lead time, the smaller the inventories it is necessary to hold in the distribution chain. But reliability is also important in affecting the levels of safety stock required (*see* **19**).

As will be seen later, the use of information technology to capture and coordinate information on sales, production inventory levels, stock movements in transit and deliveries has grown enormously in the last decade. It enables distribution managers to distribute not only their product but the information affecting this operation quickly and accurately within their own organisations, thus aiding the making of day-to-day logistics decisions. It is a truism today that 'He who holds the data runs the operation!'

19. Safety stock

No supplier willingly runs out of stock. The result is not only lost sales, but also customer dissatisfaction together with the administrative cost of raising and eventually delivering the balance of the customer's order.

It has already been shown that a small reduction in stockholding can produce a disproportionate reduction in the level of service. The reverse is also true, so that there is obviously no point in stocking up to the ceiling to meet a hypothetically possible order of several times normal demand levels. As has been pointed out, there is a relationship between mean order size, the standard deviation of the distribution of the orders around this mean, and safety stock levels.

For example, it has been demonstrated that a safety stock comprising the mean demand for the product (over a given reordering cycle) plus 1.64 standard deviations from that mean will give a customer satisfaction level of 95 per cent. In other words, it will be possible to satisfy immediately 19 out of 20 of the customer's orders.

However, the longer the lead time, the greater the probability of an out-of-stock situation arising. It is thus usual to take this factor into account as follows. When the lead time is greater than one period the standard deviation of demand over lead time is:

$$1.64 \ \sqrt{L} \times \bar{x}$$

where x = mean demand (e.g. weekly)
     L = lead time (in weeks)
     $\bar{x}$ = standard deviation of mean x.

Unless lead time is very short or almost instantaneous, it will always be necessary to trigger an order before stock has run down to safety stock level.

20. Order point

The *order point* which will achieve this can be calculated from the following formula, in which the free stock (i.e. the mean weekly demand multiplied by the length of the lead time in weeks) is added to the safety stock calculated as before:

$$1.64 \ \sqrt{L} \times \bar{x} \ + \ L \times x$$

This formula is shown in graphical form in Fig. 6.3.
    The computation can of course be made measuring lead time in days or even hours.

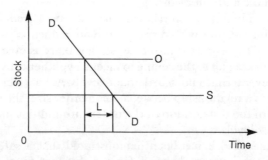

D – D = mean demand over time
$\bar{X}$ = mean demand per unit of time
L× $\bar{X}$ = mean demand over lead time
S = safety stock
O = order point
L = lead time

Fig. 6.3 *Calculation of order point.*

Replenishment policy

It is possible to apply the above concepts of safety stock (sometimes called *buffer stock*) and reorder levels to develop two models of replenishment policy.

21. Fixed reorder levels

This is by far the most common method of stock control. Because it relies on orders being triggered whenever stock reaches or falls below reorder level, and a simple method of monitoring inventory is to have two adjacent stock piles one of which represents the stock at reorder level, this model is often referred to as the 'two-bin system'. Provided that demand remains within the limit of mean plus one standard deviation the probability of an out-of-stock situation will, as already demonstrated, remain at 5 per cent and customers will enjoy a 95 per cent satisfaction level.

The amount of stock which is reordered when stock levels reach reorder point is an important inventory management consideration. Techniques, which will be described later, exist for calculating what is known as the economic order quantity (EOQ — *see* 22), and, in general, this is the amount reordered.

By dividing mean annual demand by the EOQ the length of the order cycle can be computed. This is the time which elapses between receipt of consecutive orders. Clearly this must be longer than the lead time. Ideally, the order cycle should be at least twice the lead time so that reordering can be triggered when average stock levels, i.e EOQ/2, are reached. It may be necessary, because of long lead times, production difficulties or extreme variations in demand (either seasonal or otherwise), to set a reorder quantity more or less than the EOQ, and accept the inventory diseconomies this will produce.

Three scenarios shown in Fig. 6.4 are worth exploring further in order to appreciate their consequences. The first order cycle conforms with all the standard criteria: demand is within the limits planned for, delivery of stock is accomplished within the lead time, and the EOQ is supplied. In the second order cycle, demand accelerates, and replenishment is late. This has two consequences. First, an out-of-stock situation is created, and balance orders become necessary. Secondly, when stock is received it is immediately depleted to satisfy these balance orders, so that the reorder level is reached immediately. In the third cycle, demand is suppressed (perhaps because customers, fearing a shortage, had over-ordered), and delivery after reorder is on schedule. As a consequence too much stock is held.

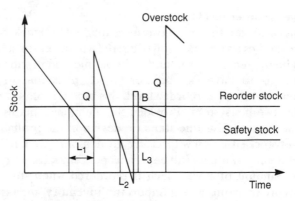

L_1 = lead time cycle 1 (standard)
L_2 = lead time cycle 2 (long)
L_3 = lead time cycle 3 (short)
OOS = out of stock
B = balance order
Q = EOQ

Fig. 6.4 *Consequences of variations in the fixed reorder level.*

Other scenarios, including worst case scenarios of large 'rogue' (or unexpected) orders coupled with supplier difficulties can easily be constructed. In some cases where known facts dictate the system must be adjusted by intervening and either ordering before (or after) the reorder level is reached or altering the quantity ordered.

22. Fixed reorder cycle

In some cases a customer does not have the luxury of being able to reorder and receive stock from within a fixed reorder time. Small corner shops, for example, must order their bread from the bakery's van salesperson when they call at a fixed time each morning, and, if they run out at tea time, have no means of replenishing their stock.

Equally, some large organisations operate a fixed reorder cycle. A brewery serving a rural area may schedule its dray to visit a remote public house every Tuesday and Friday, and may have agreed with the publican, based on considerations of what would be his EOQ, a standard order and fixed delivery days. The publican may then be told to expect a phone call from the brewery sales office on Mondays and Thursdays at a fixed time to check that the delivery is required and the amounts are right.

Once again if demand remains within the narrow limits of mean demand plus one standard deviation the system will cope. A one-off event, such as a village carnival, causing excess beer consumption, can easily in this system create an out-of-stock situation unless it has been predicted. Equally, poor sales, for example in bad winter weather, would cause the publican to become overstocked unless he cancelled some of his order.

The important consideration where a fixed reorder cycle exists is that the customer cannot adjust his stock by advancing or delaying his order point, but can only do so by ordering more or less than the EOQ.

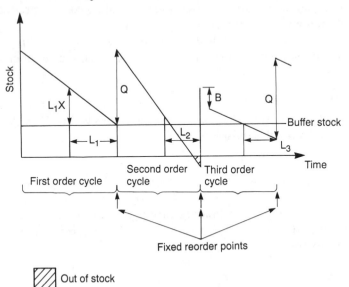

Fig. 6.5 *Consequences of variations in demand in the fixed reorder cycle.*

Figure 6.5 shows the results of poor or exceptional demand on this system. Rather than have a fixed reorder point, it is usual to have a fixed reorder level. For the sake of illustration, it is assumed that the publican did not adjust his second order after experiencing heavy demand. It is not, of course, always possible to raise balance orders — when a pub is out of stock of beer this represents lost sales which cannot be recovered. It may even represent lost trade as the level of satisfaction of the 'regulars' may be so badly eroded that they take their custom to the Red Lion across the road!

23. Economic order quantity

It has already been mentioned that there are two costs associated with ordering stock — the acquisition costs and the holding costs. It is possible to determine an optimum order size — the economic order quantity (EOQ) — such that if orders of this size are placed then a theoretically perfect trade-off can be made between all the acquisition costs and the holding costs to produce a minimum inventory cost.

The *acquisition costs* will be fixed costs per order (in our example, S/order). If annual demand is R units, the number of orders per annum will be:

R/Q

where Q is the EOQ. (Stock turnover in weeks is thus 52 x Q/R.) The total annual acquisition cost will be:

RS/Q

Holding costs per annum will be related to the percentage inventory costs of the product (I per cent) and its unit cost (C). Since the average stockholding throughout the year will be 50 percent of the EOQ, i.e. Q/2, then annual holding costs are given by the expression:

$$\frac{QCI}{2}$$

In a recent distribution cost survey (Institute of Logistics Distribution Management, 1991) where a sample of firms' inventories valued in total at £4,697 million was taken, stockholding costs were found to account for 15 per cent of this figure, or just under £700 million and the implied stock turnover (52Q/R) was 4.5 weeks.

If we graph the way in which holding and acquisition costs behave in relation to quantities ordered we observe that, quite obviously, holding costs increase as stocks increase but acquisition costs, reflecting the economies of bulk purchase, decrease. We can also see that the total cost of acquiring and holding stock, i.e.

$$\frac{RS}{Q} + \frac{QCI}{2}$$

is at a minimum where the two curves cross, and that:

$$\frac{RS}{Q} = \frac{QCI}{2}$$

We can transpose the above equation to obtain:

$$2RS = Q^2CI$$

thus:

$$Q^2 = 2RS/CI$$

and:

$$Q = \sqrt{\frac{2RS}{CI}} = EOQ$$

where R = sales per annum
S = acquisition cost per unit
C = cost of each unit
I = percentage inventory cost.

This is shown diagrammatically in Fig. 6.6.

24. An example
Using this formula we can calculate the EOQ given:

(a) price of commodity: £10;
(b) inventory holding cost: 20 per cent of (a);
(c) demand: 50,000 units p.a.;
(d) cost of placing an order: £5.

The denominator of the expression under the square root sign is CI. If C = £10 and I = 20 per cent, so CI = £2. The numerator, 2RS = 2 x 50,000 x £5 = £500,000. Thus:

$$Q = \sqrt{500,000/2}$$
$$= \sqrt{250,000}$$
$$= 500$$

We can also quite easily compute the number of orders per annum: R/Q = 50,000/500 = 100, which equate to ordering approximately twice per week. An example of this type of frequent replenishment might be potato crisps in a supermarket, where holding costs are high due to the space they are occupying in expensive retail premises.

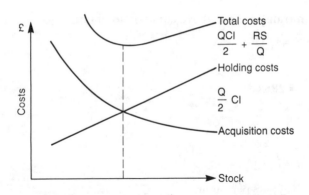

Fig. 6.6 *Economic order quantity.*

Material requirements planning

25. General
Yet another aspect of inventory management, the technique of material requirements planning involves calculating the required quantities of 'dependent demand' items (*see* **26**) and determining the timing of orders for them. This is done by working back from planned production of end-products — derived

from forecasting — to arrive at the planned acquisition and/or production of materials and parts.

26. Dependent and independent demand

The term 'dependent demand' explains the demand for a particular item — be it a component, item of material or subassembly — which is in turn dependent upon the demand for another item of which the former is an integral part. For example, in the assembly process, the demand for electric motors in tumble driers will depend on the number of tumble driers planned for production in a given period.

Such items and components will display a different pattern of demand, and therefore ideally require different methods of inventory control, than 'independent demand' items which are produced for their own intrinsic value. An example of an independent demand item would be a standard component which is manufactured and sold to industrial customers for various uses, the demand for which is geared directly to its own sales rather than to sales of another item of which it is an essential part.

Traditional methods of inventory control of such dependent demand items, such as the order point or order level, tend to lead to overstocking as the control mechanism focuses on the individual part or component only, not on the demand for the end-product into which the part will fit.

27. Material requirements planning (MRP)

Material requirements planning, however, is based on precise calculation and timing of orders, including both the point at which they are issued and their delivery lead times. Such calculations can be complex, particularly when a given part may be required for more than one subassembly or end-product, each of which may have widely-varying demand patterns.

In general, MRP is best suited to batch production, where the demand for both the end-product and its constituent parts is less consistent. Because of this, it is production-led rather than being controlled by inventory levels, and materials are ordered in 'product sets' according to the number of line items to be batch produced.

To operate an MRP system, accurate and comprehensive information is required on the following:

(a) master production schedule giving details of planned production over specified time periods;
(b) a breakdown of product structures (constituent parts) and bills of material (individual component quantities required);
(c) lead times for all parts and materials;
(d) details of uncommitted stocks and orders due in respect of relevant items.

With all this information to be collected, collated and presented in usable form, it is not surprising that MRP readily lends itself to computer application. Non-computerised systems have been applied although they are rather time-consuming.

27. Just-in-time (JIT)

'Just-in-time' is the concept of meticulously planned logistics and distribution operations, which helps reduce stocks, lead times and, therefore, costs. With such increased pressure on supply chain management for greater efficiency, it is crucial that materials and components are at the right place at the right time.

JIT creates a 'pull' mechanism in supply systems, whereby materials and products are drawn through the chain by demand and orders for products and commodities, rather than being pushed through to form work-in-progress and buffer stocks, etc. The main prerequisites for its implementation are short, dependable lead times and high levels of quality. These ingredients then remove the need for stockholding for reasons of unpredictable demand, interrupted or delayed supply and poor quality.

The forerunner of JIT was the Toyota Motor Company's 'kanban' system. 'Kanban' simply means 'card', and refers to a card-based record system of inventory control similar to the two-bin system (*see* **20**), which created a pull mechanism in the supply chain. Normally, such reorder level systems tend to produce increased inventories, so how could the kanban method be an improvement?

(a) Levels of production need to be very consistent.
(b) Every product is usually made each day.
(c) Component and materials suppliers are located close to production units, hence short lead times.

(d) Kanban cards are sent to suppliers to ensure timely arrival of replenishment orders.

The basic principle of JIT is therefore to have goods and material delivered exactly where and when required, literally just in time to make the next move along the supply chain, whether it be for production/processing or distribution. This can only be achieved by detailed forward planning and extensive use of information systems. It is not merely a particular method of distribution, but a total logistics concept which, if conscientiously implemented throughout a supply chain, means drastically reducing inventory and costs, and improving levels of service.

Essentially, there are three stages or elements to JIT:

(a) Elimination of inventory and its associated costs — stocks of any kind require capital investment and insurance.
(b) Dispensing with inventory storage — its space usage, handling and management costs.
(c) Concentration on quality — defective parts and materials are wasteful in terms of resources, energy and time. A total quality approach will mean getting things right first time, every time, to avoid material waste and process delays.

These aims can be achieved by planning demand requirements into the future, reducing batch sizes and shortening set-up times. A crucial role in JIT is taken by information technology in the form of computerised information processing and communications systems. On-line, real-time systems using EDI (*see* **31**) mean instant availability of information on supply chain requirements at strategic points in the network, thus enabling faster responses.

29. Usefulness of the JIT concept
How versatile then is JIT, and how widely applicable is it? In response, it cannot be applied to every product, particularly where demand is seasonal. It is, however, still used in many areas of purchasing, inventory management and distribution. In the retail grocery trade, for example, almost all floor space has been turned over to sales, and stores and stockrooms are now virtually non-existent. Consequently, deliveries of all fresh produce are made on a once-a-day basis or, in some cases, more frequently.

The application of such principles to industry has already brought considerable benefits. Company and logistics management need to recognise that JIT is not just a relatively new buzz-word, but an extremely useful business technique.

Order processing

30. General
The order processing system triggers every other operation in the logistics and distribution management function. Whilst in theory it is possible to manufacture, import or stock a product in anticipation of sales, in practice it is obviously much more profitable and efficient to do so in the certain knowledge of future sales, or at very least, on the basis of forecasts of sales based on current and historic demand.

The effect of variations in lead times on inventory levels has already been illustrated. Clearly reductions in lead time can produce distribution economies without sacrificing customer service levels. Equally clearly delays in processing orders will extend lead times producing diseconomies.

It is thus imperative that the moment an order is placed this should trigger action to satisfy that order. A system which relies on sales representatives taking orders in the field and posting these to a head office where they are processed and forwarded to a local delivery centre must by definition create longer than necessary lead times.

31. EDI networks
At the other extreme to the sales representative in the field are the supermarkets with electronic point-of-sale (EPOS) terminals which capture information (for example, by using a bar code reader at the check-out) by brand and size. This data is then fed into automatic stock replenishing systems.

Such systems nowadays rely on electronic data interchange (EDI) between retailer, supplier and manufacturer. With cooperation between all three it is possible for replenishment orders and associated data to be transmitted between computers, thus ensuring that all *logistic requirements planning* decisions are based on the very latest intelligence.

Such networking of EDI systems is already a reality. In the UK the TRADANET system links retailers and suppliers in the grocery trade, and the European Commission have drawn up a Community Action Plan relating to the electronic transfer of data. Called Trade Electronic Data Interchange System (TEDIS) it is intended to pre-empt a proliferation of incompatible closed-trade EDI systems.

32. Information systems

Information flows are an essential part of the logistics system. Without accurate and current information the system cannot respond efficiently. Information systems serve four main purposes:

(a) They serve as a *trigger mechanism* by producing instructions/documents necessary to activate other components of the system. For example, a proportion of the lead time between a customer placing and receiving an order is accounted for by the length of time that it takes to process the order and initiate action at the delivery depot, or, if necessary further up the distribution channel at regional warehouses or factory level.

(b) They *monitor and control* the system performance, ensuring that established cost and customer service objectives are met.

(c) They *coordinate* functions both within the system and between distribution and other key decision areas of the company.

(d) They *link* the internal systems to interrelated external systems such as suppliers, customers and third-party distribution operators.

33. Order processing systems

Figure 6.7 provides a flow chart illustrating a typical computerised order processing system. A manual system would produce the same results.

Most systems will generate invoices and delivery notes (in duplicate to facilitate proof of delivery). In addition it is possible to configure systems in such a way that they create other outputs such as inventory reports, warehouse picking lists and, where necessary, balance orders. Delivery drivers may even have a computer on board their vehicles or carry laptop computers. These, together with a small printer, can generate instantaneous

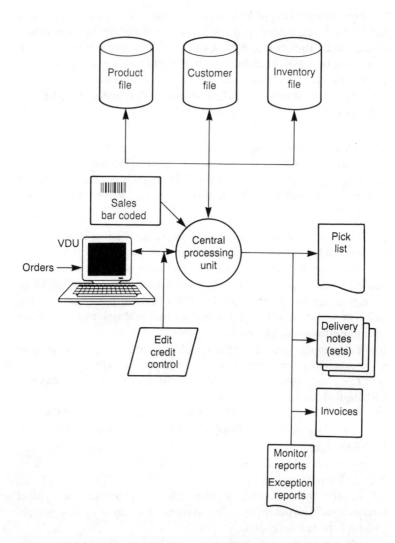

Fig. 6.7 *Typical computerised order processing system.*

delivery notes, a facility which van salesmen are finding invaluable. On return to the depot the information captured can be downloaded to a minicomputer or, via a modem and telephone line, to the firm's mainframe.

34. Demand-led distribution

Underlying the above strategies is the concept of responding as efficiently and economically as possible to customer demand. Not only does this allow customers to minimise their own stockholdings, which are often inordinately expensive in prime site retail locations, but also allows suppliers to minimise inventory costs by turning over stock quickly in the logistics chain rather than stockpiling. This naturally leads to the concept (described in 28) of just-in-time distribution, and the growth in the UK of retailer-led distribution systems.

Distribution requirements planning (*see* 16) is also obviously demand responsive, whilst materials requirements planning (*see* 27) is the complement of this where the manufacturer acts as if he were both customer and supplier of his own components and raw materials.

Given the requisite level of information in the logistics system it is even possible for orders to be processed centrally and delivery switched between warehouses or depots considering stockholdings and transport availability, thus treating all stockholding points as one 'UK warehouse' and making depot boundaries transient! This relatively new process, known as *dynamic channel selection*, is, of course totally dependent on reliable data flows.

35. Control systems

Whilst optimising the logistics function as described above is important, it is not necessarily of paramount importance. Marketing and production are also important activities which are influenced by, and in turn influence, the logistics function. There may well be direct trade-offs between, for example, trunking and local delivery costs, but there will also be indirect trade-offs between, say, lost sales and inventory savings.

An efficient information system is also invaluable as an aid in identifying, evaluating and monitoring both direct and indirect trade-off mechanisms. For example, it should be possible to measure the indirect effect on sales of reduced stockholdings or the direct effect on distribution and trunking costs of changes in the number of depots.

It is also true that although distribution has been described as the 'last frontier of cost reduction' there is no point reducing distribution costs if in the process sales revenue suffers. Conversely, if a manufacturer is making a profit margin of 10 per cent on sales, then a saving of £10 is equivalent to the profit on sales of £100, and it is often easier to make the saving than generate the sales. This concept, known as 'profit leverage', is a powerful rationale for periodic 'auditing' of the logistics function to identify any wastage in the system.

To carry out such an 'audit', it is necessary to have performance indicators to make comparisons with past performance and, where the figures are available, with individual competitors or with the averages for an industry. Examples of such indicators include:

(a) unit handling and storage costs;
(b) stock turn velocity, i.e. average inventory life in weeks;
(c) customer service levels, i.e. percentage deliveries made as complete orders from stock;
(d) average lead times;
(e) stock shrinkage measured as:

$$100\% \times \frac{\text{(Theoretical stock)} - \text{(physical stock)}}{\text{Theoretical stock}}$$

This last performance indicator raises the issue of stock integrity, discussed below.

Stock integrity

36. General

In view of the substantial investment represented by inventories and the associated costs of servicing them, managing the risks to which they may be exposed in order to retain maximum value of the investment is an integral part of good inventory management. Moreover, commodity and product condition on arrival from suppliers often feature prominently as elements in the customer service equation, therefore attention to stock integrity and minimising any risks are vital parts of good stock management.

The risks to stocks fall into four categories:

(a) *Deterioration* — merely loss of saleable/usable condition, or positive contamination or infestation by foreign matter or vermin.

(b) *Damage* — caused by poor packaging, incorrect handling, storage or transport. This can range from superficial damage to breakage beyond repair.

(c) *Loss* — due to poor stock control procedures (goods inwards, dispatch, or stock location), operator error, 'shrinkage', fire or flood. The latter two may be considered 'acts of God', but the remainder are manageable.

(d) *Depreciation/obsolescence* — brought about by poor stock control or unforeseen market changes. Again, these are largely situations where some planning and management of the situation will repay much of the effort expended.

Suggestions as to solutions to these problems are given in **37–39** below.

37. Deterioration

Essential steps are effective stock rotation procedures/systems and quality of packaging to ensure correct stock turnover sequence and protection from loss of quality over required time periods. In addition, a correct storage environment must be provided, bearing in mind the requirements of various products and commodities when held in stock. This will take account of such things as temperature, humidity, cleanness, exposure to air or natural light, and pest control.

Although many FMCG commodities are stored in a suitable temperature-controlled environment these days, it is not always appreciated that other commercial and industrial items need to be kept well protected and in an appropriate environment to maximise their condition. Even storage location can have an effect on this, as one company found after having placed certain items of confectionery on the top level of the warehouse racking below the roof lights. On eventual examination by customers, the chocolate was found to have melted — presumably in the warmth of the sunlight!

38. Damage

Packaging must be properly designed in order to keep items in marketable condition throughout the period spent in a storage environment. Also it must be of sufficient strength and durability to withstand the various physical forces to which it will be exposed during transport, handling and storage operations as it moves along the supply chain. This could be well illustrated by the trade-off between more costly, higher quality protection and reduced amounts of stock written off or sold cheaply as damaged. For some third-party operators, it could mean reduce goods-in-transit (GIT) premiums.

Formal instruction and training of warehouse staff in correct handling and storage methods, safe use of mechanical handling equipment, and effective supervision will help reduce the incidence of damaged returns from customers. A further advantage would be the acquisition and use of mutually compatible handling and storage systems and equipment, including methods of unitisation. Block stacking remains a popular storage method in many areas of logistics activity, largely for items held in bulk for short time periods. Here, quality of packaging and compatibility of handling units — usually pallet sizes — will be instrumental in ensuring that storage blocks are stable and product quality remains at the appropriate level.

39. Loss

Standardisation on effective stock control procedures, coupled with an appropriate level of supervision, is necessary to avoid re-peated loss or misplacement of items within the system. Checking of goods into the warehouse for correct quantity, condition and description will reduce, if not eliminate, errors of this nature. Fortunately, data capture and processing systems now exist to enable much faster and more accurate checking of such informa-tion on arrival of goods and materials at warehouses, factories and distribution centres. The human element, however, is still present, and the aforementioned speed and accuracy will be dependent on the skill, experience and conscientiousness of terminal operators.

Familiarisation with and, where necessary, training and frequent monitoring of such systems — whether they be manual or computer-based — is again likely to reduce this area of risk considerably. Despite the advances of information technology, it is essential to have a fallback position based on manual methods which can be used in the event of a temporary computer system failure.

'Shrinkage', the euphemism often used nowadays for pilferage, theft or fraud, is often the result of temptation among in-company staff or visitors of varying descriptions — including employees of associated transport/distribution organisations — as well as opportunist thieves from outside. Attempts of any kind must be rendered pointless by means of suitable deterrent measures. For example:

(a) Ensure a comprehensive goods-in/out checking system is enforced.
(b) All private vehicles should be parked away from warehouse premises — preferably in a separate compound.
(c) Where possible, offer cut-price or free goods to staff and possibly other selected visitors.
(d) Where this is warranted, institute random physical checks of staff and visitors entering and leaving the premises and ensure effective disciplinary action where own employees' misconduct is a factor. Also, notify other organisations and police in the event of third parties being involved.

Finally, draw up a list of fire precautions, with the assistance of fire service personnel if necessary, and acquire suitable equipment for use by staff in the event of an emergency. Where fire is a specific risk because of the presence of certain commodities, this will mean staff training in safe working procedures and appropriate emergency action. It may also mean the planning-in of certain building and equipment features in order to minimise this area of risk. Thoughtful planning at the design stage and appropriate professional advice, linked to careful building maintenance, should also reduce the risk of any damage from storm or flood.

40. Depreciation/obsolescence
Correct use of an accurate stock control system should ensure items are brought forward for order assembly or commodities are used at the right time, therefore ensuring correct stock rotation. Inventory management policy should include a regular review of all items of stock, particularly those of C classification, i.e. slow-moving items (*see* **3**). Where demand is perceived as falling, and this is confirmed as a trend, decisions by distribution or marketing management may be called for regarding continued

stockholding of such items. A major factor in this decision will be sales/usage value and stockholding costs. Accurate forecasting techniques and market intelligence will of course assist in reducing the occasions on which this may be necessary, by providing demand data as accurate and current as possible — and which will be reviewed frequently in the light of changes in the market-place.

Progress test 6

1. What is the purpose of stockholding? **(1)**

2. What common demand patterns can you identify? **(2)**

3. What do you understand by ABC analysis, DRP, LRP, JIT delivery and DCS? **(3, 16, 27, 31)**

4. What percentage of orders will normally fall within +/– two standard deviations of the mean order size? **(6)**

5. What level of safety stock should you carry to give a 95 per cent customer satisfaction level? **(19)**

6. Describe three methods of forecasting. How can forecasts be seasonally adjusted? **(8, 10, 11, 12)**

7. What stockholding costs can be saved by closing one of four depots? **(14)**

8. How are safety stocks and reorder points related? **(20)**

9. Describe the two most common replenishment systems. **(21, 22)**

10. What two factors affect economic order quantities? **(23)**

11. Give an example of an EDI network. **(31)**

12. Outline three ways in which stock integrity may be breached. **(36)**

7
Materials handling and the storage function

1. Introduction

At the interface between materials supply production/ processing and distribution, there is invariably some kind of handling operation and, in many cases, a storage facility. The extent to which this occurs is determined by the spatial relationship between raw materials sources, production/processing units, and the size, geographic spread and concentration of a company's markets. If it were a case of merely handling materials from supply vehicles to production processes, or from production lines to distribution vehicles for final delivery, then only a need for handling operations would exist. However, as a continuous flow of goods and commodities along the supply chain, without resorting to any form of holding operation, is still a target to be achieved for a large percentage of companies, then some kind of storage option must remain as part of many logistics and distribution operations. This chapter will examine a few of the more common systems in this area of logistics activity, and address some of the issues involved in materials handling and warehouse management.

2. Materials handling

At first glance, materials handling might be considered as something relatively straightforward such as moving pallets with a fork-lift truck. Although this is a classic example of such an activity, modern logistics operations have transformed the erstwhile field of mechanical handling into a much more sophisticated industrial science with a number of branches. These branches, although specialist fields in themselves, are all interdependent functions on which the total effectiveness of a materials handling system will depend.

The field of materials handling, then, comprises:

(a) packaging
(b) unitisation
(c) mechanised and automated handling systems.

These are discussed in greater detail in the sections which follow.

Packaging

3. Functions of packaging
Packaging is a function vital to most effective materials handling processes, and the need for it depends on the basic state of the commodity or goods to be handled. Some commodities, such as petrol, remain in their bulk state even after reaching the end of the supply chain, and have no need for packaging as they are transferred to the end-user in bulk. Others, like milk, or even another petrochemical industry product such as motor oil, are brought to consumers in packaged form. This form is largely dictated by the demands of the market, but is also shaped by the practical needs of efficient channels of distribution.

Basically, packaging fulfils three functions:

(a) containment
(b) protection
(c) information.

4. Containment
This ensures that, depending on the physical state of the commodity, it reaches the consumer or end-user in a convenient form and quantity. Essential for a whole range of consumer and industrial goods and materials, packaging overcomes the handling problems of such diverse products as baked beans, sauce, biscuits, most toiletries and cosmetics, as well as others such as office stationery, paints and fertilisers. What DIY customer can go to one of the large national outlets and purchase items such as nails, screws and even many tool items without having to discard some minimum amount of packaging before using them?

Thus this function of packaging is to retain items for purchase in convenient quantities for display and sale; it thus also aids merchandising and bulk purchasing. However, the basic intention is containment of the goods — a long way from the old-fashioned brown paper bag!

5. Protection

This is an essential factor in these days of high customer expectations as far as product quality and condition are concerned. Total quality is the goal currently being pursued by many businesses, and although this objective should also relate to internal processes within the organisation, quality of the good, commodity or service which is sold to the customer is paramount — whether the reason is for a sharper competitive edge, greater market share, improved corporate image, increased profits, or a combination of more than one of these.

How many shoppers would hesitate to pick up an item of bruised fruit from the display gondola of a well-known national supermarket, or a badly dented tin of canned produce from one of their shelves? Most will see such items as having lost some of their quality, and consequently select similar items which have found their way along the distribution chain unscathed. As mentioned in 6:35–38 on stock integrity, physical damage is not the only risk from which commodities should be protected by good packaging. Again, in the field of foodstuffs, the layers and protective qualities of modern packaging provided in order to retain maximum freshness and minimise the risk of any kind of contamination are considerable. But this type of measure is now typical not only of the food, drink and tobacco industry, but also of numerous others such as toys, electrical goods and, again, many DIY materials.

6. Information

The final basic function of packaging, the provision of information is equally vital both to the customer and all those handling or dealing with the product along the supply chain. For the customer, packaging provides basic information on the product — item, model, size, colour, ingredients, instructions for use and so on, some of which may be legal requirements. Furthermore, as part of the merchandising process, it can be a forceful marketing tool in helping to promote and strengthen brand identity.

From the logistics and distribution point of view, the main purpose of packaging is that of identification of the packaged product. Quick, clear identification during goods receiving, picking and delivery operations is essential to generate the required degree of cost-effectiveness and customer satisfaction in terms of order correctness, and to minimise errors. The usefulness of this function is also evident when it comes to stocktaking and replenishment routines where many items of packaging nowadays incorporate either information easily readable for use with manual systems, or some form of machine-readable code such as bar-coding.

7.   Types of packaging

The whole spectrum of packaging is divided into two main types:

(a)   primary packaging, and
(b)   secondary packaging.

These are discussed in detail in the sections which follow.

8.   Primary packaging

This type has as its main purpose containment — it is the packet or container immediately next to the product. Even so, like so many distribution issues, it is impossible to say that any one form of packaging is so limited in its function. In several areas of manufacturing and distribution, products are often presented in more than one variety of primary packaging: an inner bag or wrapper to contain the product and retain its quality, and an outer carton or other container to contain the inner wrapper, to protect it from lesser damage and — most importantly — to carry the product description and brand name and/or company logo for marketing and merchandising purposes. The usefulness of such packaging is, of course, largely limited to the materials handling function which takes place as part of production processes, and to the wider marketing aims of the company, once the commodity reaches the appropriate sales outlet.

9. Secondary packaging

Secondary packaging, however, fulfils a much wider role as far as total distribution operations are concerned. In most cases, secondary packaging consists of large outer cartons of stout, durable cardboard, which are capable of containing convenient multiples of the primary packaging units. Here, the function is mainly one of protection from the various physical risks to which the goods may be exposed during handling, storage and transport.

Along with this requirement goes the ability of such cartons or similar units to be stacked for the purposes of palletisation and/or other forms of unitisation, without damage to the primary packaging units inside. Robust cardboard cartons are a prerequisite for block storage of palletised goods, unless pallet converters are used, or metal industrial pallets. As unitisation, most particularly palletisation, is now almost universally used, such a facility in secondary packaging is vital.

Nonetheless, a considerable element of the containment and identification functions is still present, the identification function discussed in **6** being especially important during transit and storage.

In addition, secondary packaging often serves as a deterrent against pilferage, depending on the strength of fastening or method of securing cartons or outer packaging. Their bulk alone will often make it extremely difficult for complete units to be removed from manufacturing, storage and transport facilities undetected.

10. Packaging materials

In some areas of materials handling and distribution packaging materials have changed substantially in recent times, a much greater percentage now consisting of synthetic materials. Perhaps it is appropriate at this point to distinguish between the two type of packaging materials in terms of their function. The first, the purpose of which falls precisely into the containment, protection and information category, is essentially some kind of container; the second is a packing material inserted into packages to provide additional protection against the likelihood of physical damage.

The latter in many cases consists of such materials as polystyrene mouldings or granules and bubble-wrap, but large quantities of more traditional materials such as corrugated cardboard and tissue paper are still used in the distribution of books and some household items. Particularly where distribution is direct to customers from manufacturers, or distribution centres deal with small individual orders, use and choice of this type of packing material is extremely important for product quality and high levels of customer service.

In the role as protective containers or coverings, the implications for distribution of the kind of material used are much wider. Although the ubiquitous cardboard carton remains the most popular form of primary and more particularly secondary packaging, other forms have been on the distribution scene for some time. Numerous companies in transport, distribution and manufacturing now protect their unitised goods with either polythene shrink-wrap or plastic-based stretch-wrap. Both these materials have the capacity to protect cartons, bottles or other containers from water damage, dust, dirt and grime, which might adversely affect the customers perception of the product. At the same time, they bind together or keep in position cartons on a pallet and bottles, cans or tins in a cardboard tray, thereby building into the larger handling unit a greater degree of stability. Even in primary packaging, present-day synthetics play a considerable role in the form of both polystyrene-moulded packing material, or moulded celluloid as an impervious protective cover for many household and consumer items sold on convenient merchandiser cards.

11. Implications of packaging

From a cost point of view, packaging remains an interesting issue. It may lack the impact of a momentous capital project, but packaging is a multi-million pound industry, and its cost to the manufacturing and distribution industry is considerable. Many companies still tend to skimp somewhat on the quality of their packaging — to their detriment. Increased packaging costs can be justified — provided they buy stronger, more durable protection — on the grounds that they can be traded off against much-reduced claims and damages, thereby reducing administration costs, increasing customer service levels, and eventually reductions in or stabilisation of GIT insurance premiums.

Finally, the nature of packaging plays an influential part in determining certain variables in other parts of the logistics and distribution system. The volume capacity of palletised outer cartons containing packets of cereal, for example, determines vertical distances between warehouse racking beams and therefore, to a certain extent, the degree of cubic capacity/volume utilisation in at least part of the warehouse where they may be stored. The same is true of such items as bedding, duvets, pillows, etc., and many large toys. These are just one or two examples of how appropriate packaging for a product or commodity can, to a certain extent, determine the nature of a handling and storage system. In some cases, however, the reverse is true, and package sizes are determined by cost and space constraints in such areas as transport and storage.

Unitisation

12. General
The formation of multiple packages or containers into a single standardised uniform load for handling and storage purposes has become one of the cornerstones of effective materials handling and distribution systems. Rushton and Oxley in the *Handbook of Logistics and Distribution Management* (London: Kogan Page) describe unitisation as 'an assembly of individual items or packages, usually of a like kind, to enable convenient composite movement'. Unitisation creates greater efficiency of movement along the supply chain. In some cases, it may also help to maximise use of storage space.

13. Types of pallet and their uses
There is such a wide variety of handling unit currently in use that to consider them all would be a mammoth task. However, many are direct derivatives of two basic types: wooden pallets, and metal pallets, bins and cages. In the following sections we will briefly explore the nature and value of these basic types of pallet from a distribution management point of view.

14. Wooden pallets
From the original basic idea of a slatted wood platform on which packages and containers could be mechanically moved in

multiples, many different types of wooden pallet have proliferated, most particularly in size. This was largely due to manufacturing and distribution companies' individual product and packaging requirements, including the need for covered or carton pallets. This is early evidence of the product and its packaging driving the design and development of handling units and, eventually, equipment and systems.

More recently, however, irrespective of such factors as accessibility, e.g. two-way versus four-way entry pallets, a greater degree of standardisation is gaining centre stage in the theatre of handling and storage operations. Two main pallet sizes now predominate: the 1,000 mm x 1,000 mm unit, and the GKN-type 1,000 mm x 1,200 mm unit or Euro-pallet. Approaching 1992, standardisation on a single pallet size for pan-European distribution operations is an essential goal for all organisations involved, but there may well be implications for existing systems — most particularly for transport vehicle design and with regard to limits on EC weights and dimensions legislation.

Universal use of the wooden pallet has been achieved as a result of its versatility. It is an excellent handling and storage unit for most consumer and commercial products, as well as for many industrial ones. Moreover, wooden pallets are cheap in terms of individual unit cost, although a company having, say, 40,000 pallets in circulation at a replacement cost of £5 each has some £200,000 tied up in handling units alone. Even accounting for a fairly high replacement rate, owing to pallet damage, breakages and 'losses', the basic trade-off in using traditional pallets is that of high turnover versus low replacement cost.

A solution to the pallet control problem has, of course, been with us for some time — GKN's Chep pallet pool scheme. Under this scheme pallets are 'hired out' in various quantities and moved around the country. The cost of any unaccounted-for units is debited to the customer to whom they were on hire at the time in question and, with their distinctive blue colour, the combination of this ease of identity and automatic charging system ensures a greater degree of control. Continued development of the GKN scheme has also meant that their standard size unit — 1,000 mm x 1,200 mm — has eventually become more popular, helped along by more recent changes in the overall permitted dimensions of road freight vehicles.

Taking the wooden pallet to its logical development has produced the disposable pallet. In this form, it comes as an ultra-low cost item made of such materials as plastic, cardboard or polystyrene, and is intended for disposal after its one and only productive journey. Unit control is therefore unnecessary, and cost negligible.

15. Metal pallets, bins and cages

As logical developments of the original wooden pallet, these slightly more specialised units were designed specifically for the engineering and automotive industries and FMCG distribution.

Purpose-designed for operations where product weight and density tends to be high, units for the engineering and automotive industries consist of mesh-sided or post pallets with tubular metal frames and are used for castings, subassemblies, heavy cartons, etc. Other similar types of unit are solid-sided bins and stillages for smaller castings, nuts, bolts and washers. Any of these types have bases designed to be handled by fork-lift trucks or similar equipment, and to stack one on another.

Units for FMCG distribution consist mainly of the roll-cage, a lighter, higher, aluminium-framed version of its industrial relatives, which is moved on its own wheels. Designed for lightness and a high degree of manual manoeuvrability, these units are used almost exclusively in the confectionery, toiletries and cosmetics, boxed household goods and clothing businesses. Whereas industrial pallets are intended for handling by mechanical handling equipment and vehicle side-loading, roll-cages can easily be manually handled and vehicles can be similarly loaded with the assistance of a suitable tail-lift.

The main considerations with regard to such metal units are those of cost and pallet control, but with a greater emphasis on both. Their very nature makes such handling units far less prone to damage and breakage, but just as vulnerable as far as 'loss' is concerned. They are highly durable and much more expensive, representing a far greater investment in such equipment than their wooden equivalents, thus an effective control system is essential in order to minimise turnover costs.

16. Other types of container

In addition to those mentioned above, a wide variety of crates, trays, baskets and skips — mostly durable, but some of low-cost, disposable materials — exist in other slightly more specialised areas of distribution. A typical example is the intermediate bulk container (IBC) used in some areas of the chemical and rubber industries. All serve but one purpose — to increase the efficiency of handling and storage operations.

17. International units

The concept of unitisation has long been established in the field of international transport and distribution, and both air freight and surface freight operators' methods continue to be centred on industry-standardised equipment. These are discussed in the following sections.

18. Unit-load devices

Airline operators and freight forwarders move a substantial percentage of their cargo in IATA containers or unit-load devices (ULDs). Consisting of aluminium covered containers or freight cargo rafts with load-securing nets of specified dimensions and permitted payloads, they can be used for relatively small belly-hold cargoes on passenger flights or larger consignments on dedicated cargo aircraft. Yet again, the trade-off exists in the much shorter handling time required for transhipment of this kind of air freight, as opposed to the time required to handle large numbers of smaller units.

Airlines not only use such standard units for the handling and transport of freight, but also for storage and handling of galley stores and catering supplies. Standardisation is important, as these trolleys have to fit neatly into the purpose-designed niches in the aircraft. Also made from aluminium, they are both costly and highly desirable — from the point of view of airline caterers and competitors alike — therefore some kind of effective tracking system and regular audit is necessary to protect such a substantial investment.

19. ISO containers

As far as surface transport is concerned, the most popular handling and transport unit remains the ISO container. In its many forms — whether as a basic 'box' or one of the more specialised derivatives — its universal use is based on its versatility in terms of the commodities for which it can be used, and its intermodal capability of being transported by road, rail or sea.

Although 30-foot modules are still in domestic use on the Freightliner system, the international standard remains the 20-foot unit, with the capacity of fourth-generation container vessels still being measured in 20-foot equivalent units (TEUs) and 40-foot containers being the longest available. What has changed in the world of containerisation in recent years is the increased capacity — achieved not by changing module lengths, but by increasing container heights. The mid-1970s saw a move from the standard 8′ to 8′6″, and the early 1980s from 8′6″ to 9′. So that such containers could be used on the British railway network, a certain amount of heightening and widening of bridges also had to be accomplished. The development of these 'high container' routes, and the proximity of direct rail links with mainland Europe, has now provided the opportunity for many companies to take a more integrated view of logistics and distribution operations by use of containerisation.

In ISO container operations, as in many other fields of unitisation, one of the main problems is the utilisation factor. Is each handling unit accounted for at each stage of a given movement, and is its use being maximised? Like road freight vehicles, these units ideally should have 'return loads' or at least some kind of payload to take them on to another destination from which they can be profitably returned to their point of origin. International container operators continue to suffer from one-way traffic, often being obliged to transport their units empty back to where they are sure to obtain their next profitable payload. Even GKN have to transport their empty 'pool' pallets in vehicle loads in order to get them back to where they can be most profitably used.

20. Advantages and disadvantages of unitisation
The advantages of unitisation are:

(a) *Increased productivity* during the materials handling process due to handling of packages in multiples at each single movement.

(b) *Standardisation of handling units*, which contributes toward further standardisation in handling equipment, storage equipment and transport vehicles.

(c) Less damage and soiling of goods through reduced handling of packages, and the ability to cover unitised packages with an overall protective wrapping.

Disadvantages, however, are seen as:

(a) *Initial capital investment*, particularly in the more costly types such as metal pallets, roll cages and international freight containers.

(b) *Replacement costs.* Turnover, for example, in a company's wooden pallet stock can be considerable as a result of damage and breakages, to say nothing of their usefulness and high degree of mobility — which often leads to large numbers 'disappearing'. In the case of metal pallets and more expensive handling units, it is essential that logistics and distribution management devise an effective tracking system, in order to protect both the investment they represent and retain continuity of handling operations.

(c) *Imbalance of traffic and material movement*, which creates, in many cases, the problem of returning empty units.

The overall benefit of unitisation is the extent to which it is cost-effective in reducing total commodity handling and movement, and the associated costs.

Mechanised and automated handling systems

21. General

Unitisation is only the first step towards increased efficiency in the field of materials handling. It is necessary also to have suitable equipment for the easier handling of unit-loads and faster movement of packages along the supply chain. Mechanised and automated handling systems therefore include not only the various types of industrial truck which are designed for the handling and movement of unit-loads, but also conveyor systems used for the movement of packages and crane systems for high-level storage, retrieval and order-picking.

22. Materials handling trucks and cranes

In most stores and warehouses, the total operation comprises a standard sequence of activities — discharge of delivery vehicles and goods receiving, putting away of items in storage locations, their eventual retrieval for further delivery or replenishment of picking locations, and picking of line items for orders. A wide range of mechanical handling equipment has been developed to assist in many of these activities, and initially can be divided into three categories:

(a) pallet trucks
(b) lift and reach trucks
(c) crane systems.

These are discussed in detail in the sections which follow.

23. Pallet trucks

The range of trucks used for handling unitised loads starts with the basic *hand-pallet truck* — essentially a wheeled set of forks with a long handle, which looks like and operates on the principle of the hydraulic car-jack. Small, relatively inexpensive, and quite manoeuvrable, they are very useful for the handling and movement of palletised goods at ground level in depots and warehouses, and in many instances for order picking. Power is of course provided by the operator.

There are, however, two developments of the basic hand-pallet truck which add a little more flexibility to its use. First, there is the *powered pallet truck* (also known as the *pedestrian pallet truck*), which has the same function as its predecessor but is electrically powered, and sometimes has a small platform on which the operator can ride. Movements can be carried out faster using this kind of truck, and it is still a very compact, manoeuvrable tool for use in almost any kind of storage unit. Secondly, there are a number of *compact stacker trucks* in the stand-on or man-rider category, which provide the capacity to lift and stack palletised and similar items up to varying heights depending on their specification. A larger development of the powered pallet truck, they are still a very compact and versatile handling tool.

Neither a pallet truck nor a lift truck or crane, but one the use of which is restricted to ground level, is the *automatic guided vehicle* or AGV. Essentially a tow truck, these machines follow the path of guide wires laid just below the store or warehouse floor, drawing behind them a variety of unpowered trucks carrying goods and materials for storage and dispatch. Unmanned, they are remote controlled, travel at walking pace, and usually have a power cut-off device which operates if an object is detected a few feet ahead in its path — a useful safety device. Use of AGVs is normally justified only on the larger storage and warehousing sites, where travel distances from receiving areas to storage areas, and from the latter to order assembly and dispatch points, are such that use of manned handling equipment for product movement would be an expensive option.

This first category of handling equipment is relatively inexpensive in terms of both capital and operating costs, and components are fairly versatile but somewhat limited in their use. Nevertheless, their capacity for reducing handling time in many operating situations affords opportunities for significant cost reductions.

24. Lift and reach trucks

Perhaps the most-used type of mechanised handling equipment is the *fork-lift truck* or FLT — the standard workhorse of many depots and warehouses. Its most common form, the counter-balance truck is universally employed in numerous factories and warehouses for the handling and movement of mainly palletised, but also other kinds of unitised loads. Counter-balance FLTs are very versatile, and not as expensive as some of their more specialised successors, but do need a considerable area in which to move and turn, a factor which may discount their use in situations where high levels of storage space utilisation are necessary. But with their capacity to lift safely up to a height of six or eight metres, they are an invaluable piece of equipment in many depots and warehousing units. Their advantages in use are speed of movement, height of lift, manoeuvrability and choice of power source. This last point enables them to work in outdoor locations if powered by diesel or l.p.g. fuel, or indoors if electrically powered.

Reach trucks are a slight variation on the basic FLT theme, in that they can lift unitised loads safely up to heights of around 8–10 metres and, as both forks and mast have a forward movement capability, can reach into stacks and racking to withdraw pallets. With a smaller superstructure and wheelbase, they can also operate within the confines of narrower aisles than counter-balance FLTs, which makes them more desirable for high-density storage operations. A logical development of the reach truck is one which can access pallets stored two-deep in special racking. Although this seems a useful facility, it is perhaps not as common as might be expected, in spite of equipment manufacturers' claims of the high density storage which can be achieved in using such a system.

Essentially, FLTs and the reach truck derivatives are *free-path machines*. This means they can operate and transport unitised loads anywhere on a factory site, materials store, warehouse or distribution centre, mainly because their safe working load demands that their lifting operations are limited in height, and they are thus fairly stable.

However, in order to run an effective high-density storage operation, some form of free-path equipment is required which can handle storage and retrieval at even higher levels. To fulfil this role, a more specialised and highly stable machine has been developed, which can store and retrieve pallets at high levels and use even narrower aisles, as the truck's forks can pivot to right or left and the machine itself cannot and does not need to turn. These are often referred to as *turret trucks*, *high-rack stackers* or *very narrow aisle trucks*. Although they are considered to be free-path machines and can move anywhere, pallet-lifting operations are restricted to aisles only, and outside these aisles speed is normally much reduced. Alignment in aisles and floor flatness are both crucial elements in the safe operation of these machines, and they are usually guided between sets of racking by guide-rails at floor level, or wires situated below floor level. With some types, power is transmitted to them by the guide-rails, which further limits their capability when manoeuvring in open areas.

When operating above eight metres, some measures are required to ensure safety and accuracy of unit-load location and withdrawal, as the operator at ground level is too remote to exercise such fine judgment. This is usually achieved by marking the telescopic masts at driver level to denote a certain height has been reached, or by providing a miniature camera located at fork level which relays a picture of the fork position to a mini-TV in the truck cab.

Further variations on the free-path high-level truck consist of a number of *order-picking trucks*, many of which transport the operator up to the required level for picking purposes. A small platform, which can carry both operator and appropriate handling unit, is incorporated into the design for this purpose.

All the vehicles described in this section are essentially free-path items of equipment which are capable of at least limited use anywhere in a storage or distribution complex. The latter classes of truck are noticeably more expensive in capital terms than the less sophisticated ones, but perform a more specialised role, and are intended for high levels of productivity.

25. Crane systems

Finally, at the more complex end of the materials handling technology spectrum, are the fixed-path crane systems used in high-bay storage and retrieval operations. These can be of the operator-controlled, order-picking crane variety, or the remote-controlled stacker crane type. The operator cab or lifting mechanism moves up and down a vertical mast, which itself runs on fixed, dedicated rails at both floor and ceiling levels in its own aisle, and cannot operate outside it. Each aisle in such a high-bay storage unit, therefore, needs its own dedicated crane, thus making for a very capital intensive operation.

Whether of the operator — or remote-controlled variety, very high levels of utilisation must be achieved with this kind of equipment in order to obtain acceptable unit storage and handling costs.

26. Automation

Many of the types of industrial truck mentioned have been easily adapted to use advanced communications technology. It is not uncommon for manufacturers to offer minicomputer terminal facilities on fork-lift, reach and turret trucks in order to speed up the process of information transfer during storage, retrieval and order-picking operations. In quite a number of cases, these activities are virtually paperless, thanks to direct communication between materials handling equipment and a store or warehouse's computerised stock-control system. Truck operators can use mini-terminals to receive instructions and confirm task completion, and digital readings in order-picking cranes tell the operator which location to move to for their next pick or put-away. With the combination of engineering and computer technology, advanced materials handling has become an essential part of both the modern storage and warehousing scene, and the most effective, integrated supply-chain operations.

Automatic storage and retrieval systems (ASRS) consist of computer-controlled handling equipment in what are often unmanned, high-bay storage areas; they are still largely limited to a small number of installations. Capital costs can run well into the millions and, as well as the need for very high levels of productivity, there should also be as little danger as possible of obsolescence or redundancy of the system within the planned payback period. Such high levels of sophistication in a handling system can often carry with them a high degree of risk, therefore careful research and analysis at the planning stage is essential.

27. Conveyor systems

Where the requirement of a handling system — or part of it — is a fast, continuous flow of packages or unit loads rather than their placing precisely in a given position, the most effective method of achieving this is by use of a conveyor.

Conveyor systems can be relatively small and simple where the requirement is merely to bridge a gap in part of a storage, picking or materials handling operation. In such businesses as manufacturing and parcels distribution, however, some conveyor networks are very extensive, providing a comprehensive set of routes for materials to flow through and around factories, hub depots and warehouses. Many incorporate such facilities as laser readers for data capture, multiple junctions for diverging tracks, and tilt trays to divert cartons and packages to the appropriate destination on the system.

As with trucks and cranes, there are different types, each of which suit a particular kind of operation. These types are initially determined by two factors:

(a) source of movement
(b) type of bed or movement medium.

These are discussed in detail in the sections which follow.

28. Source of movement

These types of conveyor are broadly divided into two categories:

(a) *Gravity-fed or unpowered conveyors*. The former type is used for material flows from an upper to a lower level, and no power is required as the force of gravity creates the desired movement. The latter provides horizontal movement over short distances, where momentum or the number of packages in train will maintain flow.
(b) *Powered*. This type of conveyor is necessary where horizontal or upward movement is required. In the case of upward movement, incline of the track will be restricted for the purposes of safety and efficiency, and cross-slats may even be provided to hold packages in position during ascent. Power may be continuous or intermittent depending on consistency or density of material flow.

29. Movement medium

These types of conveyor are broadly divided into four categories:

(a) *Belt conveyors*. This type of conveyor is usually in the 'powered' category, and generally comprises a wide, durable belt forming a continuous moving surface which can be used for flows of a wide variety of packaging units. Powered rollers around which the belt revolves at each end provide the drive. Paper-wrapped parcels and other bagged items are best suited to belt conveyors on account of the smoothness and continuity of the movement surface.
(b) *Roller conveyors*. Here, the conveyor bed itself is formed of innumerable short aluminium or stainless steel rollers, revolving on spindles set in the side-frames of the conveyor track. This type may be powered or unpowered, and is again suitable for the handling of wide variety of packages. Where junctions occur on the system, however, packages and cartons can often become caught and create a blockage, even with the presence of guide-rails or directing ploughs. It is also possible for paper-wrapped parcels and polythene-bagged items to become damaged if they snag on part of a system under power, hence cartoned goods and similar rigid items tend to be more suited to this type of equipment, particularly where they are weighty.
(c) *Skate-wheel conveyors*. Consisting of rotating plastic wheels set at intervals on spindles revolving in the track-bed side-frames,

these types of conveyor are mainly in the unpowered category, and are useful only for the movement of cartons or similar packaging units with a continuous, rigid base. Being of less robust design than the average roller conveyor, they are perhaps best suited to relatively lightweight picking and packing operations, where the conveyor will be subject to the minimum amount of wear and tear.

(d) *Overhead conveyors.* Moving away from the more conventional type of packaging unit, handling of such items as hanging garments in polythene covers or other fabric or light cartoned goods in sack or pouch unit-loads requires a totally different approach. To meet this need, conveyor technology has designed systems which are usually suspended from ceilings in the form of a stout metal track, inside which runs a continuous wire cable to which are fixed at intervals load-bearing hooks. Numbers of hanging garments, unit-load sacks, loaded trays or other small items which are relatively light can then be hooked on to the conveyor for movement to a predetermined point in the system. Like most other conveyor networks, aerial conveyors follow main flow routes around and through manufacturing and distribution facilities, and provide a useful alternative to ground-level systems in that often, a great deal of useful working space is saved at floor level.

30. Advantages and disadvantages of conveyor systems

The advantages of conveyor systems are:

(a) A capability for very high rates of throughput. However, this will often depend on the need for labour to feed and clear the system. A minor operational hiccup which often occurs is accumulation of packages toward the end of the conveyor. This creates 'line pressure', particularly on the last few items, making it difficult to extract them and sometimes causing damage to packaging.

(b) Low running costs in comparison with the number of items handled. Powered conveyors may be needed only at certain times of heavy or timed flows, and gravity systems of course need no external power source at all. The former type will generate a certain amount of momentum in moving items once in operation, thereby making best use of available power.

The disadvantages of conveyor systems are:

(a) The capacity to move goods along fixed routes only. Most larger conveyor systems consist of fixed networks to deal with dense and/or continuous flows through manufacturing or packaging processes, from a production line to loading bays or from a reserve storage or picking area to order assembly. Mobile conveyor equipment also exists for use in a number of situations and places, frequently in loading bays and distribution centres to move goods quickly from load assembly areas to vehicles, or from vehicles to receiving areas. It is usually fairly light and can be manually moved around to wherever it is required next, as the need dictates.

(b) Occupation of large areas of floor space in the case of ground-based systems, which might hinder other parts of the handling and storage operation. A decision would be required at the planning stage as to what might be the most effective use of such space before committing the organisation to what might well be a costly white elephant!

(c) The initial cost of an extensive system can be very high, particularly when taking planning, installation and commissioning into consideration. However, as with many other large items of capital expenditure — if properly planned and specified, the initial investment should be recovered by virtue of more cost-effective materials handling over the period of the payback.

A large and complex conveyor network represents — as stated above — a substantial capital investment, and demands a good deal of planning. Its justification and introduction should be realistic, as should the expectations management have of its performance. If it has been designed around accurate specifications as regards system performance requirements then, assuming the technology is right and any bugs have been ironed out, it should be able to cope effectively with the demands placed on it, including any forecast expansion of product ranges and customer demand.

As with many components of logistics and distribution systems, the main trade-off is one of increased efficiency of material flow against capital and operating costs, but careful design and maintenance are necessary to ensure this is achieved. A poorly designed or maintained system can result in thousands of pounds annually of additional cost, whether in the form of extra staffing or lost productivity.

The function of some conveyors is simple and straightforward, merely providing a link between separate functions or points in a supply chain. A typical example, and one of the shortest types of conveyor to be found, is the large roller-bed conveyor which transfers full pallet loads from road vehicle trailers onto warehouse floor areas in a matter of two or three minutes. More sophisticated systems can constitute a comprehensive materials flow system, which is capable of identifying, sorting and directing unit-loads in order to assure their safe arrival at the required point in the handling, storage and transport operation and — ultimately — the final consumer. Whatever their size and complexity, whatever the amount of capital investment they represent, or however basic they may be, in principle they are a vital link in the supply and distribution chain, and an item of equipment that many factories, warehouses and distribution centres could not function without.

Storage and warehousing

31. The need for warehouses

Why is it that many companies' logistics and distribution operations still require storage and warehousing facilities in order to function effectively? Why is so much, in terms of buildings, capital equipment, human resources and management expertise, utilised in costly stockholding units such as depots and distribution centres?

Conventional wisdom justifies the existence of warehousing activities on the following grounds:

(a) Optimising production cost savings by permitting long production runs, and minimising set-up and changeover costs. This will help keep manufacturing and processing costs down through economies of scale.

(b) To provide a buffer between the rate of supply and manufacture, and demand. Supply of raw materials and production operations can be planned in advance, based on forecast demand for an item or commodity, whereas actual demand from customers and consumers can be unpredictable and will fluctuate. Some form of stockholding operation will add the flexibility required to overcome this problem. In the event of a sudden unexpected increase in sales demand, raw materials or components supply failure, or breakdown in production, inventory held in stores and warehouses can be used until the problem is resolved or an alternative source is found.

(c) The creation of 'anticipation inventory'. Many products and commodities — particularly in the consumer goods markets — have a seasonal demand pattern, where the demand profile has a marked peak over a fairly short period of time. In order to make provision for such demands, and yet maintain consistency in levels of production, stocks to service such demand need to be built up over an extended period. Typical examples might be wines, spirits and beers for Christmas and New Year festivities, antifreeze for motorists' winter needs, sun-tan preparations for the summer holiday season — and of course all the raw materials required for these production processes.

(d) Maintenance and improvement of customer service levels. The closer stocks are located to demand areas, the greater the availability of line items to fulfil individual orders, and the shorter lead times can be. Where the spatial relationship between points of supply and demand is more distant, providing high levels of customer service is both more demanding on the distribution system and more costly. By creating trade-offs with the transport function — such as bulk transport and deliveries, giving noticeably lower unit transport costs — logistics and distribution management can use stockholding points to support customer service levels in a more cost-effective way.

(e) To facilitate break-bulk and order assembly operations, where large bulk quantities are broken down into smaller individual orders before onward transit to customers. This aspect of storage and warehousing can also be readily linked to the need for accurate checking and recording of receipts, stocks and despatches, thereby monitoring progress of material along the supply chain.

In addition to these reasons, there is a need for companies at all times to protect their investment in all types of inventory and manufactured goods. The best and most convenient way to achieve this is often seen as the provision of a secure and suitable environment such as a warehouse or storage unit, where the risk to inventory from damage, deterioration and unauthorised removal will be minimised.

37. Warehouse networks and locations

On the basis that the need for some kind of stockholding operation has been established, the next stage is to consider and plan the form it will take. The first step in that process is to choose between centralised or regional distribution. This process has been reviewed in 4:4.

38. Centralised distribution

This relies on the holding of stock at a single or very small number of locations, often a factory or manufacturing complex warehouse. In the retail trade — its grocery and supermarket sectors in particular — this form of stockholding is interpreted as 'centralised' holding of line items and ranges from all suppliers at their own or contractor's regional warehouse, for consolidation and final delivery of multi-product loads direct to individual outlets. This is a distinct departure from the former type of system, where inventories are centrally located relative to the geographic spread of a company's market. This fact, coupled with organisation size in terms of turnover, market share, available resources and even corporate objectives, will determine whether or not a company opts for a central stockholding policy, or something more geographically dispersed.

39. Regional distribution

The trend which has emerged over the last 15–20 years has, in many areas of business and industry, been toward a regionalised distribution network. Led again by the grocery and retail trades, the pattern has been one of establishing large stockholding units in a company's main market areas, with a view to optimising transport and warehousing costs and improving customer service by shortening lead times. Regardless of whether these regional warehouses or distribution centres are operated by the retailer or their third-party distribution contractor, most have conformed to what has become a standard pattern in respect of building type and location, equipment, methods of operation and style of management. Most of them are referred to as *regional distribution centres* (RDCs) and are set in out-of-town locations on industrial estates or greenfield sites close to motorways, where land was initially cheap, local authority rates low and labour rates were less costly than in the conurbation areas.

40. Centralised vs. regional distribution networks

There are advantages and disadvantages in both centralised and regional distribution networks.

Centralised stockholding and distribution often leads to high transport costs and longer lead times. However, it is a more economic method of distribution both in terms of establishment costs (buildings, staff, vehicles, etc.) and costs of inventory, as there is a direct relationship between inventory levels and the number of locations at which it is held. (The square root law calculation for this purpose is dealt with in 6:**14**.)

Regional networks, on the other hand, incur high establishment and inventory costs, but generate the benefits of lower transport costs and higher levels of customer service. This is illustrated by Fig. 7.1 which shows a simple trade-off model used to determine the optimum number of depots in a network. As can be seen, primary distribution or trunking costs increase as the number of distribution centres in the network increases, while secondary distribution or final delivery costs reduce as each additional regional distribution centre is that much closer to any given customer in its designated market area. The lowest point on the total cost curve therefore indicates the optimum transport and warehousing cost — hence the optimum number of regional centres from a purely cost point of view. Other factors may, however, play a part in determining the final decision. For example, the desired level of customer service may dictate a greater number of warehouses in the network than the optimum, which is based on cost alone.

Once decisions have been made relating to the type and extent of the warehousing network, then a more precise, cost-effective location must be identified for each unit. Again, the ultimate objective of this exercise is to optimise transport and warehousing costs, and maximise customer service. When the capital costs of establishing such a unit and the operating costs are taken into consideration, the total will often run into millions of pounds. Therefore the correct choice of location must be arrived at scientifically — not by rule of thumb! Depot location theory is again examined in some detail in Chapter 9 employing the technique of assignment theory. However, in practice this is now mostly done by computer modelling.

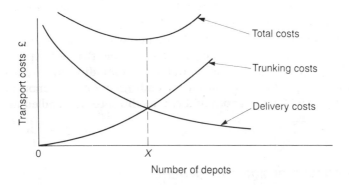

Fig. 7.1 *Relationship between depot costs and transport costs.*

41. Siting factors

Besides deciding on the most cost-effective location for warehouses and RDCs, a good deal of thought and planning must go into the selection of the actual site. Factors for consideration will be:

(a) Availability of suitable land not only for the warehouse itself, but also for vehicle parking and manoeuvring, other ancillary facilities, and potential future expansion of the unit.

(b) Proximity of the site to motorways and other transport links, as well as ease of access to delivery areas.

(c) Any existing funding or concessions from local or central government in connection with the development or running of the centre.

(d) Access to and for a suitable labour force to operate the distribution centre, preferably with relevant or related experience.

(e) The area of the proposed site must be considered from the point of view of environmental legislation relating to goods vehicle operation, and from a security viewpoint.

Even more detailed considerations regarding the building

itself will need to be reviewed. Can the company afford a new purpose-built distribution centre, is a standard modern-style industrial unit sufficient for their needs, or do financial constraints limit them perhaps to a converted factory or older warehouse building? For organisations in a healthy financial position, the dilemma may be whether to purchase/develop a property of their own, or to rent a suitable building for an agreed period.

In the final analysis, it will depend on what the company can afford, what is available in the chosen area and the more specific needs of the storage operation in terms of building size, vehicle access, equipment to be installed, and a suitable warehousing environment for the goods and commodities to be handled and stored there.

Warehouse design and layout

42. General

Having looked at some of the more important factors relating to the building and its location, the arrangement of facilities and equipment inside a distribution centre — vital to its efficient operation — need to be considered. Design and layout depend largely on three factors:

(a) basic purpose of the facility (*see* **44**);
(b) most appropriate storage regime (*see* **45–49**);
(c) type of storage equipment used (*see* **50–55**).

43. Main objectives of effective warehouse management

Before examining these factors in detail it is essential first to consider the three main objectives of effective warehouse management:

(a) *To make maximum use of space*. Use of volume capacity or 'cube' is vital to efficient storage unit design and operation. For reasons of cost, most warehouses are designed for maximum use of height, as building upwards does not cost as much as increasing floor area (*see* Fig. 7.2). Nevertheless, other factors are also instrumental in achieving high space utilisation, such as choice of storage and handling equipment. The extent to which aisles and other working areas of storage unit floor space can be minimised in order to use more space for actually storing goods, will help reduce unit storage costs. Therefore selection of high-bay racking and narrow-aisle handling equipment, for example, will provide the opportunity for high-density storage, and consequent low unit costs.

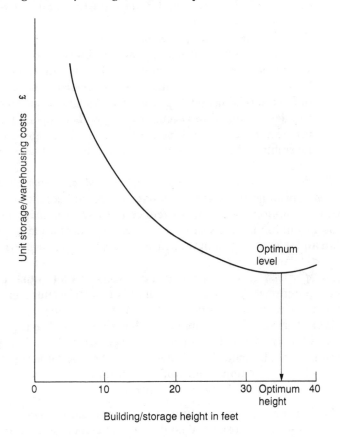

Fig. 7.2 *Warehousing — unit cost per storage height.*

(b) *To minimise movement.* This will also therefore minimise time and cost. This objective should relate not only to total movement within the storage unit, but in addition conflicting movements which might cause congestion, delays and perhaps even accidents. A desirable solution — if possible and practical — is to have a one-way flow within the building or complex. As a result, two basic storage/warehousing models have emerged:

(i) *Through-flow*. Flow is one-way, material or goods entering at one end of the storage unit and being dispatched from the other. This system is most suitable for a factory, plant store or warehouse, where the point of entry of material into the store, e.g. the end of a production line, is fixed and not easily changeable.

(ii) *'U' flow*. Here again, the general flow of material is one-way, entering and leaving the warehouse on the same side of the storage area. In practice, of course, there would be a number of bays or vehicle docks, divided into clearly defined receiving and dispatch areas. A slight variation on this design sometimes occurs where goods receiving bays are located along one side of the building, and load assembly and dispatch bays are located along the adjacent side.

(c) *To minimise the amount of handling to which goods and materials are subjected*. This objective once again has the aim of keeping down costs, but additionally it aims to reduce the risk of damage and maintain minimum levels of product quality. Careful planning, design and selection of equipment are the key factors in achieving this particular objective.

(d) *To effectively control movement and storage*. Good, workable control systems which monitor movement of materials into, out of and within a warehouse or distribution centre are essential.

Identification of consignments both arriving and leaving, by means of both manual recording or electronic data capture methods, should permit a high degree of operational accuracy. Likewise, information controlling storage and retrieval operations should minimise stock control errors.

Within the constraints of these objectives and the two basic models illustrated, more detailed design and layout depends to a great extent on the three factors listed in **42** and discussed in more depth in the following sections.

Purpose of the facility

44. Basic purpose of the facility
The kind of operation to be carried out in order to fulfil its

role in the company network is one of the most influential factors in the design and layout of a storage or distribution unit. Such facilities take various forms, depending also on the nature of the materials to be handled and stored. For example, is it a bulk materials handling and storage operation, or one dealing with unitised products? Examples of the former might be:

(a) Petrol or other oil-based products which are brought in to distribution depots by rail or pipeline, kept in bulk storage tanks, and distributed in bulk by road tankers. No store or warehouse building is therefore required.

(b) In a slightly different way, milk distribution is carried out from dairies, where again road tanker vehicles deliver the liquid in bulk for pasteurising and testing, bottling and cartoning, prior to onward delivery in the form of daily door-to-door, multi-drop operations or bulk unitised deliveries to cash-and-carries and supermarkets.

Moving to the other end of the scale, the operation might be totally unitised, as with many FMCG distribution centres, with palletised products being delivered in bulk, stored for varying periods of time, and eventually used to fill orders from retail outlets or customers. To a great extent, this type of operation is of a break-bulk nature, but one which incorporates a substantial storage element in order to fulfil its planned purpose in the company's scheme of things. Both this, and the previous two examples, demonstrate how stores and depots can have a dual function — as points for storage of necessary stocks, and points for distribution of goods and materials to other parts of the organisation, to the next stage along the supply chain, or direct to customers and end-users.

Many distribution centres, however, are run as 'stockless depots', carrying out only part of this latter role in that they serve purely as transhipment points where there are no — or only very temporary — storage facilities. Their activities are characterised almost entirely by the break-bulk and order-consolidating nature of the operation. A typical example of this kind might be the distribution of automotive components, where these are collected by contractors' vehicles or brought in by suppliers, re-sorted into full loads, and distributed to plant locations on a daily basis. This forms a 24-hour cycle, based on JIT manufacturing and distribution techniques, where any parts which remain will soon be accounted for and transported to the appropriate location as soon as possible.

Among all storage and distribution units, there will be varying degrees of storage, handling and distribution activity at each, and the degree of each will be designed to suit the individual company's purposes. Furthermore, the design of the unit will be determined by those purposes, and the layout planned accordingly.

45. Receiving and dispatch operations

Irrespective of the basic nature of any warehouse or depot, receipt and dispatch of goods and materials are both important processes — and as such require careful planning and control.

It has already been said that accuracy of order fulfilment is often a measure of the customer service level. For this, and other reasons relating to good internal control, operational accuracy is an essential component of effective warehouse or distribution-centre management. This process begins when deliveries are made to the stockholding unit or transhipment point.

Well-planned procedures for the checking of commodities on arrival — to determine correctness of delivery location, item identity, quantity and any other important criteria — is where good inventory management begins. Whether checking is carried out by visual inspection and consignment details manually recorded, or item information is captured and recorded electronically, the objective is to ensure that only correct items are received and that only their correct description is transmitted on to the warehouse information and control system.

These principles apply equally to order assembly and dispatch where, again, mechanisms should be in place to ensure that orders have been correctly processed. Furthermore, this not only requires checking of the line items and materials themselves, but also of accompanying paperwork. Just as in-coming delivery notes may form the basis of the data transferred to the warehouse information system — once goods have been checked against it — so consignment notes may well be used as the source of information in telling the stock management system what has been dispatched.

One final comment here on receiving and dispatch operations

relates to quality control. Much emphasis is now placed not only on accuracy of deliveries and consignment information, but also physical quality of all items. Accordingly, an appropriate level of quality management should be built into checking procedures as mentioned above, to ensure that operational accuracy and product integrity and quality are achieved simultaneously.

Storage regime

46. Most appropriate storage regime
Choice of the most suitable storage system will be based on:

(a) stock location
(b) stock rotation

although these will, in turn, depend on the demand profile of the product/commodity range.

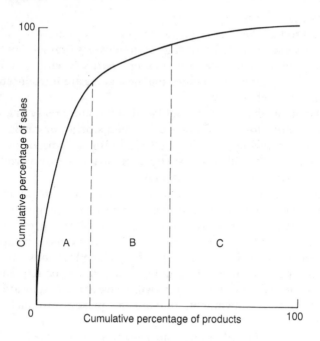

Fig. 7.3 *A typical Pareto curve.*

Calculation of the latter requires application of the 'ABC analysis' technique described in 6:**3**. The results of the calculation demonstrate whether the demand profile of a given range conforms to a typical Pareto curve (*see* p.123). An example of this is shown in Fig. 7.3 where 80 per cent of product demand is represented by only 20 per cent of the range. Accurate analysis using this technique will reveal which are the fastest moving items in the range and which are the slow movers. Inevitably there will be some in neither category, which can be classed as 'medium demand' lines.

Location and rotation of stock will now be discussed in greater detail.

47. Stock location

Once an ABC classification has been completed, planning of stock locations can take place, using one of two basic methods — fixed location and random location.

Fixed location storage

This method applies where particular line items occupy the same individual locations in the storage system over sustained periods of time and without alteration, except perhaps when product ranges are expanded or changed and new items are introduced or existing ones deleted.

The main advantage of fixed location is that it is easy to learn and remember for warehouse staff. When storing or retrieving goods, or carrying out stock-checks after a period of familiarisation, staff will know exactly where to go to store a product or pick a line item for order assembly.

Fixed location storage then is a straightforward, practical system, and suitable for smaller, less complex storage operations. It will be mainly controlled by means of a manual system, e.g. stock cards or tickets. It is, however, used in many larger, more complex stores and warehouses, but normally for picking locations only. In this way, items on picking lists and instructions can be sequenced to match the order in which pickers will arrive at product locations, thus minimising movement, maximising pickers' productivity, and maintaining one-way flow of the picking operation.

Variations of fixed location storage are sometimes referred to by two other terms — *popularity storage* and *zoned storage*. In the former the most popular line items are located in the same storage area; in the latter, similar products or items are located in close proximity to each other. Popularity storage therefore is based on the demand or usage value of an item, whereas zoned storage is based on intrinsic product similarity.

Random location storage
Using this storage regime, any product can be stored in any location — there are no designated areas or slots for individual line items. It can more easily accommodate changes in product ranges without reorganisation as with fixed location systems.

The drawbacks of implementing such a regime are, first, the difficulties in locating stock as positions are constantly changing, and there is no point in operators attempting to familiarise themselves with such a fluid system. Secondly, more attention needs to be paid to the actual recording process, to ensure accurate, effective stock control. Errors and inaccuracies might lead to stock being misplaced, or excess time taken to put away or retrieve it.

Nonetheless, random location has a considerable benefit in that it minimises movement, hence time and cost, in storage and retrieval operations. The nearest suitable location is always chosen for each stock move, whether the staff are putting away or selecting items for order or replenishment of pick-faces.

Random location is therefore a more sophisticated regime, and nowadays is widely used in many larger storage and warehousing operations. Coupled with current computer technology, it is frequently planned, operated and controlled by a suitable stock-control program, where the system database and selective capability enable both storage and retrieval operations to be carried out with a high degree of efficiency and accuracy. In many cases, random location regimes are used for bulk or reserve storage only, where the area involved is considerable, and the opportunities for minimising operator travel distance are much greater than in order-picking operations.

48. Storage identification systems
Whichever method of stock location is used, some form of check on the correctness of each move that takes place is essential. In a smaller store or warehouse it may not be particularly difficult

to locate stock items — even if members of staff may not have remembered exactly where they have been put. Even the need for locations to be identified by some kind of number or code may not be all that necessary. However, in larger, more complex units, the latter is an absolute necessity. If an extensive store used a fixed location system, much time could be wasted in searching for specific items or suitable places in which to store them — with random location the problem would be multiplied out of all proportion.

For any storage system to work effectively, therefore, a location coding or identification system must be devised. Moreover, if a large storage and distribution unit employs random location of stock — particularly computer-controlled — the capability to double check put-away and retrieval moves will more than likely be built into the stock control program. This will usually take the form of a check-digit for each storage location, and to which it is unique. Only when the correct check-digit for the specified location is keyed into the computer system will storage or retrieval of the correct item be confirmed on the stock database. Where it is possible for operators to select the correct item, but not from the correct location and perhaps out of stock rotation sequence, this kind of checking mechanism is invaluable.

49. Picking operations

The significance of effective receiving and dispatch operations at a storage or distribution location has already been established. Similar criteria should, however, apply to order-picking activities. In many instances, order picking is a very labour-intensive part of warehouse activity, and as such needs to be carried out in an efficient manner.

A standard method of achieving such efficiency is to design picking areas based on fixed-location storage. This enables pickers simply to follow a one-way system around racking or other storage locations, retrieving items for order-assembly as required. A further implication of this kind of operation is, of course, that picking lists, labels or documentation will show line items in the same order as their storage locations. Changes in sequence would only be required whenever new introductions were made to commodity ranges, or slow-movers, declared obsolete were removed from stock.

The alternative kind of retrieval operation utilises fixed-picking or order-assembly stations, and mobile storage media such as carousels or automatic picking cranes. Yet again, the essential element is maximisation of pickers' time spent actually retrieving items and assembling orders. Fixed-location storage often remains an important element, as faster-moving items need to be located centrally in large, vertical carousels, around chest height in horizontal ones, and closest to picking stations in automatic systems, in order to achieve maximum picker/machine productivity.

Picking operations can be broken down into four main elements:

(a) movement between locations
(b) time spent on paperwork/list
(c) any waiting time (instructions/replenishment)
(d) actual picking.

In order to maximise actual picking time, in addition to the above points, it is necessary to avoid congestion. This is usually best achieved by separating waves of picking and replenishment activity, either by carrying them out simultaneously in different areas of the warehouse, or in the same areas but at different times. Furthermore, the importance of effective warehouse information systems to support picking operations cannot be overstressed, with timeliness and accuracy among the key factors.

50. Stock rotation

As the second element of many storage regimes, stock rotation is often equally as important as stock location. Obvious examples in which stock rotation is absolutely crucial are in FMCG distribution, in the food, drinks and tobacco (FDT) categories and, to a lesser extent, in medicines, toiletries and cosmetics.

Competitive edge is frequently about customer service level, major elements of which are not only product availability, but also product quality. In the food industry, this often means freshness. All foods and drinks have a defined shelf-life before their condition starts to deteriorate, and most supermarket chains will have agreed a maximum acceptable shelf-life for all products with their relevant suppliers in their efforts to maintain product quality standards and consistently meet customer expectations.

However, within a product's shelf-life there are minute degrees of freshness, and the strategy of food manufacturers and retailers is to utilise this factor to enhance their marketing position. Food legislation in more recent years has also made the display of 'sell by' or 'best before' dates mandatory in the case of so many everyday food items. Therefore it is necessary for distributors, wholesalers, and retailers to rotate their stock and sell the freshest first not only from the viewpoint of good business practice but from a legal point of view also. The two main methods of stock rotation are discussed in the following sections.

51. FIFO

Most FMCG supply chains are operated on the basis of 'first in, first out' or FIFO stock rotation, where freshness and product condition are paramount for commercial and legal reasons. Even where big supermarket chains are not involved, branded product manufacturers like to ensure their products are consumed at their best, which means good, effective stock rotation. It is important to stress, however, that FIFO storage is not restricted to FMCG products only. Many consumer durables distributors and retailers, and both 'trade' and retail outlets for automotive parts, need to rotate their stock to reduce any losses which might result from obsolescence. The effects of advancing product technology and differentiation are felt just as much in the field of stock management as are customer expectations and demands.

In order to achieve complete FIFO rotation, all lines in stores and warehouses must be accessible at all times, and this has obvious implications for the planning of both layout and equipment.

52. LIFO

Whereas a FIFO system is most suited to commodities which have a limited shelf-life within which they retain their merchantable quality, a 'last in, first out' or LIFO regime is used for products or materials where their usable quality does not deteriorate at all, or only very marginally. LIFO stockholding systems are typically used by such businesses as steel stockholders, quarry operators and the wines and spirits industries, where length of time in controlled forms of storage effectively increases product quality, and is a prerequisite for the more expensive, top quality lines.

LIFO can also be used in parts of an otherwise FIFO system. Bulk unitised movement of fast-moving items — sometimes colloquially referred to as 'garbage in, garbage out' — entails storage of large quantities of unitised products for short periods of time only. During this type of operation, methods of storage with low levels of accessibility are often used, resulting briefly in LIFO selection of the product at the point of retrieval.

Storage equipment

53. Type of storage equipment used
The necessity for any kind of storage equipment is initially governed by whether such storage will be in bulk or unitised form.

Bulk storage, whether of raw materials, part-processed commodities or finished products, will often utilise large, high-capacity silos, storage tanks or containers, from which quantities will be drawn according to the demands of production, processing or distribution. The need to store large quantities and the very nature of bulk handling — in that it often needs to be a more flowing, continuous operation — dictates the need for the kind of equipment used. Emphasis here is much more on storage units and associated flow control systems rather than additional items of capital equipment for materials handling purposes only.

Despite this general rule, there are a number of bulk materials which are kept in stockpiles in open depots. Many building and construction materials come into this category, where such items as aggregates, gravel and sand are bulk stored at ground level, and require mechanical plant and equipment for their transfer onto road vehicles for distribution.

Since unitised products cover such a wide range of goods and materials, the need will vary considerably, not only as to whether some form of storage equipment will be required at all, but also as to the most appropriate type for the purpose.

54. Block stacking
The simplest and cheapest method of storing unitised items is that of *block stacking*. Goods most frequently stored in this way are palletised, whether on conventional wooden pallets or more

specialised metal ones. Other varieties of handling and storage unit can also be block stacked, provided the stacks created are physically stable, and the packaging or storage units are capable of withstanding stacking pressures.

The main criteria for the effective use of block stacking are either square, flat-topped pallet loads or securely nesting unit-loads, durable packaging, and either a high turnover rate, or the need for a low degree of accessibility to the stock. These latter points should eliminate problems of stock accessibility which may include both the retrieval of stock items and physical stock checking.

The advantage of block stacking lie in its inherent cheapness in not requiring capital equipment for actual storage purposes and in the high levels of space utilisation that can be achieved. This latter advantage is, however, often eroded during the stock turnover process by 'honeycombing' — the creation of gaps in storage blocks by the retrieval of items for dispatch. These gaps often cannot be refilled because of the necessity to retain access to items at the back of the part-empty row.

Block storage is frequently used in brewery distribution and many bulk stores such as factory warehouses. A further benefit of the method is the degree of flexibility it gives in that block positions can be moved around the storage area as they are not tied to fixed locations by racking or shelving positions.

55. Shelves, bins and racks

Among the most common forms of storage equipment are shelving, binning and racking. These three basic types are used for a wide range of products in many areas of industry.

Shelving and *binning* are the most popular means of storing smaller, lighter items such as automotive parts and accessories, electrical components and books. In many cases, these will be in cartons or other forms of light packaging, although the smallest items such as nuts, bolts, screws and washers in engineering or similar stores may be stored loose in bins. In their various types, they provide a high degree of stock accessibility and — where use can be made of additional mezzanine floors above ground-level storage — high levels of space utilisation. Connected by steps, these floors and their respective sets of shelving can be accessed by stores staff without the need for specialised, high-capital equipment to assist them in their storage, retrieval and stock-checking duties. In many cases, light, mobile steps or picking platforms are used at ground level to access the higher reaches of shelving units. High-rise shelving, accessed by fixed-path order picking cranes, is a logical extension of this kind of storage medium where very large numbers of locations are required for relatively small, easily handled items.

Racking systems come in a variety of forms and are discussed in greater detail in the sections which follow.

56. Adjustable pallet racking

Because wooden pallets are the most popular unit-load in use, *adjustable pallet racking* (APR) can be found in an overwhelming percentage of storage and warehousing units. As its name implies, such racking can be assembled and adjusted to accommodate a wide range of pallet sizes. However, as pallet bases have to a great extent become standardised, the need for adjustment will relate mainly to the vertical distance between racking beams in order to take pallets of a particular height.

Indeed, this factor itself may have implications for warehouse layout — particularly where there is a considerable variation in pallet heights — as locations of certain line items may have to be planned and fixed, even in a random location bulk storage area. The alternative would be to create all spaces to accept maximum height pallets, but this would result in a substantial loss of space utilisation.

Relatively speaking, APR is an inexpensive method of storage in capital terms, but this depends on the height of racking used. Up to around eight metres, a lifting height within the capacity of many current reach trucks, APR racking is the most acceptable method of storage and no specialised handling equipment is required other than the aforementioned reach trucks. Above an eight-metre lift height, although free-standing APR will continue to support palletised goods, narrow-aisle trucks will be needed for storage and retrieval operations. Not only are these machines more expensive in capital terms, they require more specialised training of operators, and either guide-rails or under-floor wires in the aisles to ensure the trucks do not deviate from an absolutely straight path between the racking.

Also adding to the cost of such high-rack operation is the

construction and finishing of the warehouse floor to ultra-level standards. This is because suitable stackers operate at such heights that, were the floor not within supplier specifications, the trucks might become unstable when being operated. All this serves to demonstrate that, in spite of equipment manufacturers' claims of much-reduced aisle widths and something in the order of 30 per cent less storage area needed for high-rack operation, there are still trade-offs to be considered — in this case, mainly in the area of overall cost.

57. Variations on APR

A similar situation arises concerning the possible benefits of *double-deep racking*. This is APR in which pallets or unit-loads are stored two-deep either side of access aisles. This method of storage creates something like 33 per cent more pallet positions in a given storage area, a fact which, on the face of it, implies that unit storage costs should be lower. In spite of this apparent advantage, access to stock is restricted as rearmost pallets cannot always be accessed at first reach due to the pallet in front. An obvious solution is to store pallets in pairs, but this can have implications for stock rotation.

Drive-in and *drive-through racking* are further variations on the APR theme, where the pallets are supported cantilever-style between racking uprights. Although these methods provide high-density storage, drawbacks of drive-in systems are the stability of the racking which has no lateral supports when viewed from the front, and the time taken to store and retrieve pallets, as well as possible damage to the racking itself. It could also be said that access to stock is a problem, but this type of racking is normally only used in 'garbage in, garbage out' operations, that is for temporary storage of unitised products in bulk. Hence the logical place for this type of racking would be close to receiving and dispatch areas for short-term storage of fast-moving products, where handling movement in terms of travel distance can be reduced to an absolute minimum.

58. Other racking systems

The most flexible kind of racking system, relative to store or warehouse layout, is *powered mobile racking*. Operating on rails in the floor, it too maximises use of storage space by permitting the creation of only one or two aisles between the banks of racking. Most important here is retention of the required degree of access to stock items, and the careful planning of effective picking sequences.

High-bay storage is a further extension of the high-rack method, but one which requires a much greater commitment in terms of capital expenditure. For purposes of stability, racking supports are usually part of the structural steel building framework, in addition to which storage and retrieval equipment will be of the fixed-path variety of stacker or order-picking cranes. This kind of capital-intensive system might be used for high-density storage in areas where land is particularly expensive, or where site development is restricted and movement to another site is not an option for consideration. Circumstances best suited to its use are often those where high-density storage of high-value items forms a major part of the stockholding operation. For such a system to be cost-effective in the long term, the product ranges must have a good, secure future in order to achieve the payback on such an expensive and specialised facility.

59. Carousels

The final main category of storage equipment in popular use is the carousel which, as its name implies, is based on a kind of storage 'roundabout'. The operator remains stationary whilst controlling a revolving system of storage locations which bring the required product location to his or her workstation. Carousels are of two types: horizontal and vertical.

In a horizontal carousel a long assembly of light, wire-basket or similar containers, which are collectively of sufficient depth to reach from floor level to just above average operator height, revolve round two end supports in a horizontal plane. These are often used for small, easily handled packages or cartons such as medicines, cosmetics, etc.

The other type is the vertical carousel. These often resemble a large metal cupboard with an open access panel extending their full width just above waist height on one side. Again the operator is stationed by the access panel and controls the movement of all storage trays inside. These revolve around inner shafts at the top and bottom of the installation.

60. Summary

The preceding sections give an indication of the wide variety of storage equipment which is available. They give rise to an equally wide range of differences in store or warehouse design and layout. Basically, however, most warehouse and storage facilities where receipt, stockholding, order assembly and onward dispatch are the major functions will be built along essentially similar lines.

Stockless logistics

61. Are warehouses obsolete?

Notwithstanding the continuing use and development of warehouses, distribution centres and their networks, there is a considerable body of logistics management opinion busy questioning their purpose and usefulness. It is now a well-accepted fact that in order to achieve fast, smooth movement of goods and materials along the supply chain, high-speed, if not instantaneous, transfer of information concerning that movement is vital.

Techniques such as optimised production technology and just-in-time (JIT) distribution have brought into question the advantages of storage and distribution centre networks from the viewpoint of manufacturing industry. The installation of electronic point-of-sale (EPOS) equipment in so many retail outlets provides 'on-line' transfer of sales information from shops and stores to distribution centres and suppliers, enabling logistics and distribution managers to track actual demand on a daily basis.

From a financial point of view, company senior management are debating the benefits of large sums of capital tied up in safety stocks, and storage and warehousing complexes, and their associated running costs. Mobile warehousing has become an accepted practice by many companies, using demountable equipment ferried between factories and distribution areas for delivery by smaller locally based road vehicles.

Not only is the search for an effective alternative being cost and technology driven, it is also being propelled by moves toward greater integration throughout the supply chain. Barriers created by the traditional independence of manufacturers and retailers are in the process of being broken down; greater trust and the freer flow of information is drawing organisations in each sector closer together. Although new centres are still being opened as business opportunities are created and logistics operations reconfigured, it remains a strong possibility that even the state-of-the-art warehouse and distribution centre of the 1990s may become a casualty as the business and technology revolution continues its progress.

Progress test 7

1. What are the three main sub-functions of materials handling? **(2)**

2. In what ways do the containment, protection and information functions of packaging help in logistics and distribution? **(3–6)**

3. Explain the difference between primary and secondary packaging. **(8–9)**

4. Describe the purpose of the following:

    (a) a four-way entry pallet;
    (b) a roll-cage;
    (c) a ULD. **(13–18)**

5. What are the advantages of unitisation? **(20)**

6. List the main types of powered pallet and lift trucks. **(22, 24)**

7. Indicate the kind of conveyor you would use for:

    (a) hanging garments
    (b) cartoned goods
    (c) computer equipment
    (d) aggregates. **(27, 30)**

8. Give at least four reasons for having warehouses and storage facilities. **(31)**

9. Indicate the benefits of:

    (a) centralised storage;
    (b) regional storage.   **(38, 40)**

10. Why should warehouse managers try to maximise use of space and minimise movement?   **(42)**

11. What is a storage regime?   **(46)**

12. Explain the benefits of (*a*) high-bay storage and (*b*) carousels.   **(58, 59)**

8
Transport and fleet management

Transport considerations

1. Compatibility

A vehicle must be compatible with the way (road, rail, etc.) upon which it operates. For example, a major problem associated with the Channel Tunnel is the 'Berne' loading gauge of continental freight waggons, which are both too wide and too high to pass BR platforms and signals or through our bridges and tunnels, despite the fact that the bogies on which they run are the same rail gauge ($4'8\frac{1}{2}''$) as BR (*see* Fig. 8.1).

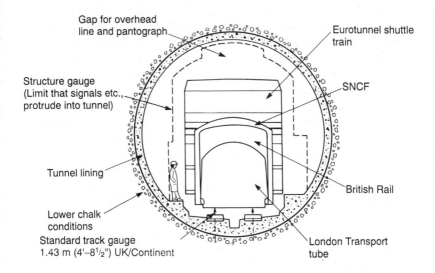

Fig. 8.1 *Comparison of Channel Tunnel loading gauges.*

In the long term the way can be upgraded to accommodate improvements in vehicle design and technology. In the 1960s the growth of the motorway network in the UK provided the stimulus for an increase in the legal maximum gross vehicle weights (GVW) of goods vehicles from 24 to 32 tons, and the present maximum of 38 tonnes is a compromise between the EC limit of 40 tonnes and UK limits imposed by present bridge strengths. A major programme of bridge strengthening by highway authorities will permit the government to bring the UK and EC limits in line by 1999 when the present 'derogation' (or UK exemption) from this EC law expires.

2.   Lorry bans

The operation of large goods vehicles is, however, often inappropriate in congested urban areas, as was demonstrated by the Wood Committee whose report in 1983 on heavy lorries in London resulted in the present London lorry ban.

3.   Combined transport

There is considerable interest at the moment in combined transport which is receiving a great deal of attention by the EC. In March 1991 the Transport Minister of Luxemburg, who was then President of the Council of Transport Ministers, singled the topic out as paramount in the development of a Common Transport Policy, and Karl van Miert, the Commissioner for Transport, asked member states to initiate a programme of cooperation between road and rail operators.

Charterail is a good example of a combined transport initiative. It represents an investment between the public sector BR and private sector vehicle and trailer manufacturers and operators aimed at developing a 'road-railer' vehicle which can be transferred from road to rail with the minimum of on-site load handling equipment. It has been formed specifically to meet the needs of the fast-moving consumer goods (FMCG) trade. Although BR has a minority interest in the company, it operates outside the railway culture. It is managed entirely by distribution professionals and has a fiercely market-led philosophy.

Charterail acts as prime contractor, taking care of the total distribution of goods from producer to retailer, subcontracting the required rail facilities from BR, as well as some of the collection and delivery to and from railheads in unique road-railer vehicles which can be loaded onto special rail 'low bogie' waggons without the need for expensive container or swap body handling equipment.

On the Continent it is possible to transport fully loaded semi-trailers on rail bogies by providing either a 'pouch' or depression in the rail waggon's bed (the SNCF 'Kangaroo' system) or 'low loader' rail waggons with small rail wheels (the DB 'Combi' system), but neither of these solutions is feasible in the UK with our smaller loading gauge. It is for this reason that the Charterail-type solution, discussed above, is developing in the UK. Of course, such road-railer combined transport would have no difficulty in running on the wider continental loading gauges.

For the foreseeable future, however, it is most likely that containerisation will continue as the dominant form of combined transport.

4.   Importance of road-based movements

Movement of freight by road in the UK accounts for over four-fifths of the tonnage lifted and over two-thirds of the tonne/kilometres. Any transfer from road to rail would have environmental benefits, and section 8 of the Railways Act 1974 provides for infrastructure grants for private sidings where these can achieve such transfers in environmentally sensitive areas.

These grants have recently been extended to cover schemes based on the use of inland waterways, and any transfer to rail likely to relieve traffic on roads which have not in the past been considered environmentally sensitive. Some hauliers and distribution companies have transferred their trunking operations to rail using Speedlink, the single waggon-load express railfreight service, but BRB abandoned the service in May 1991. However, it is likely that individual speedlink movements might in future be provided by private rail waggon operators. Indeed, one such operator, Tiger Rail, which moves trainloads of its waggons from Cornwall to the NE and Scotland, already offers a private Speedlink-type facility on this corridor.

The so-called road lobby, in arguing for greater investment in roads, often claims that even if rail-freight tonnage increased by 50 per cent this would have a negligible effect on the numbers of lorries on the road, but this argument ignores the very significant reductions which would occur in long-distance freight movements by motorway, and the changes in the composition and deployment of operators' fleets, with smaller and more environmentally friendly urban vehicles being used much more efficiently. At present over 30 per cent of all long-distance freight vehicles are running empty!

Vehicle selection

It is obviously important to select the right vehicle for the job. The type of operation and the type of load are the two most significant factors.

5. Type of operation

Long-distance work, both national and international, utilising motorways and trunk roads requires reliable, robust vehicles able to sustain high average speeds. With medium distance, local work and multiple deliveries, or combinations of these operations, factors such as manoeuvrability and transmissions and brakes able to sustain constant stopping and starting assume more importance.

6. Type of load

Heavy loads dictate the use of vehicles with well-built chassis and bodies, whereas, when the volume or bulk of the load rather than the weight decides the capacity of the vehicle, lighter models may be chosen. However, operators are always mindful of the adverse effect on payload of too heavy a vehicle, but fortunately, nowadays, manufacturers and bodybuilders are able to supply light but strong vehicles, such as aluminium-bodied tippers and box vans and 'tilts' (curtain-sided vehicles and trailers with load restraining cross beams which can be custom sealed for international ('TIR') journeys and work).

It is equally necessary to use specialist vehicles for various types of traffic, for example tankers for fluids (powders, liquids and gases), tippers for bulk aggregates, and insulated or temperature-controlled vehicles for loads which are temperature sensitive, such as frozen and chilled foodstuffs, chemicals with low 'flashpoints', and hot foods such as liquid chocolate.

7. Type of body

In the UK manufacturers tend to supply chassis on which bodybuilders can mount specialised bodies to operators' specifications. Some UK vehicle importers deal in continental manufacturers' vehicles which are more often supplied complete with body, but even importers usually give operators a chassis or chassis-cab option to choose between.

In the range of small and medium goods vehicles (below 3.5 t and 7.5 t GVW respectively) there are many standard box van or pick-up models available.

Curtain-sided, tipper and refrigerated bodies and the kind of traffic for which these are suitable is described in 6. One of the most versatile body types is the simple flat platform which enables pallet loads to be fork lifted on and off from the rear and sides. Some 'flats' may be curtain-sided or have sliding doors for easy access, and there are even today refrigerated curtain sided 'reefers' used for bulk transfer of frozen food.

As well as being able to load, unload and 'turn round' vehicles quickly, it can be very advantageous to have the vehicle available for such purposes without tying up the tractive unit which will be used to power it. There are three ways of achieving this:

(a) By using 'demountable bodies' which can be left at the loading bay and lowered onto the vehicle chassis when filled (or emptied).
(b) By using standard ISO containers and 'skeletal' vehicles onto which the containers can be placed by crane or other container handling systems, and then locked securely to the vehicle by the use of twist locks.
(c) By using either trailers or semi-trailers (*see* below).

8. Types of vehicle

The three types of road vehicles are rigid, articulated or road train.

Rigid vehicles

Rigid vehicles can be operated in the UK up to a maximum of 30 t GVW on four axles. They are generally more manoeuvrable than articulated vehicles or vehicles and trailers, and, when weight rather than bulk is the main selection criteria, are the natural choice. Separation of vehicle and motive power can if necessary be achieved by the use of demountable bodies.

Articulated combination vehicles

Articulated combinations comprise a tractive unit, which is in effect a short-wheelbase rigid vehicle, with a turntable or 'fifth wheel' onto which the front of a semi-trailer can be coupled so that at least 20 per cent of its weight is imposed on the tractive unit. 'Artics' as they are known can operate up to 38 t GVW on a minimum of five (often six) axles in the UK and 40 t GVW in continental EC states, and by trailer swopping can deliver great operational efficiencies and productivity gains. They are, at 16.5 m maximum overall length, with 13.6 m maximum length semi-trailer, less manoeuvrable than rigids and have a regrettable tendency to 'cut in' on corners and roundabouts, and to 'jack-knife' on wet and icy roads, although this latter risk is today much reduced by the use of automatic braking systems and load sensing devices.

Draw-bar trailer combination vehicles

Draw-bar trailer combinations are more popular on the Continent than in the UK, but their popularity is growing with distributors who have to handle light, bulky packaged articles (for example, foam, cereals or potato crisps) since their overall platform space (15.65 m at 18.35 m maximum length) is actually greater than can be achieved by articulate operation. However, this is distributed between the rigid and trailer, and is thus of no use for the carriage of indivisible loads like long girders. They corner better than artics, with the trailers faithfully following the drawing rigid vehicles, but are more difficult to reverse into confined spaces. However, draw bar trains can be broken up with the trailer being left at a convenient depot or changeover point for later distribution once the load on the rigid vehicle has been distributed.

This type of vehicle is especially useful if demountable bodies can be swopped between drawing vehicle and trailer, and enables hybrid trunking (with full road train) and delivery (with separated vehicle and trailer at destination) operation. Draw-bar combinations are at present restricted to 32 t overall GVW.

Even greater operational flexibility can be achieved by the use of a 'converter dolly' (effectively a single axle with a draw-bar and 'fifth wheel' attached) to convert a semi-trailer into a composite trailer. This can then be used as the trailing vehicle in a draw-bar combination for the trunking part of the operation, then the rigid vehicle can deliver its load, and the semi-trailer part of the composite trailer can be used behind a locally out-based tractive unit to deliver the other half of the load.

Legal requirements for safe operation

9. General

Road freight transport was deregulated in 1968. There are no controls over the quantity of vehicles which a distributor can operate, but the quality of his operations is tightly regulated through a system of Operator Licensing introduced by the Transport Act 1968.

There is also legislation to control the construction, use and testing of goods vehicles, and the licensing and hours of work of their drivers.

10. Operator Licensing

Goods vehicles used on a road for hire or reward or in connection with the user's trade or business became, with deregulation of road haulage in 1968, subject to the UK system of quality licensing known as Operator Licensing. Exceptions were made for small goods vehicles of less than 3.5 tonnes gross vehicle weight. The main aspects of Operator Licensing are summarised below:

(a) Vehicles authorised under an operator's licence must be owned by the operator or in his possession, and the operating centre from which they are used must be specified and be within the area of the licensing authority granting the licence.

(b) The licensing authority (LA) is the Chairman of the Traffic Commissioners for each traffic area.

(c) Operator licences are vehicle specific, and operators must inform the licensing authority within *one month* of the acquisition of a new vehicle, otherwise that vehicle ceases to be authorised even if its acquisition does not result in the number of vehicles authorised in the licence being exceeded. This is known as 'operating within the margin', the margin being the difference between the number of vehicles ' in possession' and 'authorised'.

(d) There is provision for temporary detachment of vehicles to other traffic areas for a maximum period of *three months*.

(e) An operator may not hold more than one operator's licence in any traffic area.

(f) Applicants for an operator's licence are required to furnish the LA with specific particulars which in effect become statements of intent regarding such matters as the proper maintenance of their vehicles, the observance of drivers' hours regulations and weight limits. Applicants must notify the LA of any previous convictions and of any convictions received between the making of their application and its disposal by the LA.

(g) Applications must be published by the LA and certain prescribed trade unions and employers' associations, the police, relevant local authorities and planning authorities may make objections.

(h) In considering an application the LA is required to have regard to whether the applicant appears to him to be a fit person, the arrangements for ensuring that his vehicles will be properly maintained and that his drivers will observe the drivers' hours and records regulations, and the financial standing of the operator.

(i) Except in the case where he is not satisfied on environmental grounds the LA must grant the licence if he is satisfied about the above matters. In determining the operator's financial standing he may be assisted by a financial assessor.

(j) Regulations made in 1984 as a result of an EC Directive 561/74 on access to the occupation of goods vehicle operators further provided that operators' licences should be classified as:

    (*i*) standard, national
    (*ii*) standard, national and international
    (*iii*) restricted.

A standard licence is required by operators who carry for hire and reward (road hauliers) whilst a restricted licence is necessary for own-account operation where only the operator's own goods are carried.

11. Qualifications for an operator's licence

The qualifications required of applicants for an operator's licence are that they should be of:

(a) good repute
(b) appropriate financial standing
(c) professionally competent.

An LA must refuse an application where the operator cannot meet these requirements, except that the requirement as to professional competence is not required of applicants for a restricted licence (*see also* **12** and **13** below).

12. Professional competence

An applicant will meet the requirements for professional competence if he obtains by examination a Certificate of Professional Competence (examining body, Royal Society of Arts) or holds any other prescribed qualification recognised by the Secretary of State for this purpose.

It is now no longer possible to obtain a CPC by experience. The so-called 'grandfather rights' lapsed in 1981.

13. Good repute and financial standing

EC Directive 438/89 and further regulations made in 1990 specified much tighter criteria on which LAs are to judge an applicant's good repute, professional competence and (in the case of applicants for standard international licences) their financial standing.

Conditions may be attached to a licence requiring the operator to inform the LA of any specified changes in the organisation, management or ownership of his business.

14. Sanctions

An operator's licence, unless revoked or prematurely terminated, remains in force for *five years*, or until such later time as an application by the operator for a renewal of the licence, which is treated as an application for a new licence, or any appeal under that application to the Transport Tribunal, is disposed of. An LA may, without prejudice to the outcome of the application for the full licence, grant an interim licence pending the determination of an application.

On application by an operator and (unless the variation sought is 'trivial') having published this, an LA may vary the operator's licence by the addition or deletion of specified vehicles and trailers, altering any condition (*see* above) or converting the licence from a restricted licence to a standard national or standard international licence.

An LA may revoke, suspend, prematurely terminate or curtail

an operator's licence if during the preceding five years the holder
has been convicted of prescribed 'relevant' road offences or has
not complied with the statements of intent made when the licence
was granted. Revocation is mandatory where the holder of a
restricted operator's licence has been convicted within five years
of a second offence of using this for hire and reward.

15. Disqualification

When an LA revokes an operator's licence he may also
disqualify the holder from obtaining or holding another operator's
licence, either indefinitely or for such time as he thinks fit.

He may direct that if whilst such a disqualification is in force
the disqualified person controls or is a director of a company, or
is a member of a partnership which holds an operator's licence,
the licence in question shall be liable to revocation etc.

16. Inquiries and appeals

An LA may not make an order of revocation, suspension,
curtailment, termination or disqualification or attach a condition
without first holding a public inquiry if the operator requests this.

He may also direct that the order does not take effect until the
time limit for any appeal to the Transport Tribunal has elapsed
or any such appeal is disposed of. If he refuses such a stay the
operator may apply to the Tribunal for a direction and the
Tribunal must give its decision within 14 days.

17. Environmental conditions

Section 69 of the Act (which prescribed LAs' disciplinary
powers) was extended by the Transport Act 1982 to impose
environmental conditions on the operators of goods vehicles. The
provisions of sections 69A–G are of vital importance to transport
operators, including industrialists with their own in-house
transport. They are summarised as follows:

(a) The operating centre from which the vehicles authorised in
the operator's licence will be operated must be specified in the
licence, and applicants may be required to give the LA particulars
of the use which they propose to make of this.
(b) A statutory objector may object to the grant of an operator's
licence on the grounds that the operating centre is unsuitable on

environmental grounds. Owners and occupiers of land in the vicinity of the operating centre may also make representations to the LA on the same grounds if the use of the operating centre could prejudicially affect their use of, or enjoyment of, their land.

(c) However, where there is no material change in the operating centre or the use made of this the LA may not refuse an application for a renewal of the licence on environmental grounds other than on the specific grounds that the parking of the authorised vehicles at the operating centre would cause adverse effects in the vicinity.

(d) An LA may instead of granting an operator's licence as applied, modify the grant by specifying on the licence only such places as are not unsuitable for use as operating centres. The grant of an interim licence is without prejudice to any subsequent grant of a substantive licence.

(e) An LA may attach prescribed environmental conditions when granting an operator's licence regulating the number, type and size of vehicles to be authorised, the parking arrangements and the hours of operation. He may vary or remove these at any time.

(f) If he is precluded from refusing an application because there has been no material change in the operating centre or operations he may only attach such conditions if he first gives the operator the opportunity to make representations to him with respect to the effect of these on his business and he must then give special consideration to such representations.

(g) An operator may apply to vary his operating centre or the environmental conditions on his licence but such an application will be published by the LA and could be subject to the same objections and representations as a substantive application.

(h) There is a provision if the operator requests this for the LA to give an interim direction that his licence should continue in force until the application for the variation or any appeal arising out of his decision is disposed of.

(i) An application for an operator's licence or for any variation (either the addition or deletion of specified vehicles or an environmental change) must be published by the applicant in a local newspaper circulating in the locality affected, otherwise it will automatically be refused by the LA.

(j) An LA may revoke, suspend, curtail or prematurely terminate an operator's licence on the grounds that the operator has breached the conditions controlling the use of his operating centre, subject to the existing section 69 safeguards of public inquiry and continuance up to appeal.

18. Objections and representations regarding environmental conditions

Environmental objections and representations must be made within a prescribed period and in a prescribed manner. These, and the considerations which the LA is required to have regard to, are set out in regulations and include:

(a) the nature and use of the land in the vicinity;
(b) the extent to which the grant of an application would result in a material change in the operating centre or its use adversely affecting the environment in its vicinity;
(c) any planning permission relating to the land;
(d) the number, type and size of authorised vehicles and the arrangements for the parking of these;
(e) the nature of the use of the land as an operating centre;
(f) the times of use; and
(g) the means and frequency of vehicle ingress and egress.

For the purpose of disposing of environmental objections an LA may consider an application for an operator's licence or a variation to an operator's licence in respect of each operating centre separately (i.e. centre by centre).

Appeals against the refusal of an LA to grant an operator's licence, or by his decision to revoke, suspend, curtail or prematurely terminate, may be heard by the Transport Tribunal.

19. Vehicle construction

The Road Vehicle (Construction and Use) Regulations 1986, together with the 1989 Lighting Regulations, prescribe minimum standards for the construction of goods vehicles. They cover such matters as their weights and dimensions, braking efficiencies, equipment and lighting. Increasingly, the legislation applies EC Regulations or Directives.

Vehicle Examiners employed by the Vehicle Inspectorate (an executive agency of the DTp) are empowered to conduct fleet inspections and roadside checks on goods vehicles and to issue prohibition notices where defects are found.

20. Drivers

Drivers of most vehicles over 3.5 gvw must comply with EC Regulation 3820/85 on their hours of work. Goods vehicles are fitted with tachographs which are used by their drivers to record their journeys and work, and traffic examiners of the VI are empowered to examine tachograph charts at roadside checks or at operators' premises.

Operators have a responsibility to ensure that their drivers comply with the regulations and to retain charts for inspection.

The limits on the hours of work of drivers are as follows:

Maximum aggregate driving without a 45 minute break —
4 hours 30 minutes
Maximum daily driving — 9 hours
Maximum fortnightly driving — 90 hours
Minimum daily rest — 10 hours
Minimum weekly rest — 45 hours

There are, however, relaxations in these rules to cover split daily rest, extended daily driving or reduced weekly rest, but in most cases, where these relaxations are claimed the driver is required to compensate by taking additional rest within the prescribed periods.

21. Unified vocational licences

Entitlement to drive a large goods vehicle (LGV) is contained in the new EC unified vocational licence. Drivers who pass a 'vocational' (LGV) driving test now no longer have separate ordinary and HGV licences, but instead receive the new European licence with Category C (LGV) entitlement. Existing HGV drivers will, on the expiry after five years of their HGV licences or on reaching the age of 45 when medical re-examination is required, no longer receive a replacement HGV licence from the Traffic Commissioner, but will on 'renewal' receive a replacement European driving licence with Category C entitlement from the GVLC at Swansea.

Category C + E entitlement allows the driving of non-rigid LGVs such as 'artics' or 'drawbars'.

22. Disciplinary powers

Traffic Commissioners do, however, retain the disciplinary

powers which they have always had over LGV drivers, and may recommend to the Secretary of State that drivers who are convicted of offences in connection with the driving of an LGV, such as drivers' hours or overloading offences, or of offences which reflect on their ability to drive, such as drunken driving, are not fit persons to hold Category C entitlement.

Transport performance and cost considerations

23. Fleet costing

The ways in which fleet costs can be recorded, computed and analysed are dealt with fully in Chapter 12.

It is paramount that operators should know their costs, not only as an essential prerequisite to be able to price their services (even where 'price' is an internal transfer cost between interdepartmental budgets) but also as a means of monitoring the profitability and efficiency of the distribution operations.

24. Performance indicators

Mention has been made of distribution efficiency indicators (6:**35**). Within the narrower transport function it is possible to devise similar meaningful and well-tried indicators. The following list illustrates this, but is by no means exhaustive:

(a) Operator costs and revenue per vehicle
(b) Operator costs and revenue per mile
(c) Miles per driver
(d) Miles per vehicle
(e) Tonnes per driver
(f) Tonnes per vehicle
(g) Revenue as a percentage of turnover
(h) Revenue per vehicle
(i) Vehicle utilisation/availability
(j) Vehicle capacity/availability.

Routeing and scheduling

25. General

The principles of both manual and computer-aided scheduling

are fully discussed in Chapter 9. However, the importance of good scheduling should be obvious. It is no exaggeration to say that poor vehicle and load scheduling can destroy the profitability of a distribution function.

26. Importance of competent staff

Drivers often have, or are given, a quasi scheduling function in that they can rearrange the sequence of their deliveries to take account of changing circumstances such as congestion, queues of vehicles at delivery points, traffic diversions and early closing days. Many schedulers are ex-drivers promoted because of their skills in this direction, their often encyclopedic knowledge of the geography of their delivery area and the idiosyncracies of the firm's customers.

Employers are increasingly realising the value of such competent staff and initiating driver, clerical and supervisory training programmes embracing these and other important associated issues such as customer care.

If an operator were to lose all his fleet in a workshop fire he could, by hiring vehicles, be providing a service of sorts again the next morning. However, if his staff left him or took industrial action, provision of any sort of service would be virtually impossible since, even if a driver agency could supply replacement staff, their knowledge and understanding of his products and customers would be sadly lacking!

Good drivers and good schedulers are invaluable, and, in the short term, irreplaceable.

'Make or buy'

27. General

Having answered the question of which methods of transport are most suited to the needs of their logistics operation, many companies must then address the 'make or buy' decision — whether to own and manage their own logistics and distribution operation, or whether to buy in such services from a specialist operator.

The bulk of UK distribution transport is undertaken by road, along with a not insubstantial percentage of raw materials transport. Consequently, it is important for managers involved with logistics and distribution to be aware of the options open to them as far as operational areas suited to road transport are concerned.

For many years, road transport has been divided into 'own-account' and 'hire and reward' sectors, depending on whether the goods were carried in connection with one's own or someone else's business. Traditionally, the former firms owned and operated their own vehicle fleets, until the idea of dedicated transport services provided on a contractual basis by specialist contractors really started to gain popularity during the 1960s and 1970s. The following decade continued the trend of increased use by manufacturers and distributors of specialist transport and distribution services as a means of acquiring vehicles on contract hire, or buying in contract distribution packages in the form of the bespoke, comprehensive and often dedicated services which are now a familiar feature of present-day logistics and distribution operations.

Benefits accruing from the use of such specialist, third-party services, fall into four categories:

(a) No capital outlay
(b) Specialist management
(c) Economies of scale
(d) Costs and cost control.

These are discussed in detail below.

28. No capital outlay

No capital outlay is required for vehicles, equipment or infrastructure when a client company is buying in a specialist transport or distribution service, unless it is seen as a positive financial advantage to the manufacturer/distributor/retailer. (This latter issue will be dealt with in more detail in the section on financial management.) As a result, a company's financial resources can be concentrated on the core activity of the business, thus eliminating an element of opportunity cost and improving ROI. For organisations in a healthy cash position, this particular issue may not carry too much weight, but for others, it may mean the difference between maintaining or improving the quality of operations and customer service, or losing their competitive edge.

29. Specialist management

Specialist management of logistics operations by professional transport and distribution operators releases client company management to concentrate on the mainstream business activity. Thus many operational and legal requirements, including such often delicate issues as distribution staff wage negotiations and industrial relations, become the responsibility of the third-party contractor. In this way, specifically logistics-related problems are left to be dealt with by the contracting company, relieving client firms of unwanted pressures, and enabling them to carry on with the area of business with which they are most familiar.

30. Economies of scale

These exist where a manufacturer or retailer uses a third-party contractor with an extensive network of services and/or depots. Using this network as a basis, consistent or improved levels of service can be achieved even where peripheral collection/delivery areas are involved, e.g. far north/west and south-west UK, most particularly if client companies do not demand a dedicated service. General distribution of more than one client company's goods together makes contractors' operations more viable, and achieves a more realistic cost for their customers. This applies equally to any storage and warehousing operation as well as transport.

31. Costs and cost control

These are of considerable importance in any business, which means that an important benefit of any contracting arrangement must be the extent to which such a vital management function can still be effectively carried out. Transport and distribution contracts will be agreed within certain parameters of commodity flows, capacity to be moved and required service levels. It is on this kind of understanding that contractors will present their customers with a monthly or quarterly account for services during that period. This makes for easier accounting and budgeting within the client company, with the exception of such items as fuel and excise duty. Contract distribution costs, for example, would therefore be known in advance, and enable manufacturers for instance to budget more accurately for that particular service.

32. Disadvantages of third-party operations

Despite the 1970/80s increase in favour of third-party operations, there remain one or two potential disadvantages:

(a) Loss of control
(b) Contractor's commitment
(c) The profit element.

These are discussed further below.

33. Loss of control

Loss of control of logistics operations by the client company is often cited as a major disadvantage of third-party contracts. Loss of *direct* control inevitably results from such a commercial arrangement, but very few customers neglect to exercise a high degree of indirect control over their logistics and distribution activities, even when they are in the hands of logistics industry professionals. Such circumstances as the high degree of competition in this sector of business, consequent flexibility of contracting companies and the close relationships which often develop between client and contractor during the course of long-term contracts of this nature tend to negate the validity of the 'loss of control' issue.

34. The contractor's commitment

This might be seen as a distinct disadvantage from the other side of the agreement. This commitment takes the form of substantial capital investment in buildings and equipment (some of which can be highly specialised), vehicles and staff. The ever-present risk of non-renewal of contracts means that the possibility of disinvestment and redundancy remain in the background, and most reputable operators would rather maintain a favourable corporate image untarnished by such things which might indicate poor management or ill-advised decisions.

A highly specialised distribution centre could well be difficult to dispose of in the wrong circumstances, and even a dedicated transport fleet might realise a fraction of its true value in times of unfavourable trading or recession, or if the client company decides to reduce the scale or change the direction of their logistics and distribution operations.

35. The profit element

This has for some year been the traditional answer given to third-party companies' sales executives by many potential contract hire and distribution customers as their reason for not taking the 'contract' route. 'Why should we pay a specialist firm's profit percentage when we could do it cheaper?' If manufacturers and retailers could re-create high-quality distribution systems in-house, the costs involved would technically be lower as they would no longer be paying a contractor's percentage. But would the trade-off prove worthwhile? Detailed analysis and comparison of distribution costs would be needed in order to try and ascertain to what extent, if any, savings made through a return to 'own-account' operation would be swallowed up by change-over costs and substantially increased management and administration.

As a result of recession, the pendulum is starting to swing back in favour of in-house transport and distribution operations. Some companies are withdrawing from contract facilities, and utilising whatever resources exist within the organisation. However, as technology, specialisation and the search for higher quality continue to affect business and industry strategy, can leading firms afford to be without such a specialised service as an integral part of their competitive edge? Some large national companies have sought a compromise in putting their own systems and staff into contractors' depots — or vice versa — which helps in the exercise of control and reduces the element of profit charged by contracting companies. The question business managers must ask themselves is, can we survive without a professionally run logistics operation, and is there a positive trade-off between a third-party contractor's profit percentage, and a state-of-the-art logistics system which gives our customers the service level we have targeted to give them?

The discussion regarding third-party operation will continue, and no doubt the changing economic and commercial climate will influence the balance of the argument. Other issues remain concerning provision of transport services to industry, such as that of methods of vehicle and fleet acquisition — by purchase, leasing of one or more of the contract methods mentioned above. These matters will, however, be dealt with in Chapter 12 on financial management.

Progress test 8

1.   Should the vehicle fit the way or the way be made to fit the vehicle?   **(1)**

2.   What do you understand by combined transport? Give an example.   **(3)**

3.   Three factors comprise the selection criteria for vehicles. What are these?   **(5, 6, 8)**

4.   Identify three common types of goods vehicle.   **(8)**

5.   What are the three prerequisites of an operator's licence? **(11)**

6.   Who may object to an operator's licence application?   **(10)**

7.   How are environmental considerations accommodated within the UK system of operator licensing?   **(17)**

8.   What are the main legislative controls over:

   (a) vehicle construction and use;   **(19)**
   (b) drivers' hours, records and licensing?   **(20, 21)**

9.   What do we mean by 'make or buy'?   **(27)**

10. List and explain three main advantages of third-party transport.   **(27)**

11. What arguments would you use to support 'own-account' operation?   **(32)**

9

Information technology in logistics management

Use of IT in logistics

The most up-to-date integrated distribution systems employing techniques such as just-in-time delivery, dynamic channel selection, materials resources planning and distribution requirements planning could not function were it not for the instant availability at every point in the supply chain of accurate data on the current sales, production, inventory and transport situation.

1. Real-time systems

The ability to access current data the moment it is captured is an important product of modern information technology systems and is known as 'real-time' computing. For example, in some of the most sophisticated systems, the moment an item is sold at the supermarket check-out this information is captured via a bar code reader and can then be read immediately anywhere in the distribution chain by means of EDI systems. Computer speaks to computer via local, area, national and, in some cases, international networks. The movement of goods along the supply chain is reflected by corresponding movements of information.

2. IT as a management tool

It has been observed that 'he who holds the data runs the business', and that 'information is power', but an equal truism, much overquoted, is 'garbage in, garbage out'. What these sayings illustrate is that accurate and reliable information is today a prerequisite of management. Despite this, however, information technology is still only an aid to management, it cannot and should not be expected to replace management. As a management tool, information technology can be employed in a variety of ways, explored in the following sections.

3.   IT as a control mechanism

For example, very efficient software (computer programs) exists, and can be bought 'off the shelf' (or customised to specific distributors' requirements), for carrying out the inventory control function. This may be interfaced with other systems to produce invoices, balance orders, picking lists, replenishment stock orders and a host of other related functions and 'reports'.

The sheer amount of information generated by IT systems can easily overwhelm a manager, but this apparent disadvantage can be turned to advantage by programming the system to produce one of the most useful of all management tools, the *exception report*. Parameters within which the distribution system will normally operate can be identified and set, and the software written in such a way that only significant divergences from the norm will be reported.

4.   IT as a planning tool

Control would of course not be possible without the existence of a plan against which to measure performance. Every organisation should have its own *corporate plan*, comprising an overall 'mission statement' (e.g. 'to serve the UK market with 95 per cent delivery within two days of ordering') and the objectives which flow from this (e.g. the transport function might be required to operate with less than 10 per cent vehicle downtime). Exception reporting, based on a comparison of real-time data and objectives then becomes an obvious *performance monitoring* tool.

Performance indicators have already been referred to (some examples, such as stock turn velocity, were given in Chapter 6 on inventory management), and it will again be obvious that information technology systems are well placed to monitor overall performance in this way.

Planning is a continuous process, and plans are frequently modified in the light of the results of the sort of control monitoring processes described above. Further aspects of planning are considered in the following sections.

5. Operational planning

At a quite mundane level, the organisation's day-to-day activities have to be planned — this is known as *operational planning*. Load planning is one such activity which recurs on a daily basis. Again software exists to facilitate and speed up tasks such as order processing, load selection and vehicle routeing.

As already mentioned inventory and stock control programmes are nowadays commonplace in large warehouses, and in some instances, computerised or computer-aided load picking is employed. Consignment tracking using technology such as bar code readers is now the norm in large parcel distribution companies.

6. Tactical planning

Medium-term adjustments in a distribution organisation's operational plans often have to be made. For example, it is frequently necessary to deal with seasonal fluctuations in demand. Thus, for example, the system known as *dynamic channel selection* can be employed to deliver to the same customer from different depots at different times depending on inventory, transport or production constraints.

Such recasting of plans over a timescale of a year or less are usually referred to as *tactical planning*.

7. Strategic planning

Information technology can be of enormous advantage in formulating strategic plans to cover periods of, typically, between one and five years. The making of important decisions such as the siting of a new depot or the provision of additional warehouse capacity is so much easier if the effects of different location strategies can be tested using computerised simulations.

Which customers can best be served from which depots can also be tested and decided using a well-developed operational research technique, the 'assignment model', and so versatile are these techniques that they are increasingly today being used to make tactical decisions.

The remainder of this chapter explores some of the more common uses of information technology within the industrial logistics function.

The depot siting problem

The optimum site for a depot can be determined by taking into consideration the factors listed below. However, the actual site chosen may well be a compromise arrived at for any number of different reasons, including availability of land and finance.

(a) Accessibility from the point of view of vehicles using the depot.
(b) Availability of labour locally.
(c) The value of land in the desired location.
(d) The availability of land, bearing in mind current needs and possible expansion.
(e) Proximity to the markets to be served.

It is possible to construct mathematical models to simulate some or all of the costs and benefits of the above constraints, but the results obtained from such models when actual data is used are merely a guide to management decision making — the reasons for the final choice of site may be more pragmatic than scientific.

One of the most popular depot siting models is the gravity model. If we imagine that a number of urban areas are to be served from one depot, and that each area exerts a pull on the depot proportional to the average weight of deliveries to be made there, then it is easy to construct a mathematical model which will suggest the ideal site from which total delivery costs, related to tonne mileage, will be minimised. Suppose we lay a map of the area on a table, drill a hole through the map and table whenever there is a major concentration of customers, and through the hole pass a string to which is attached a weight proportionally equivalent (e.g. 1 g to represent 10,000 kg) to the average weekly demand for goods around that concentration. If all the strings are then knotted together, and the weights allowed to dangle freely below the table, the knot should locate itself on the map at the optimum depot site (*see* Fig. 9.1).

Nowadays, computer programs can be designed to simulate the above physical model, and to print out the co-ordinates of the ideal site. Undoubtedly, if we used such a program to identify the best site for a Lancashire/Yorkshire depot, the computer would suggest somewhere on the Pennine Moors! Management would then have to decide in which nearest Pennine town (e.g. Huddersfield or Oldham) to look for a suitable site. In this case, ease of access to the M62 trans-Pennine motorway would be an important factor.

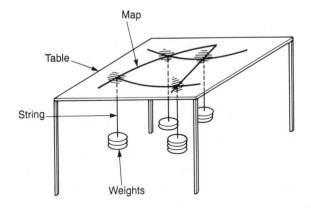

Fig. 9.1 *'Gravity' depot siting model.*

Inventory management

8. IT and inventory management

Chapter 6 on inventory management discussed different statistical forecasting techniques, ways of determining economic order quantities and of controlling inventory (either on a fixed reorder cycle or fixed reorder level), and order processing systems. Each of these functions has been computerised and suites of the appropriate software are freely available commercially to carry out any of the tasks associated with each function. In some cases the software is 'generic', i.e. capable of being utilised in a variety of logistics situations; in other cases it has been 'customised' to a particular operator's requirements.

9. Essential features

The essential features of all information technology applied to inventory management is that it generates databases recording (often in 'real time' as explained in **1**, but if not, on a batch processing basis, i.e. at frequent time-intervals — nightly, weekly, etc.) stock levels, receipts, deliveries, invoices, picking sheets, replenishment orders, etc.

The output generated by one system is also frequently the input of another 'interfacing' system. Thus sales and forecasting, production plans, deliveries and invoicing, reorder and economic order levels all affect each other. Obviously the better the information technology systems are coordinated and 'networked' with each other within a system, the more efficient that system will be.

10. Electronic data interchange

In addition, as explained in Chapter 6, information captured by suppliers or customers and exchanged with them can be of mutual benefit to all parties. In fact, allowing customers to access the suppliers' databases, perhaps by on-line services such as Prestel, can ease their task in ordering replenishment stock and provide a powerful incentive for them to do so through the supplier who gives them this facility! Mention has already been made (6:31) of the EDI systems in the field of industrial logistics management which have been developed for this purpose.

Perhaps the greatest benefit is that in freeing captured information instantaneously to all interested parties (manufacturer/supplier, warehouser, distributor and retailer) the potential to reduce costly high stockholdings at all points in the chosen distribution channels can be fully realised. To cite a well-understood example, JIT delivery systems could not function without the backing of efficient EDI.

Allocation of customers to depots

11. The problem

It is obviously important that customers are allocated to depots in such a way that delivery costs are minimised. This can be done in a number of ways, basing our allocation decision on any of the following criteria:

(a) What is the nearest depot or factory?
(b) What gives the cheapest total costs?
(c) What are the customers' requirements *vis-à-vis* stock held?
(d) What is the current allocation?

Very often existing factories, depots and stocks are located at historic sites and new markets have grown up in 'greenfield' areas which these were never planned to serve. To make matters more complicated the market originally served from these 'historic' sites may be contracting or even have totally disappeared!

A situation such as this gives rise to a classical problem, variously described as the *transportation or assignment algorithm.*

12. Illustration

The problem can be illustrated in the following manner:

Suppose that a manufacturer or distributor has three distribution depots (A, B, C) from which he plans to deliver to four hypermarkets (a, b, c, d). The grid in Fig. 9.2 shows the costs (pence per unit) associated with delivering one unit of production from any particular depot to any particular hypermarket, according to the supply and demand schedules below.

		Hypermarket (demand)			
		a	b	c	d
Depot (supply)	A	8	9	6	3
	B	4	11	5	10
	C	3	8	7	9

Fig. 9.2 *Delivery costs.*

Supply schedule (000s tonnes/month)		Demand schedule (000s tonnes/month)	
Depot A	17	Customer a	15
Depot B	20	Customer b	16
Depot C	18	Customer c	11
		Customer d	13

NB: Supply = Demand = 55,000 tonnes/month

The costs associated with each cell in Fig. 9.2 reflect the relative difficulty of each link. They will generally correspond in magnitude fairly closely with distances between depot and hypermarket, and in fact this figure is often used as a 'proxy' for cost, so that a minimum tonne/km schedule is computed. Similarly, running times between depot and hypermarket can be used as proxies to calculate a minimum time schedule.

13. Optimisation of the allocation

To achieve as low as possible a total cost the distributor must make maximum use of those cells (boxes) at the intersection of rows(depots) and columns (hypermarkets) which have the lowest costs. After this has been done the total cost can be computed. If these are still too high an attempt can be made to reallocate between customers so as to reduce costs. The technique is thus, like the savings method of minimising mileage between a finite group of customers discussed later in the chapter (20), iterative.

As with the savings routeing method there are also mathematical techniques for solving this problem. These can be incorporated into an algorithm which can be repeatedly worked until an optimum solution is reached.

For all optimisation problems there are two approaches, described as 'exact' and 'heuristic'. Exact procedures, as implied, always give the optimal solution, whilst heuristic procedures are essentially rules of thumb, or trial and error systems, which will usually give a good if not optimal solution. The two commonest techniques used for solving the depot siting problem are known as:

(a) *Vogel's Approximation Method* (VAM), which gives a basic feasible solution, often as good as (b) below, and usually within 5 per cent of this, and
(b) *the shadow cost method* of optimising an assignment problem. This is a particular case (the Simplex model) of the well-known mathematical approach known as linear programming.

14. Vogel's approximation method

Using VAM, the initial basic solution arrived at for our hypermarket allocation problem is given in Table 9.1.

Table 9.1 VAM solution to allocation problem

Depot	Store	Assignment	p/unit	Cost £
C	a	15,000	3	450
A	b	4,000	9	360
B	b	9,000	11	990
C	b	3,000	8	240
B	c	11,000	5	550
A	d	13,000	3	390
	Total	55,000		2,980

15. Shadow cost method

However, when the optimisation routine, which employs the linear programming technique (Simplex Model) of minimising 'shadow costs', is applied to this initial basic feasible solution, a saving of £180 can be identified involving making the following +/– exchange of assignments:

+9,000 Ba +4	–9,000 Bb –11
–9,000 Ca –3	+9,000 Cb +8

The net saving is given by:

$$
\begin{aligned}
& 9,000\ (Ba - Bb + Cb - Ca) \\
=\ & 9,000\ (4 - 11 + 8 - 3) \\
=\ & 9,000 \times 2p \\
=\ & £180
\end{aligned}
$$

The optimum assignment is thus as given in Table 9.2.

Table 9.2 Optimum solution to allocation problem

Depot	Store	Assignment	p/unit	Cost £
B	a	9,000	4	360
C	a	6,000	3	180
A	b	4,000	9	360
C	b	12,000	8	960
B	c	11,000	5	550
A	d	13,000	3	390
	Total	55,000		2,800

Algorithms such as VAM and Simplex are nowadays incorporated into computer programs which are capable, given the data representing an assignment problem, of producing a minimum cost solution.

Goods vehicle scheduling

16. The problem

Goods vehicles do not as a rule serve the same customers at the same times every day and the demand for them is generally highly unpredictable,. Goods vehicle scheduling is thus extremely *demand responsive* over short time intervals. This means that distribution managers must plan goods vehicle operations at two different levels:

(a) at the *strategic* level in terms of long-term resource allocation, and

(b) at the *tactical* level in terms of daily fluctuations in customer demand and driver and vehicle availability.

A simple objective, such as minimising vehicle distances, can conflict with other valid aims affecting aspects of customer service, driver and vehicle utilisation, and costs. Other constraints such as traffic congestion and delivery restrictions can further complicate matters.

17. Approaches to solving the problem

Despite the complexity of the problem attempts to arrive at solutions have been made, and some of these have resulted in significant advances in our understanding of logistics problems. Initially mathematicians using the science of operational research developed 'pencil and paper' techniques which addressed problems such as minimising distance travelled between a variety of locations.

Many of these techniques could be expressed as *algorithms*, i.e. a set of sequential steps or instructions which, if followed, would produce a solution. Algorithms are the raw material of computer programs. They are generally *heuristic* (i.e. the result of trial and error) because the size of the problem is not conducive to the production of totally efficient algorithms which can take into account the many compromises involved, for example between maximising speed by routeing vehicles along motorways or minimising distance by using ordinary roads (*see* Fig. 9.3).

18. The IT solution to the problem

Today IT is increasingly being employed to address the goods vehicle scheduling problem. However, it is increasingly being recognised that the ability of a human familiar with a network to identify sensible journeys and diversions, cannot adequately be replicated by a computer, and mainly for this reason computer-aided scheduling packages ('menu-driven' by the scheduler) often today continue to eclipse the fully computerised scheduling package in which data is simply input and the 'optimum schedule' then output without any scheduler/computer interaction.

The earliest applications of information technology to vehicle scheduling used large mainframe computers incapable of responding to schedulers' fast-changing requirements. The systems developed were of some use at the strategic level, for example to plan a fixed daily delivery round for a bakery, but found little application outside such large users.

The situation has changed rapidly of late as a result of the current availability of:

(a) powerful low-cost minicomputers bringing near mainframe

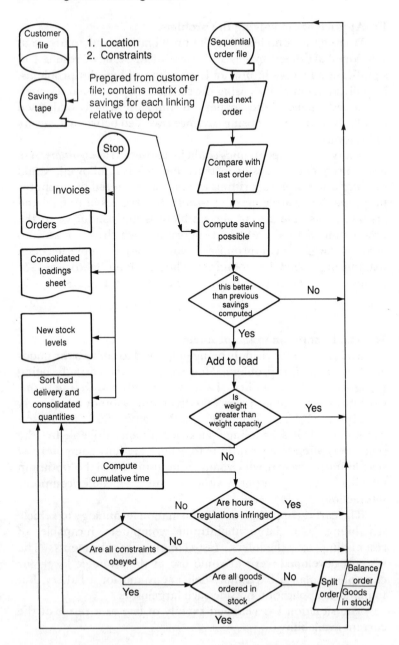

Fig. 9.3 *Computer routeing flow diagram.*

processing speed and capacity directly into the workplace. These can operate as stand-alone or networked systems, and
(b) easily updated and accurate road databases which can be used as the basis of a company's computerised scheduling.

Traffic clerks and schedulers who plan the utilisation of vehicles are key personnel whose efficiency can have a direct bearing on the economic performance of the undertaking. Modern information technology can remove the drudgery from their task, helping them to arrive quickly at initial feasible solutions and to test these by amending or fine-tuning their schedules and observing the results.

19. The routeing/scheduling problem

The vehicle routeing/scheduling problem involves supplying a given quantity of goods in vehicles of known capacity. The drivers may be required to make collections and deliveries simultaneously or to perform either of these tasks separately. They may be engaged on local or long-distance deliveries. It may be necessary to schedule a 'night out' for the driver, or for drivers to exchange vehicles and/or trailers.

Routeing problems fall into two groups in accordance with possible procedures adopted for their solution:

(a) *Link oriented.* All premises along discrete links or 'edges' (roads) connecting 'nodes' (junctions) must be capable of being served. Refuse collection, newspaper, post and milk rounds are good examples of linked work.
(b) *Node oriented.* By far the most difficult problem, this involves the connection of a number of 'nodes' (customers' premises) in the most economical way possible.

In both cases optimum solution is achieved by minimising distance or time.

A number of theoretical approaches to routeing have been developed over the years. It is not essential to understand the mathematics of these routeing 'models' to apply them — computer programs incorporating them are fully documented with all the necessary steps spelt out, and the manual application of relevant techniques is clearly and concisely described in accompanying manuals and numerous texts.

Routeing models most commonly fall into one of three categories:

(a) one-stage solutions;
(b) two-stage solutions;
(c) incremental improvement methods.

These are discussed more fully in the following sections.

20. One-stage solutions

The savings method, developed in 1963 by Fletcher, Clarke and Wright, is the most common one-stage solution and is still used today as the basis of many manual and computerised load planning systems. Well-known scheduling programs such as ROUTEMASTER use this method. (We will look briefly at some of these later.)

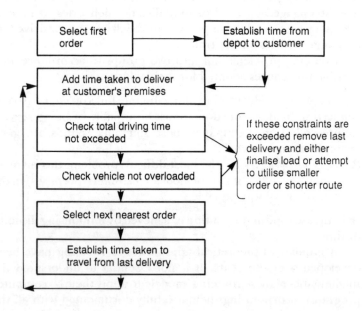

Fig. 9.4 *Fletcher, Clarke and Wright 'savings method' algorithm.*

21. Two-stage solutions

A common technique first ranks customers according to the angle created between the depot and the two most distant customers within a sector, and then the sectors with the least angle are selected until the capacity constraints of the vehicle are reached. Linking customers in this way on the boundary or circumference of the delivery area tends to create greater distance savings than making links along radial routes, and leads to arc or circumferential routes, not unlike the petals of a flower.

A second stage in the process might be manual or computer-assisted routeing of the vehicle between customers within the arc using the savings method.

22. Incremental improvement methods

An initial basic feasible solution is first developed using an alternative model and then a stepwise or iterative exchange sort is carried out on this solution. The basis of early attempts at the solution, such as the TRASAL (Travelling Salesman) program, it gives the scheduler the facility to exchange the position of one customer in the delivery chain with every other customer in the chain and to observe the effects of the exchanges on distance, enabling the scheduler to answer the question 'What if . . . this customer were served earlier/later'.

As a generalisation, the more exact the method is claimed to be, the more expensive it will be in computer time and computer memory space occupied.

23. Manual routeing and scheduling

The problem, once again, consists of determining on a daily basis the loads, routes and schedules for a number of vehicles and drivers operating from one or more depots. It is a tactical problem which usually varies each day, unless the customer demand pattern is fairly constant in which case fixed delivery rounds can be established.

Purely manual systems usually involve a traffic clerk, often an ex-driver with intimate knowledge of the delivery area and customers, planning a day's work for each driver. Orders are stacked in racks corresponding to discrete areas, and loads are assembled by selecting orders for clusters of customers in adjacent areas.

24. Types of route

Normally, the patterns of demand will generate one of three common types, although many routes are a hybrid of two or more types. These are illustrated in Fig. 9.5.

(a) *Arc routes* link customers in an arc shape at various distances and in the same general direction from the depot. Generally the driver will leave on one radial route, deliver to a cluster of customers and return along an adjacent radial route.

(b) *Area routes* link customers in concentrated areas or link clusters of customers in areas remote from the depot. Considerable 'dead mileage' (*see* below) is often involved in shaping these routes.

(c) *Radial routes* link customers situated along radial roads to and from the depot. These are essentially linear — for example, a driver routed to a port with an export order may have spare capacity on his vehicle and be given one or two extra deliveries to make en route.

25. Deliveries off route

Where two or more deliveries are slightly off route, a useful rule of thumb is to *sum the distances to each diversion by alternative routes, ignoring the common, and unavoidable distance between the two deliveries*. For example, in the network shown in Fig. 9.6, where deliveries have to be made en route to customers at A, B, C and D, if the driver delivers first to C, the total diversionary distance is $6 + 8 + 8 = 22$ miles, and if he delivers first to D it is $5 + 8 + 7 = 20$ miles, a saving of 2 miles.

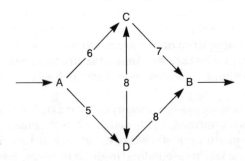

Fig. 9.6 *Off-route delivery network.*

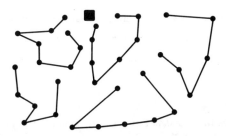

Arc or circumferential routes

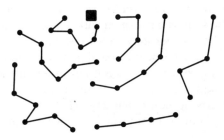

Regional routes

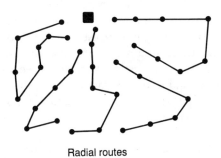

Radial routes

Fig. 9.5   *Types of route — note the differing degrees of 'dead mileage' involved.*

Summing the distances off route to the diversions, and ignoring the common distance D–C (8 miles):

Via C then D = 6 + 8 = 14 miles

Via D then C = 5 + 7 = 12 miles (preferred route)

Saving   2 miles

26. Dead mileage

All routes have a *stem* comprising 'dead mileage' between the depot and the first delivery. This represents non-productive driver time. Some operators prefer to build this in at the start of the day, effectively running to a distant customer first, and working back in towards the depot. However, there may be a fuel penalty in this in so far as the stem is performed with a laden vehicle.

Conversely, a driver may have to wait to unload if he arrives too early at a customer near to the depot, and could better utilise his time driving to a more distant customer in the early hours before traffic builds up and, further minimise the risk of exceeding his statutory driving hours that day. This sort of decision is best taken in the light of the circumstances which are known to prevail.

27. Assumptions

Once the nucleus of a load has been built up, a scheduler can check the weight or volume against the vehicle capacity, the distance to be travelled against constraints such as drivers' hours regulations and trade union agreements, and make subjective allowances for known congestion black spots, weather conditions, etc. He may then add to or subtract orders, substitute one order for another, or adjust the delivery order. In doing so, a number of *assumptions* have to be made:

(a) There is a legal limit to the length of the drivers' working and driving day. Routes must reflect this, even though some routes may be for more than one day.

(b) Vehicles have limited capacity.
(c) All deliveries must be feasible, i.e. within customers' earliest and latest delivery times.
(d) Vehicles either return empty or with scheduled back loads.

28. Load planning

The two main *objectives* for good load planning are:

(a) to minimise costs by minimising:
   (i) mileage — this will reduce variable costs, and
   (ii) fleet size — this will reduce fixed costs;
(b) to make the most efficient use of staff and vehicles.

Many other *factors and constraints* also have to be considered. Table 9.3 provides a useful checklist.

29. Computer-assisted vs. manually adjusted scheduling

Whilst no computer can be programmed to remember every idiosyncrasy of every customer or of the area served and no computer program can replicate all the variables which a scheduler must consider or compensate for his detailed knowledge of an area, it is possible for computers to be used to produce initial basic feasible solutions at least as good as the scheduler's first stab at the problem.

Such programs can also take away the tedium of calculating aggregate distances and volumes/weights, and allow the scheduler to amend the initial route and see the effects of this instantly displayed. It is also as well to vet the load before the goods are placed in the vehicle (usually in reverse delivery order — first in, last off).

A good scheduler or driver can usually spot potential delays (such as customers scheduled for first delivery who always open late!) and will be able to make cosmetic changes to the load to overcome such problems. (Another example would be knowledge of motorway repair works causing temporary delays at peak hour, which can be circumvented using a parallel road network.)

Table 9.3 Checklist of factors and constraints on load planning

Vehicles	–	number and type
	–	capacity
Manpower	–	number of staff
	–	types of driving licences
	–	training undertaken by staff
	–	union agreements
	–	shift patterns and working hours
	–	rota patterns (work allocation)
Customers	–	order pattern
	–	location
	–	delivery point facilities
	–	opening/closing times
	–	day/night delivery
	–	return loads/return empty cases/return empty vehicle
Company	–	customer service policy
	–	running speed/operating policies/agreements
	–	product characteristics
	–	depot locations
	–	return load policy
Environment	–	road pattern/network
	–	weather conditions
	–	legal restrictions

Data requirements for distribution-based IT systems

30. System 'inputs'

Whilst the 'outputs' of distribution-based IT systems are impressive — real-time inventory figures, stock location and picking lists, loading schedules, depot siting analyses and delivery routes, to name a few — these do not just appear once a program is written and installed on a computer. Programs require data input on which to operate, and, indeed, the computer will invariably cease to execute the programme and ask (usually by means of an on-screen 'prompt' such as '?') for any missing data which it needs.

31. Elements of the database

Customer databases usually already exist for sales, ordering and invoicing purposes, but frequently have to be amended or updated to make them 'relational' to scheduling programs. They may have to be manually input into a computer if they only exist as hard copy (e.g. as a cardex index) and they have to be in a form readable for the program.

There are three items of information which are critical:

(a) spatial or locational data;
(b) assignment of the customer to a supply depot;
(c) operational data.

These are discussed further below.

32. Spatial data

Spatial data specifies customer location, either by reference to:

(a) postcode,
(b) Ordinance Survey grid reference,
(c) reference to a gazetteer of place names.

Commercial software (for example the program MATCH-CODE, which can be accessed 'on-line' by using a telephone, modem and the BT Prestel service) can convert postcodes to grid references.

There are also some very comprehensive geographical databases available commercially, which query entries such as 'NEWPORT' (there are ten Newports in the UK!) and invite a supporting input from a menu of alternatives such as 'GWENT?', 'I.O.W?', etc.

Simple routeing programs can compute distances between grid references geometrically and apply a 'curvature factor' (often in the order of 120 per cent) to this distance 'as the crow flies' to approximate to actual distances. Commercial programs, discussed in **39** below, contain more sophisticated utilities.

33. Assignment to depot

Assignment of customers to depots can be on a permanent or temporary basis, or, as described in Chapter 6 on inventory management, where dynamic channel strategies are employed, on a tactical day-to-day basis.

34. Operational data

Operational data will contain the details (size, weight, composition) of orders and constraints such as early closing days, opening and closing hours and special delivery instructions.

35. Commercial databases

Using a reliable commercial geographical database avoids having to make crude approximations. Most commercial databases can accommodate grid reference, postcode or gazetteer locational inputs and nearly all contain some if not all of the following features:

(a) Customer specification — by grid reference (to nearest 100 km), postcode or name (village, town, suburb, even well-known pubs like 'Scots Corner' on the A66).
(b) Link specification — road number (A627), road class (A, B, minor), motorway, dual carriageway, rural, urban, hilly, etc.
(c) The ability to assign different travel speeds to different classes of link.
(d) The facility to establish complex links between places separated by natural barriers such as estuaries, mountain ranges, etc., or to avoid nominated locations (such as specified motorway roadworks) and to calculate distances over these diversionary routes.

Most commercial databases are regularly updated by the software houses in cooperation with the Post Office and motoring organisations (RAC, AA). Many contain graphics facilities so that the road network can be displayed on the screen and the scheduler can interact with this by the use of light pens or a 'mouse pad'. Well-known commercial geographic database matrices include ROADFILE, ROADNET and VISIT.

Monitoring performance

36. Methods of monitoring performance

As well as being able to prescribe the work of a driver and vehicle, it is also of enormous benefit to be able to monitor their performance.

Tachograph analysis is one way of doing so retrospectively, and there are useful programs on the market which interface with tachograph analysers so that the data from the analysis can be captured and displayed in spreadsheet fashion. Such programs lend themselves to *exception reporting* where drivers' hours infringements can be highlighted and reported and warning letters to the drivers generated.

Many operators also install cab radio or 'cell-phones' to enable them to keep in touch with their drivers and vice versa.

37. Vehicle locational systems

A comparatively recent innovation is the use of vehicle locational systems, where, through the interception of signals generated by local transmitters or, increasingly nowadays, satellites, a 'geodetic fix' of the vehicle's position can be reported and even displayed on a map on the operator's VDU. This may well be the same map as that used by the commercial routeing program so that planned and actual locations can be compared in real time!

The spy-in-the-sky is replacing the spy-in-the-cab, and, inevitably, there is likely to be a re-run of the same industrial relations problems which the tachograph and in-cab radios caused in their infancies before drivers and their unions realised the ways in which such systems might benefit and protect them as well as increasing overall operational efficiency.

Penetration of IT into industrial logistics management

38. Survey findings

In 1989 the Institute of Logistics and Distribution Management produced a 'Special Distribution Industry Survey' on *The Management of IT* which contained some surprising findings:

(a) The survey discovered rapid growth in the use of IT, with expenditure on IT at just under 2 per cent of turnover. A comparison was made with expenditure in other sectors, namely:

(*i*) financial services: 3–4 per cent;

(*ii*) manufacturing and retail: both 1 per cent.

The second, low, figure was significant since the report also identified lower expenditure on IT (and a lower number of terminals per employee!) in food retailing than in specialist distribution companies.

(b) On a more positive note EDI appears well established, with the distribution industry clearly leading in this field. Bar coding and stock location systems were reported to be dominant amongst companies' stated planned innovations. Most companies surveyed were using personal computers either networked throughout their organisations or linked to central mini or (less often) mainframe computers.

(c) The average number of staff employed in the IT functions of respondent firms (average size 1,300 employees) was just less than ten, with a trend away from off-the-shelf packaged software towards bespoke systems either developed in house, by consultants or through parent companies.

(d) The most extensively computerised applications were invoicing, accounting and inventory management, and the least computerised applications were vehicle routeing and fleet management, and, where these systems had been introduced, they were on average less than two years old.

(e) Operational planning programmes such as fleet management (including vehicle replacement) and distribution planning (including depot siting) were the applications which most used packaged software.

The survey gives an interesting snapshot of the use of IT in distribution. It is clearly growing apace, but at different rates and in different directions in different parts of the industry.

39. Inventory control and IT

It is hardly surprising that inventory control emerges as the favoured IT application. These systems differ from most other systems in that they are capable of making decisions rather than merely aiding managers by providing information on which they can base their decisions. Indeed it has been argued (*see* '*Management Today*', May 1991) that they work best when human intervention is kept at a minimum!

The same article makes the point that, whilst in theory inventories can be reduced or even eliminated by fashionable techniques such as just-in-time (JIT) and materials resource planning (MRP), commercial reality dictates that in a competitive world the need to give a speedy reliable service makes the carrying of a certain level of stock essential to a smooth and efficient operation. This means that in practice, therefore, inventory control continues to be essential to the management of supply and production.

40. The human factor

Finally, to return to the premise 'GIGO (garbage in, garbage out)', postulated at the start of this chapter, it is still true to assert that computers alone cannot manage and that distribution managers must still make important decisions, although these may well be computer-aided.

However, the integrity of the data contained in modern systems is increasingly improving with the elimination of much human and keyboard error by the use of bar codes, EDI and the sophisticated input checks which are contained in today's programs. (A good example is the check digits at the end of product codes which should equate to the sum of the figures in the code.)

Users of IT can therefore be increasingly confident of the systems which are now employed and are continuing to be employed in the field of industrial logistics management.

Progress test 9

1. What is a 'real-time' system? **(1)**

2. How can IT aid managers? **(2)**

3. How can IT assist in making planning decisions? **(4)**

4. Explain the use of IT in:

   (a) depot siting;   **(p.160)**
   (b) customer allocation;   **(11–15)**
   (c) inventory management.   **(8–10)**

5. Explain how the concept of the 'savings' algorithm enabled a routeing model to be developed.   **(20, Fig. 9.4)**

6. How can schedulers be assisted by IT?   **(21)**

7. Identify three common types of route.   **(Fig. 9.5)**

8. What constraints does a scheduler face?   **(Table 9.3)**

9. How completely has IT penetrated the industrial logistics function?   **(35)**

10. How can IT assist with the problem of vehicle location? **(37)**

10
Human resources management

Human resources management as a business function

1. Introduction

Industrial materials management, transport and distribution comprise what many people now regard as total business logistics, and have traditionally been capital-intensive operations. As such, one of the reasons for the focusing of management attention on these areas has been the reduction of costs — Peter Drucker's well-known 'last frontier'. But this area of business activity has also been — and largely remains — a labour-intensive operation. Despite the advent of modern techniques in the storage, handling and movement of both materials and information, supply chain management still requires large numbers of people to plan the operation, to carry out the tasks and, most of all, to manage it as an integrated process for the benefit of the organisation and the customer. The role of personnel management in developing the most effective policies relating to recruitment and selection, training and development of staff in such a vital business function is therefore crucial.

2. Recent changes

During the last 10–15 years, a much greater emphasis has been placed on the more effective management of human resources. This has been reflected in changing management styles, the higher profile adopted by supervisor and manager training and development, and the reappraisal of 'people management' as a business function. Amending the title of a functional head or department's responsibility from 'Personnel' to 'Human Resources' has, in many cases, been a good deal more than just a cosmetic change. It has been an in-depth exercise in reviewing the role of that particular business function, and the re-examination of the company's policies and style of management concerning employees at all levels.

Human resources management (HRM) now comprises a wider range of responsibilities concerned with attracting, engaging and parting with employees. Such areas as manpower planning, remuneration and working conditions, training, and administration of pension schemes and retirement arrangements under a variety of circumstances, remain very much a part of functional activity. But, though job and person specifications, selection and recruitment, staff appraisal and development, and some aspects of discipline remain part of good human resources management, there has been a shift in the balance. The role of many such managers has become, in some ways, much more that of a 'staff' manager or adviser to 'line' managers. As the field of human resources management has broadened, so 'line' managers have become more involved in its specialism, and often nowadays need to possess some of the skills which were previously regarded as very much the province of the personnel or human resources professional.

3. HRM and logistics

But where should this review of human resources management in a logistics context begin? Perhaps the most appropriate starting point would be to consider the role and responsibilities of logistics management itself. In order to do this, an assessment of the importance and position of logistics within the corporate framework is a prerequisite. Where do materials and distribution management feature in the average company's strategy? How important to its goals is effective, integrated supply chain management? To answer these and other related questions, it is necessary to examine briefly the process of evolution undergone by both organisation structures and transport and distribution management over the last 20 years or so.

4. Logistics within the corporate structure

No attempt could be made to position logistics management correctly in an organisation's structure without an understanding of the role it would be expected to fulfil within that company's overall business strategy. Most companies would see that role as effectively planning, managing and developing the smooth, continuous and timely flow of goods and materials through the supply chain. But to what end? What do businesses hope to achieve by adopting and fostering such a concept? Perhaps increased sales, greater market share, improved profitability or enhanced corporate image. In turn, these corporate objectives are themselves achieved through firms having a sharper competitive edge than their competitors — which, in many cases, means raising and maintaining levels of customer service.

This latter conclusion points to logistics and distribution management being a customer-oriented activity, and therefore a sub-function of what in many companies is now marketing. Chapter 1 describes such integrated operations as a recent phenomenon, where previously their component activities were the responsibility of different business functions. The more traditional company structure (see Fig. 10.1) is an example of the

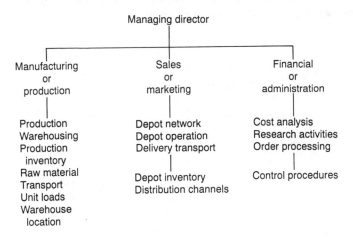

Fig. 10.1 *Traditional company structure.*

organisational framework which existed in many firms up to the last 15 years or so. In such a format, materials management was the responsibility of manufacturing/production, transport, storage and distribution might be within the remit of production or sales management, and any associated administration procedures fell squarely into the lap of finance and administration departments. Thus the effectiveness of logistics and distribution was severely limited, being split across business functions with often widely differing objectives. It might also be considered as having — in this context — a rather ancillary role, like many 'staff' functions.

5. Development of logistics as a corporate specialism

Following developments in overall business philosophy, industrial relations and physical distribution, the latter began to emerge as a specialism in its own right. Along with personnel (now referred to as human resources management) physical distribution management came, over a period of time, to be represented either at a senior level of management, or in some cases — and more importantly — at board level. This gave rise to the more recent and extended structure now adopted by many larger companies (*see* Fig. 10.2). Here distribution management became a distinct 'line' management activity in its own right. It became more effective through the integration of its sub-functions and development of the synergy effect.

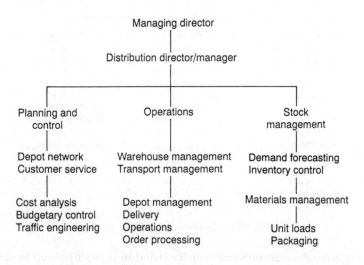

Fig. 10.2 *A recent, extended organisational structure.*

As mentioned above, evolution of the new corporate framework was based partly on the emergence of physical distribution management as a discrete discipline, driven to a certain extent by companies more completely embracing a market-oriented business philosophy. Personnel or human resources management became more significant within the organisation, partly as a result of pressures generated by the industrial relations climate of the 1970s, but also as part of the universal search for a more effective management style overall. In doing so, it coincided neatly with the evolution of the new area of corporate responsibility — integrated physical distribution management.

6. Total integrated business logistics

Modern business cannot stand still. If it is to become and remain successful, it must develop. And so the process has continued over the last decade — and still continues up to the present day and beyond. Whereas, previously, forward-thinking businesspeople and managers were preaching the gospel of the 'total distribution concept', now the goal is total integrated business logistics.

Here firm links must be forged between materials management and physical distribution management, between suppliers and customers, between manufacturers and retailers. In many cases, driven by such factors as globalisation of industry, the search for total quality, and continuing rapid advances in information technology, this has already started to happen in the larger and more aware organisations. Many companies, however, still adhere to their more conservative structures, methods and relationships — presumably considering concepts like logistics management as 'flavour of the month' (or year) ideas, which will eventually lose favour.

7. Role of human resources management

What then is the role of human resources management in this next stage of corporate evolution? Even in the more recent company structure, it is possible for quite rigid chains of command and lines of communication to exist. Areas of responsibility are often highly departmentalised. Is the answer to reconfigure the corporate structure once more, a task for company senior management? Or perhaps to redraw the job descriptions of logistics supervisors and managers, thereby giving them certain areas of joint responsibility? The principle would be that, by doing so, a truly integrated logistics team could then be developed.

Greater intra-organisational cooperation is, however, only part of the answer. The capability now exists for companies to exchange ideas and information with an immense degree of speed and freedom — to their mutual benefit. Again, some are already doing this, but others must generate the will and the trust to become more involved with each other, and use the advantages to develop truly integrated supply chain management.

Development of the modern logistics manager

8.   Role of transport and distribution managers

Having taken an overview of logistics at the corporate level, the next step is to examine the development of the modern logistics manager. A major factor in this process has been the evolving role of transport and distribution managers in the last two decades.

Of greatest significance to an aspiring transport or warehousing manager in the 1960s was experience in the industry and the job. A high degree of practical experience and task management was needed. Staff-management was often achieved through autocratic styles or past experience in the job — many transport and warehouse managers had been drivers and warehousemen, then foremen and perhaps assistant managers, before reaching full manager status. Qualifications had a certain amount of credibility in the eyes of the industry — but no more. Professionalism, in an area of activity that always seemed to be the 'Cinderella' of business and industry, had only limited value — it didn't necessarily get lorries out on time, make drivers productive or improve warehouse utilisation.

Nevertheless, over the following 25 years, the role of similar managers was to change tremendously, driven by six major factors or events as discussed in the sections which follow.

9.   Legislation

The Transport Act 1968 was seen as a logical change of direction in the regulation of the industry. A new quality-based operator licensing regime supplanted the old quantity licensing system. Stringent maintenance standards and professional competence of operators and transport managers became, over a short period of time, mandatory targets for all road hauliers and transport contractors. The licensing procedure was changed, vocational licences were introduced for drivers of vehicles exceeding 7.5 tonnes gvw, annual plating and testing became part of fleet maintenance programmes, and the prospect of licensing for transport managers loomed on the horizon.

Within a short space of time, managers in the industry had to familiarise themselves with a host of new provisions relating to day-to-day vehicle and fleet management, and impending changes to their own status.

10. World oil crisis

In the wake of the 1973 Arab-Israeli war, fuel costs rose sharply — an alarming trend which continued for some time. These increases fed through to the cost of living during the 1970s, affecting not only transport costs, but those of labour, vehicles, inventory, land and buildings.

This introduced, if not increased, the need for effective cost control as part of the transport/distribution manager's day-to-day responsibility. In spite of greater control over inflation during the 1980s, the cost element of logistics and distribution remains one of the main areas for management attention, as consumers continue to demand consistent quality and value for money — and companies seek to maintain their competitive edge. High interest rates have been a feature of central government's monetary policy in order to try and control inflation, and this has tended to exacerbate the cost control problem.

The result of these events has been a need for logistics and distribution managers to be highly numerate, with a considerable awareness of financial matters generally, and of some specific techniques in particular.

11. Industrial relations

Due largely to the domestic political situation and rapidly increasing inflation, trade union power mushroomed during the 1970s, aided by several pieces of employment legislation. The result was numerous successful demands for increased wages and improved working conditions — but in many cases, without any corresponding agreement for increased productivity. Not only did this trend reveal itself in higher labour costs, but also in a more aggressive industrial relations environment. Although many managers in the field of transport and distribution had been accustomed to fairly tough bargaining and staff-management scenarios, such a development strengthened the need for industry professionals to have in their everyday armoury a working knowledge of the new legislation, and experience of putting into practice a more assertive style in managing their human resources.

12. Commercial pressure

As a result of changes in the commercial and consumer environment since the 1960s, there has been increasing competition in all areas of business. A significant part of this change has been the retail-led distribution revolution — starting in the grocery trade with the supermarket chains and continuing its progress via out-of-town shopping facilities and DIY and homeware hypermarkets. Availability of growing ranges of all kinds of products and commodities, either immediately or within ever-shortening lead times, has increased the customer service level expectations of the average consumer.

Added to this, the beginning of both the 1980s and the 1990s has seen recession bite into the UK's industrial and commercial fabric. As companies seek to increase or, in many cases, maintain market share, logistics and distribution managers have come under pressure to improve their function's performance.

13. Information technology

While all these things were happening, computer systems were increasingly becoming a very successful management tool. Electronic data processing systems had started in most firms as a more efficient method of calculating payrolls, and producing wage and salary slips, along with certain accounting documents and financial information. The previously mentioned changes brought about increased pressure for much faster collection, analysis and transmission of information, to assist in streamlining all aspects of business and industry.

Operational research techniques also aided the development of computer programs which could be used to help solve some of the day-to-day operating problems of distribution management, and serve as a strategic planning aid in systems development, improvement and expansion. Computerised stock control systems, programs to optimise the location of logistics facilities and numerous others soon became part of both daily decision making and long-term business planning. Knowledge of such systems and their applications was fast becoming a requirement for the aspiring distribution manager.

14. The European dimension

Although international road transport operations had developed considerably during the 1960s — mainly into Europe and the Middle East — a positive step toward even closer ties with continental countries came in 1973 when UK membership of the EEC was finally confirmed. Distribution had, until then, been largely road-based, whereas some of our EEC partners in the Community were decidedly pro-rail. How would this affect throughout-by-road transport and distribution?

As it happened, continued involvement in Europe did little to change industry's operating methods — although many companies turned to using Freightliner containerised transport in the mid-1970s to minimise the effects of high fuel and road transport costs. In the early 1980s, however, two significant developments were mooted, which would greatly affect logistics and distribution strategy — the planned building of a fixed link across the Channel, targeted to open in 1993, and the concept of a 'Single European Market' to be achieved by 1992.

Since the planned realisation of these twin ideals, many logistics and distribution managers have had to consider their function in an increasingly international context. With manufacturing and distribution industries taking on a European, if not global perspective, managers in logistics functions have been developing a consciousness of their imminent wider role on the international scene.

15. The modern logistics manager

Taking all these changes together with those at the corporate level, how were companies to find suitable candidates for these new management positions? What kind of people would be likely to be able to fulfil the role of a modern logistics manager? Many existing managers had grown with the job, and had adapted to the needs of the new discipline; many had to be trained in the skills and aptitudes required by a successful manager in logistics. This latter process is still continuing.

During the evolution process, the spectrum of physical distribution activity itself has changed and broadened. No longer is it limited to those areas it occupied at the beginning of the decade. Logistics management — as it is now frequently known — is now a highly specialised area of company management, comprising materials management and physical distribution management. Many businesses now see their physical commodity movements in terms of total business logistics, using such techniques as distribution requirements planning and 'just-in-time' methods. Aspiring managers must therefore be well-qualified to undertake such a complex role.

Staffing in the logistics industry

16. General

Despite the great strides already described in the application of IT to the distribution industry and the automation of many materials handling functions, it remains a labour-intensive industry. Warehouse staff continue to hand-pick goods even where automation brings goods to them rather than their having to walk to the picking location, and drivers still drive both trunk and delivery vehicles even if they no longer load them themselves!

17. Size and scale of the industry

Official statistics give some clues to the size of the industrial logistics industry, but the way in which they are collected and reported makes it difficult if not impossible to arrive at a total labour figure. The Registrar General's classification of employment contains a category of Transport and Communication employees, of which in 1986 when *Transport Statistics* (HMSO) was last revised there were 1,442,000. Deducting the 431,000 post and telecommunication employees this leaves just over one million transport workers. Some of these (144,000) were employed by BRB, including Railfreight, and 196,000 were in road passenger transport.

Of the remainder, 232,000 were in road haulage and 439,000

in 'other' (mainly own-account) road transport. These figures include only inland transport and exclude port, airport, airline and maritime employees, many of whom are involved in international distribution.

It has been estimated that very roughly one-third of distribution in the UK is 'retail-led', one-third provided by hauliers as a 'bespoke' or dedicated service, and one-third provided by manufacturers' and suppliers' 'own-account' transport. But this tells us little about total numbers of employees. For example, what proportion of the 232,000 employees in the road haulage sector are directly engaged in distribution? Half a million might be a reasonable estimation of the number of employees in the own-account and retail-led sector, where it is known that productivity is not so high as in the haulage sector, but how many other jobs the industry directly supports in warehousing, vehicle manufacturing and repair and at the 'interface' with retail distribution (e.g. in the warehouses/ stockrooms attached to supermarkets), it would be impossible to say.

Official statistics also classify employees by function, such as managerial, supervisory, operative and clerical. In the logistics industry the number of operatives is relatively high.

Distribution management

18. General

There are strong arguments for managing the distribution function as a whole, with the appointment of a distribution director at board level.

Not all organisations, however, accept this logic, and in some cases distribution is treated as part of the marketing function, or even the sales function, whilst in other organisations the traditional departmental boundaries between transport, ware-housing, inventory management, production, etc., still prevail. However, this is becoming less and less common as the enormous trade-offs and economies which can be made between these functions when their management is coordinated becomes appreciated.

19. Divisional management structures

Some distribution organisations have a divisional structure, with the overall management of each division being arranged either on a federal basis (i.e. by geographical area) or a product basis (e.g. foodstuff, fashion, etc.). At each division and sub-division (depot, warehouse, etc.) there will be found a divisional general manager and 'line managers' controlling day-to-day direct management functions, such as the transport manager or the depot engineer.

At head office there will also be overarching specific management functions with a chief traffic manager, a chief engineer, etc., who will have oversight of the equivalent divisional operations but not day-to-day responsibility, and other supporting 'staff' managers such as personnel, finance, industrial relations, marketing and distribution.

20. Contract distribution and franchising

Because distribution is such a specialised function separate from, and often seen as detracting from, the mainstream activity of a company (be it manufacture, trading, retail or supply of services), various ways of hiving off the activity without losing overall control have evolved. One method of achieving this is *contract distribution* where a specialised company such as Excel Logistics will quote to take over the entire physical distribution of a company, providing its own warehousing, vehicles, staff and logistics.

Other 'solutions' rely on relieving the company of some of the burdens of distribution, such as industrial relations problems, legal compliance (e.g. goods vehicle operator licensing, drivers' hours and vehicle maintenance), and the financial problem of capital tied up in distribution (vehicles, buildings, computer hardware, etc.) which might be more profitably invested in the mainstream business.

To this end companies might 'franchise' their deliveries to owner-drivers, either (as many ready-mixed concrete suppliers do) selling the vehicle to the driver, or using contract hire vehicles. Similarly with retail-led distribution which relies on manufacturers bringing in supplies in bulk to the retailer's own distribution hubs, it is a short step from this scenario to franchising out the 'hub' operations to one or more different bespoke distribution companies (perhaps retaining one hub 'in house' as a cost comparison monitoring exercise).

The net result of many of these strategies is that employees in the distribution industry are often not employed by the organisation whose goods they deliver, but by their agents, or indeed often by specialised distribution employment agencies.

21. The need for management skills
Logistics management is nowadays no longer a function which can be exercised by a driver promoted to dispatch manager working from a portakabin in the yard. It is a highly sophisticated function demanding well-trained and competent specialised managers.

Managers obviously need the same general skills as in any other management role. These have been identified by the CBI and BIM in their well publicised Management Charter Initiative (MCI) as:

(a) Managing resources — both physical and human
(b) Managing finance
(c) Managing enterprise.

22. Qualifications
The MCI has set out three levels, Certificate, Diploma and Masters, roughly appropriate to supervisory, middle and top managements.

Professional bodies such as the Chartered Institute of Transport (CIT) and the Institute of Logistics and Distribution Management (ILDM) have developed their own certificate and diploma programmes roughly in line with the MCI, and there are degree programmes giving, for example, full exemption from the final examinations for corporate Membership of the CIT, and higher degree programmes such as the MSc in Transport and Distribution run by Salford University in conjunction with Huddersfield and Birmingham Polytechnics and the CIT, and the MSc in Distribution and Logistics at Cranfield School of Management.

23. Managerial qualities required

Distribution managers must be numerate, able to handle complex operational research problems using the latest IT, be good communicators and possess staff-management and leadership skills. They must have an entrepreneurial approach to this highly competitive industry, a sound grasp of financial management principles and in addition be able to recognise the financial consequences of their decisions.

24. The role of supervisors

Supervisors are paradoxically both the most dispensable and most crucial personnel. IT is today eroding their 'post office' role. When senior managers can view progress and results on their desk-top VDUs they may feel that they have no need of supervisors reporting to them — providing their workforce can be sufficiently motivated to manage their own areas of responsibilities as autonomous work groups.

However, the role of senior managers is to plan and if they are forced to take on the supervisory control function as well this decreases their effectiveness. Thus supervisors will always be required but will have to develop more democratic leadership roles rather than their old authoritarian roles as controllers. Distribution is still very labour-intensive with many employees (e.g. drivers) remote from continuous supervision. Pyramidal organisation structures today are becoming 'flatter' with shorter chains of command, and 'wider' with supervisors having wider spans of command. Whilst this inevitably results in less layers of management, nevertheless the same competences of being able to manage human, financial and physical resources will always be paramount in distribution.

25. Operative training

As their titles imply, drivers and warehouse and clerical staff etc. usually have a well-defined function to perform. It is easier to carry out an analysis of the training needs of their jobs in terms of the knowledge and skills which they require to perform those jobs competently than it is in the case of managerial and supervisory staff. For the latter, often the training needs emerge as a result either of their 'falling down' on some aspect of the job or of an employee assessment process.

Operative training programmes can be devised to input the necessary knowledge and skills, often by simply providing 'on the job' training where the trainee is a supernumerary working alongside a qualified trainer. In other instances 'off the job' training can be arranged with the firm's own instructors or by using outside educational and training providers, such as commercial driving schools.

The replacement of Industrial Training Boards as the providers of funding for training by local 'employer-led' Training and Enterprise Councils (TECs) has meant the channelling of grant aid for operative training into programmes which seek to increase employees' work-based competences, or their ability to perform work-related tasks in line with specific performance criteria.

A National Council for Vocational Qualifications is working with examining bodies such as the Royal Society of Arts Examination Boards (RSA), City and Guilds of London Institute (CGLI), and the National Examination Board in Supervisions Management (NEBSM) to restructure their qualifications in performance criteria terms and to accredit trainees more on a continuous assessment basis than by using traditional time-constrained examinations.

Ironically, the Certificate of Professional Competence (CPC), despite its title, is still a traditional examination based on a menu of objective test questions, but the reasons for this are connected less with the examining body (the RSA) and more with the wording of the Brussels Directive on access to the occupation of road transport operator!

The RTITB became totally self-funding as a training provider, RTIT plc, in 1992, it no longer has any powers to raise a training levy or make training grants. It already acts as the secretariat for a new industry-led body, the Road Haulage Industry Training Standards Council (RHITSC), which will set training standards for most operatives in the industrial logistics industry. For the first time since 1964, the own-account sector comes into its scope. (Further reference to the training role of RHITSC is made in **30** in the context of driver training.)

Road staff

26. General

Men have always outnumbered women amongst the ranks of professional delivery van and lorry drivers. It is not too difficult to understand both the undeserved 'macho' image of the job and, conversely, why it is that we are now seeing a larger, though as yet not significantly larger, cohort of women vocational drivers.

27. Driver 'culture'

Even those whose task it is to recruit and select professional drivers often know little of their culture, values and ideologies. The reasons for this are not hard to see. Drivers are, for most of their working day, their own boss. It is this independence which flows naturally from their general remoteness from *direct* supervision which is for many the main attraction of the job. Workers who conform to McGregor's Theory X preferring to be directed rather than being self-directed, do not as a rule end up as professional drivers.

Professional drivers know that they are 'on their own' most of the time. Whether they are faced with rescheduling their deliveries en route to accommodate a five-mile motorway tail-back, or confronting an unhelpful warehouseman at a delivery point, it is, in the first instance, their own resources on which they have to depend. This explains their love/hate relationship with tachographs and cab radios, which, whilst offering them the ultimate back-up which they acknowledge they may one day desperately need, are still perceived as 'spies in the cab'. When drivers, their unions and their employers eventually appreciate that satellite technology now enables an undertaking (albeit at prodigious cost at present) to locate their vehicles to within the nearest 100 metres, what bizarre negotiations might well take place!

28. Unionisation

Drivers are notoriously difficult to organise, not just for their employers, but also for trade unions. And yet a high proportion of them are unionised, many in closed shops. There is a long and strong tradition of collectivism, of belonging to a fraternity, the romantic notion of being 'gentlemen of the road', and of doing nothing to upset that fraternity. They belong to general and industrial unions like T&G, URTU and RMT, yet they behave in many ways like elitist craft trade unionists. Hence the surprising solidarity of the 1978 lorry driver's strike, and, in a more general way, the almost total observance of picket lines, no matter whose (nurses', miners', printers' or dockers'), by practically all drivers, whether employed by own-account operators or hauliers.

Underpinning all this is the vague realisation they have of their paramount importance to their employers. Indeed, their perception of this fact can sometimes be keener than that of their employers!

29. Recruitment and selection

The hard fact is that drivers are the ambassadors of transport operators. They are the first point of contact between the customer and the operator.

For this reason, if for no other reason, their selection and recruitment should be conducted meticulously. Sadly, this is not universally the case, although the days are probably passed when drivers would be taken on in the haulage world without even their driving licences being checked, and then given their 'notes' and the keys of a £30,000 vehicle. But greater care in screening applicants has more often occurred at the insistence of the insurance companies than for sound commercial reasons.

Too few undertakings make a driving test part of their selection procedure, or more to the point, conduct driver selection interviews even half as rigorously as the interview they give to an applicant for a clerical vacancy.

30. Driver training

The possession of a vocational LGV driving entitlement, whilst obviously an important prerequisite, is not alone sufficient to guarantee that an employee or potential employee will perform satisfactorily in the job. As already discussed in the general context of operative training (*see* 25), employers need to look for other task-based competences, and, where these are absent, attempt to remedy the omission. An obvious deficiency in many cases is training in customer care.

Persuading the average highly resourceful and independent driver that he may have a training need of any sort is not the easiest of tasks, but unless he himself perceives the need he will not be motivated to re-train.

And yet clearly, many drivers do have quite specific training needs. The problem is that these often relate to task-based competences, or rather, lack of competences. Although convincing them of the need for training is never easy, fortunately quite traumatic events in road transport, such as the approach of 1992 and competition from foreign cabotage operations, are already persuading the more perceptive driver of a need for fundamental change.

A good example of such change is the introduction of the new unified European driving licence, the details of which were explained in 8:21, to replace the UK two-tier ordinary/vocational licence. The number of classes of HGV licences is reduced, for example appearing to 'de-skill' HGV Class 2 drivers now that Class 3 drivers obtain entitlement to drive all rigid goods vehicles. Conversely, new drivers of draw-bar combinations will need to take a test of driving entitlement similar, but not identical, to the old Class 1 HGV driving test, thus creating a new elite. Despite inevitable and entirely understandable trade union protests, the logic of a single licence, and of a 'super' HGV licence for both artics and draw-bars, is irrefutable.

The message for the driver is clear — handling a large vehicle is but one necessary competence, albeit a paramount one.

31. Agreement on training needs

There are inherent difficulties in reconciling employer and employee perceptions of training needs. The new Road Haulage Industry Training Standards Council, which represents the trade associations and the trade unions, is struggling to reach agreement on industry standard training recommendations. Nor is it easy to follow up such recommendations in a volatile labour market, the subject of the following sections of this chapter.

Driver employment

32. Labour turnover

Labour turnover has always traditionally been high amongst drivers — there seems to be something of the nomad in their make-up. Recent high levels of unemployment have reduced the turnover level, but whilst employers in some parts of the country are able to build up a stable workforce, others, especially in the more prosperous SE, still have difficulties. And, with the demise of training in road transport and the 'privatisation' of the RTITB (which, as already pointed out, unlike the RHITSC only covered hauliers' training needs), there are undeniable skill imbalances in the industry. Employers need to understand the labour market for drivers and to be able to draw up realistic manpower plans to pre-empt as far as possible, any such future imbalances.

33. The micro labour market for drivers

Some undertakings have responded by offering drivers 'single status' agreements. The driver is put on the staff, enrolled into the pension scheme and paid a salary. The winding up of the Road Haulage Wages Council in 1980 gave rise to many local agreements on consolidation of earnings and single status.

However, not all employers can afford an expensive 'core' driver workforce which is effectively a fixed overhead. The notion of drivers as 'hands' to be taken on or shed as the fleet grows or shrinks dies hard. So there emerges another class of driver — some would argue a second class — in what has come to be termed the 'peripheral' labour market. Amongst these are part-time drivers, agency drivers, owner drivers, franchisees and drivers employed on precarious temporary contracts. These are discussed further below.

If the recruitment, selection and training of 'core' employees in many cases leaves much to be desired, it totally fails in most instances to match up to good practice in the 'twilight world' of peripheral employees.

34. 'Part-time' drivers

Part-time drivers are often doing a second job or are 'unemployed'. Frequently they are part of our 'black economy'. Their attraction to an employer is that they are an easily tapped pool of reserve labour. There is rarely a commitment to anything more than minimal training of part-timers.

35. Agency drivers

Employment agencies have proliferated during the present

recession. They seem to attract particular occupations such as secretarial staff, computer operators, draughtsmen, nurses, catering staff and, of course, drivers. Some like Manpower and Overdrive actually specialise in placing drivers.

The activities of such agencies are controlled by the Employment Agencies Act 1973 under which they may not charge drivers for registration, but make a charge to the employer with whom they place them. Some agencies even hoard a 'core' of reliable drivers whom they have found they can trust, paying them unemployment fall-back pay and holiday pay, and providing rudimentary training in customer care and record-keeping. But they also have a register of casual or 'peripheral' labour on whom they can call.

The legal position with regard to driver agencies is confused. The Transport Act 1968 (relating to goods vehicle operator licensing) defines the user of the vehicle, who must hold the operator's licence, as the driver, or the person whose servant or agent the driver is. The Transport Tribunal, in a historic ruling in 1985 (the Gordon Wright Appeal) gave its blessing, however obliquely, to the employment of self-employed drivers, when it held that the test of who 'employs' a driver for licensing purposes is who 'controls, hires and fires' the driver, not whether he is liable to account for his tax and National Insurance.

36. Owner-drivers

Owner-drivers, who actually drive their own vehicles rather than the operator's vehicles, are of course still 'users' of the vehicle and must hold the operator's licence (and the CPC). The ready-mixed concrete industry employ many owner-drivers, who drive vehicles which they acquire from the operator under a hire-purchase or leasing agreement, but which are tied to the operator whose 'barrel' is mounted on the vehicle. The industry has a good record of safety and operational training of its drivers, and maintenance and commercial back-up for them.

37. Franchised drivers

Increasingly drivers are franchised to operators. Interlink and ANC, for example are two well-known large parcels operations relying on franchisee owner-drivers to perform collection and delivery services. Often this is done with vehicles just under the 3.5 tonne operator licensing threshold.

All franchisors, be they Macdonalds or Dynarod, rely on standardisation of service levels and procedures, so training of franchisees is an essential and usually well-conceived operation. Sound selection of franchisees is also paramount to a franchisor's success, and great care is usually taken of this aspect of the business.

38. Drivers on temporary contract

Temporary contracts to meet peaks of seasonal demand will always be a feature of transport and distribution. The Post Office Christmas mail is a prime example. In this case drivers are asked to do very little except drive. Not so the temporary mail-order driver recruited in pre-Christmas or pre-Whitsun peak times. There a much more detailed job description exists and consequently a greater training need.

Part of that need is to make sure that the driver relates to his customer, liaising with mail-order agents, often housewives, who are frequently out at work, and their 'helpful' neighbours over collections, deliveries and balance orders. Tact, efficiency and a good customer care attitude are called for.

39. Pay and conditions

An employer asks a lot of his drivers, but does not always value good drivers as much as he values an asset like a new lorry. As a minimum, pay and conditions commensurate with what is expected of a professional driver must be offered. The 'monkeys and peanuts' syndrome is very true, and monkeys can crash vehicles and alienate customers only too easily.

In the UK drivers' working conditions lag far behind those of their continental counterparts. The European truckstop is closer to a Crest Motel than a UK transport cafe. And 1992 is on the horizon. If drivers have not yet made the comparisons, they will.

But good pay and conditions are not everything. Hertzberg has pointed out that these 'hygiene factors' are only a prerequisite, and that employees will only be motivated if the 'satisfiers' are right. These include such factors as recognition, responsibility and job enrichment.

Incorporating these into the driver's contract of employment is one of the major challenges facing the distribution industry today.

Human resources planning

40. General

It is important that the future staffing needs of the industrial logistics industry should be met. One way of ensuring this is for employers to prepare rolling staffing plans.

The starting point is obviously a *staffing inventory* of the existing staff, but this alone is insufficient, since mere numbers or establishment counts fail to describe the workforce in any meaningful way so far as future requirements are concerned.

41. Staffing audit

This is necessary to establish what qualifications and skills exist, and what the anticipated 'survival rate' of the workforce is. The former exercise could, for example, pinpoint a future skills shortage (e.g. of LGV drivers), whilst the latter could point to a loyal but ageing workforce with an anticipated heavy retirement pattern in the coming years. Reference has already been made to the instability of the labour market for professional drivers, and the ways in which operators can seek to 'fine tune' this by supplementing their 'core' driver workforce from the 'peripheral' LGV driver labour market.

The plan must also seek to quantify as far as is possible the future staffing requirements, taking into account factors in the employer's corporate plan such as anticipated growth or retrenchment, new markets, new technology and competition.

42. Labour market assessment

Equally important is an assessment of the labour market to anticipate the future supply of employees. This is a difficult exercise, involving looking at demographic trends (e.g. the lower numbers of school leavers in the 1990s, the growth of part-time employment and numbers of female 'returnees' coming back into the labour market after motherhood), economic trends (including unemployment) and labour legislation, such as the new rights which part-timers would have if the UK embraced the European Social Charter.

Any obvious mismatch, e.g. skills shortages in areas such as computing, must be addressed by appropriate personnel strategies, for example:

(a) training and retraining
(b) recruitment
(c) transfer
(d) promotion
(e) termination — either involuntary (illness, death, personal circumstances) or planned (redundancy, voluntary severance, early retirement, etc.).

Figure 10.3 illustrates the complete staffing planning process.

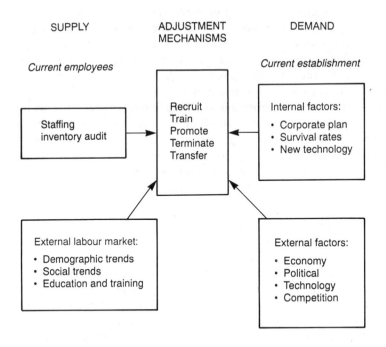

Fig. 10.3 *The staffing planning process.*

Industrial relations

43. General

Many operatives are members of trade unions (*see* **28**), for example TGWU (drivers), URTU (drivers and salesmen), USDAW (retail distribution). The extent of trade union penetration depends on the particular branch of distribution and on historical factors — for example, the bakery industry is traditionally unionised.

44. Closed shops

The closed shop or union membership agreement (UMA) under which an employer agrees to employ only members of a particular union in a well defined 'bargaining unit' (such as a depot) is common in the industry. Where it exists it tends to cover operative grades and is a post-entry agreement — in other words the employee does not (as is often the case in engineering, for example) have to be a member of the union to be employed but undertakes to join if employed. It also tends to have the tacit support and encouragement of management, who value negotiating with only one union.

However, the provisions of the Employment Act 1988 prevent an employer dismissing an employee for failure to belong to a union and effectively emasculates closed shops in law, if not *de facto*. Additionally, the European Social Contract, in defining a right to belong or not to belong to a trade union, would, if embraced by the UK, have the same effect.

45. Wages councils

The number of wages councils which traditionally fixed minimum operative wages in many industries, and which embraced many distribution employees (e.g. road haulage drivers), is now significantly reduced, surviving only in one or two areas of low pay such as catering, baking and retailing. Local agreements on wages and conditions have replaced national negotiations in most areas of employment within the logistics distribution function. Some area agreements, for example for road haulage drivers, still have a 'knock-on' effect on wage negotiations in large distribution companies.

46. Wage levels

The introduction of a national minimum wage, were it to come about as a result of political change or European intervention, would have an immediate effect on distribution costs but would probably not affect employment levels significantly as all competitors would be equally affected.

Although operative wages in transport and distribution tend to be at or near the national average, there are wide variations from the mean. Distribution employees tend to be better paid than their counterparts in road passenger transport or rail transport, and the incidence of overtime working remains relatively high, thus driving up average earnings.

47. Industrial relations at managerial level

Managers in logistics distribution rarely belong to trade unions, except in some large organisations like BRS where strong trade unionism survives from nationalisation days. Salaries of distribution managers are generally higher than in other areas of employment in transport, which partly explains low trade union membership at this level, and careers in the industry are becoming popular with graduates with the recent development of a number of first and Masters degrees in transport and distribution at centres such as Huddersfield and Birmingham Polytechnics and Salford University.

Progress test 10

1. What is the approximate size of the road haulage industry compared to the size of the UK distribution industry? **(17)**

2. What do you understand by 'retail-led' distribution? **(17)**

3. How can the distribution management function be integrated into an organisation's corporate structure? **(18, Fig. 10.2)**

4. Distinguish between:
    (a) contract distribution
    (b) franchising

    (c) owner-drivers

    (d) own-account operation

    (e) bespoke distribution.   **(17, 20, 35, 36)**

5.   What three skills does a distribution manager require?   **(21)**

6.   What is the role of NVQs in driver training?   **(25, 30)**

7.   What is the purpose of a CPC?   **(25)**

8.   What essential element of a driver training programme is most frequently neglected?   **(30)**

9.   Explain the legal position of agency drivers.   **(35)**

10. How do UK and 'continental' drivers' pay and conditions compare?   **(39)**

11. What are the two prerequisites of a staffing plan?
(40, 41, Fig. 10.3)

12. What are the internal and external inputs in a staffing plan?   **(Fig. 10.3)**

13. What is a closed shop? Why are closed shops strong in the road freight transport industry?   **(44)**

The economics of logistics

Economics and change

1. What is economics?

The basis of economics concerns the micro-theories of exchange, scarcity, choice and the factors of production (land, labour, capital and entrepreneurial skills). Macro-economics, on the other hand, is the application of these micro-theories in the market-place. They are clearly revealed in the logistics industry through the effects of supply and demand, pricing policies, location factors, and economies of scale, to name but a few aspects.

2. The changing landscape

Since the early 1960s the central areas of many towns and cities have changed dramatically. The old linear high street shopping areas gave way to modern new developments including the growth of indoor shopping centres incorporating many of the familiar multiple stores. New bus stations and multi-storey car parks were constructed. Low density private housing estates were built in preference to high density council housing. Traditional heavy industry together with cotton and woollen manufacturing declined or disappeared. In their place industrial estates with single storey, high technology, capital-intensive factories and plant mushroomed, predominantly on the periphery of urban areas rather than near to the commercial areas and central business districts. This led to areas of neglect and decay near the centres.

3. Changes in the consumer markets

Coupled with these changes the average household size has

reduced but the number of households has increased and the demand for single and two-bedroom accommodation continues to rise as the number of elderly people, single people or couples without children, as a percentage of the total population, increases.

More recently out-of-town hypermarkets and shopping centres have been established, normally with a major food supermarket as the focal point. This has caused many town and city centre food stores to close and relocate. The cheap land and the vast areas of free-car-parking space on peripheral sites compared with limited access and expensive land in central areas has been responsible for these moves.

Consumer markets are highly dynamic requiring careful research on behalf of the companies which serve them. Future demographic trends forecast a growing elderly population as people live longer and the birth rate remains low. A further prediction calls for more specialised corner shops catering specifically for the older age groups to be established. In conjunction with these views is the declining demand for baby food and baby, toddler, infant and young children's clothes because of the lower birth rate. Manufacturers of these products have to monitor the trends very carefully in order to respond to consumer demand. Economic appraisal is therefore essential.

Economics and the logistics industry

4.   Evolution of the logistics industry

As these developments occurred the logistics and distribution industries had to evolve. Sophisticated warehouses and distribution centres were designed and constructed which incorporated processes to cater for the increasingly complex consumer markets which have arisen. The important economic factors which had to be considered were the location of manufacturing bases, and the cost and availability of labour, land, raw materials and transport.

5.   The economics of manufacturing

A manufacturing company considers the demand for its products, carefully calculates the cost of raw materials or semi-finished goods required in the manufacturing process, together with all elements which are referred to as added value, in order to derive a selling price net of transport costs. Careful market research is undertaken to determine the likely demand for the new product, taking into consideration such factors as social trends, fashions, income, the economic situation and competition. Finally, the cost of promotion, transport and a profit element is calculated to determine the wholesale price. Only if a satisfactory rate of return is guaranteed will a company use its scarce resources to produce the product. Remember that a company has to choose how to utilise its scarce resources to best effect. This entails the use of capital, labour skills and training costs in determining such decisions.

6. Demand for goods

In this situation the law of demand becomes a reality. The law states that the higher the price of a good the lower the demand and the lower the price the higher the demand. Alternatively, if the market oversupplies, the effect will be a price reduction. This has been evident for a whole range of surplus goods during the recent recessions. Organisations, in an attempt to sell their goods, have introduced various special offers and have slashed prices. This affects profit margins and ultimately the commercial viability of the organisation itself.

7. Supply of goods

The law of supply is completely the opposite: the higher the price the higher the supply and the lower the price the lower the supply. This is because at lower prices suppliers are unable to make a profit. At a given price demand equals supply. This is called the *equilibrium price*. From this it is clear that price affects both demand and supply.

When demand is greater than supply, prices rise. Organisations respond by increasing output and new companies enter the market. There is an obvious time lag between the decision to increase supply and the finished goods becoming available. The logistics and distribution industries play a vital role here by procuring the additional raw materials or semi-processed goods to the point of manufacture and the finished goods from the point of manufacture either directly or through distribution centres to the point of sale, i.e. to the consumer markets. The timing and efficiency of this logistical operation has a crucial economic role to play.

8.   Economics of distribution

Distribution over the period described above has also undergone its own revolution. Sophisticated computer-aided warehouses and distribution centres have been established which can handle the whole range of goods from consumer durables through to ambient temperature-controlled food items. New technology has improved inventory control enabling techniques such as JIT (just-in-time) to become a reality whereby deliveries, if to a manufacturer, occur at a predetermined moment when a particular stage in a manufacturing process has been reached, or if to a retailer, when stock has diminished to a point of requiring replenishment. For this process to work effectively careful economic monitoring has to occur. The ideal situation would be zero inventory when delivery occurs.

The distribution revolution has meant lower levels of stock or parts, which ties up less capital — a scarce factor of production. The release of this capital means greater choice in the activities which organisations can become involved in.

9.   Own-account or contract hire?

A question which often involves manufacturing organisations and large retail companies is whether or not to own and operate a fleet of vehicles itself or to contract hire. There are no hard and fast rules concerning this subject. Observation among firms confirms this point. However, a number of factors are considered which assists companies in deciding which decision to make:

In favour of own account
Complete control exercised over operations including:

(a)   fleet type and availability;
(b)   maintenance and repair schedules;
(c)   fleet replacement policy;
(d)   driver recruitment, discipline and scheduling;

(e) driver remuneration, incentives and bonuses;
(f) distribution management and administration staff;
(g) depot costs, location costs and operating costs.

In favour of contract hire
Control can be exercised in other ways:

(a) contract clauses can specify many of the above points;
(b) no need to employ specialist transport staff;
(c) capital is not tied up in depot costs;
(d) where land is expensive only the main business need take up valuable space;
(e) the transport and distribution element of the business may only be an insignificant proportion of the whole, therefore why not leave it to the experts;
(f) some businesses have marked seasonal variations therefore it makes more sense to hire in distribution vehicles (or at least some of them) rather than having vehicles stood idle;
(g) some businesses are of a specialised nature which may require special vehicles, special handling and special training. This is often best left to experts, e.g. refrigerated vehicles, tankers, cranes, certain types of removal and storage.

10. Opportunity cost and escapability
These are two economic terms which organisations consider when undertaking investment appraisal.

(a) *Opportunity cost* (or *resource cost*) is the name given to the identification of any sacrifices made when choosing the best use of available resources, e.g. if project A is chosen in preference to project B. The cost of project B is opportunity foregone. In other words, the opportunity cost relates to the next best use of resources if they were not used in a particular way. A logistics company might weigh up the advantages of purchasing new production machinery compared with building a new warehouse. The value of buying the new machinery would be measured in terms of not having a new warehouse which is what the resources could have best been used for otherwise.
(b) *Escapability* is the term used to describe the net savings a company can make if a process is not undertaken and costs saved, or escaped.

Economies of scale

11. Short-run average costs

In the short term certain costs (factors of production) are fixed, for instance a warehouse may have inescapable overhead costs, e.g. business rates, insurance, security, maintenance and interest payments or rent. Other costs increase with output and these are referred to as variable costs. In economic terms a combination of these fixed and variable costs are called *short-run average costs* (SRAC).

An organisation will use certain factors of production to produce output. If a specific quantity is required the factors which prove to be the most efficient for that quantity will be used. If the amount produced is lower than that required then the average cost of each unit produced will be higher than unit cost at the exact quantity. This occurs because some fixed cost factors are not used to their greatest efficiency. Similarly, if more than the quantity required is produced then the average unit cost will rise because some of the factors become inefficient. If the quantity required varies then a different combination of factors which produces the new quantities most efficiently will be utilised.

12. Long-run average costs

In the long term, however, all costs are variable, and in the language of economics they are called *long-run average costs* (LRAC) — in financial language long-term is considered to be more than one year. In the long run when the cost and quantity of all factors of production can be varied a firm will only produce a given quantity by using those factors which are most efficient at the quantity required.

13. Economies of scale

Economies of scale refer to the effects on average costs of changes in output. They do not arise simply from spreading fixed costs over a larger output but from utilising factors of production more efficiently in the long term, though they are associated generally with larger outputs.

Economies of scale can be classified under four headings:

(a) *Managerial economies*. Large firms employ specialists to run the various functions within the organisation, e.g. production manager, engineering manager, accountants, auditors, personnel officers, stores manager, research and development, together with other line and staff managers. The scale economies arise from the specialism. In small firms certain members of staff have to, out of necessity, undertake more than one role, or tasks have to be contracted to outside specialist organisations. The use of electronic equipment such as a computer network and an internal telephone system are also examples of managerial economies in so far as they save time and avoid the need to repeat manual tasks.

(b) *Technical economies*. These arise from the use of large equipment at low unit cost, e.g. large capacity transport such as lorries, trains, ships or aircraft. In each case the maximum use of large capacity would reduce costs considerably from using two or more smaller units. Transporting heavy low-value bulk loads by rail, e.g. coal from pit to power station, regularly is more economic than transporting the same quantity by road. Production-line processes compared with hand-produced goods are further examples.

(c) *Financial economies*. Large firms utilise a variety of sources of funds and are able to raise additional share capital on the stock market. Small firms are restricted to expensive bank loans and hire-purchase.

(d) *Marketing economies*. Increased purchasing power enables large firms to enjoy bulk purchasing with substantial discounts. Similarly, large firms with lower unit costs can afford to sell more cheaply than small firms. With a larger turnover profit margins can also be smaller which reduces prices. Supermarkets employ such tactics to encourage shoppers. Large firms can afford to advertise their products nationwide and gain a national reputation. Marketing costs per unit decrease with output.

14. Diseconomies of scale

It is sometimes difficult for large firms to identify where diseconomies occur except where direct and indirect costs can be clearly established in connection with a particular process. However, managerial diseconomies are often associated with large firms. Bureaucracy is blamed. Poor communications, departmentalisation and repetition are sometimes responsible for an increase in management costs per unit of output.

Economics and price determination

15. Price — and maritime economics

The maritime industry is a wonderful example of how price affects both demand and supply. When demand is low the freight rate is low. Only the most cost-effective ships operate, and then only at low speed in order to conserve fuel on long voyages. The inefficient ships are laid up and their second-hand value drops; some are even scrapped. When the freight rate rises as a result of an increase in demand the first reaction is for the efficient ships to speed up. This effectively increases supply as the number of journeys now being completed in a given time period rises. This is one of the few areas where an increase in supply can be almost immediate whereas generally a time lag exists in which a shortage usually occurs sending the price up higher. As the freight rate continues to rise due to a continuing increase in demand the second effect is for the inefficient ships to re-enter service. The second-hand value of ships rises and if a sustained high freight rate is anticipated then new ships will even be ordered and built. The whole situation is extremely volatile.

16. Pricing policy

Price discrimination exists in the distribution industry although in a slightly different fashion from the passenger industry where the definition is 'for the same unit of travel to be charged at different rates'. A typical example in distribution is found in the small parcels trade. Certain national carriers convey small parcels, normally up to a maximum weight of around 25 kg, based on weight rather than distance travelled. The secret of economic success depends upon complex calculations and the volume of traffic. A typical systems network is based on a number of radial depots dotted around the country and a central hub depot. On a daily basis radial depots collect small parcels for next-day delivery. These parcels are sent by vehicle to the hub depot where they are sorted and sent on to their final destination (or nearest point) by the vehicles returning to their radial depots.

Such matters as heavy loads on certain journeys can be anticipated by the use of a network computer which monitors details of every small parcel. In such a network, the total cost of the entire operation can be calculated and an estimate made of the volume (number and weight) of parcels likely to be carried. In reality once this volume has been reached the operation moves into profit. The volume figure can be calculated on a daily, weekly, monthly and annual basis. This form of price discrimination favours the long-distance parcels at the expense of the short-distance ones. Generally, most nations' postal systems are operated on the same cost basis.

17. Elasticity

The term elasticity refers to the flexibility suppliers and consumers have as far as choice is concerned when a change, e.g. in price or income, occurs. It is a measure of the responsiveness to this change. The formula for elasticity is:

$$\text{Elasticity} = \frac{\text{Proportionate (or percentage) change in quantity}}{\text{Proportionate (or percentage) change in determinant}}$$

There are four types of elasticity in common use:

(a) *Price elasticity of demand* (PE$_d$)(often called 'own price'). It shows the responsiveness of quantity demanded to a change in price. Formula:

$$\text{PE}_d = \frac{\text{Proportionate (or percentage) change in quantity demanded}}{\text{Proportionate (or percentage) change in price}}$$

For example, if an increase in the freight rate (price) of 20 per cent causes a 10 per cent reduction in quantity demanded (tonnage), the price elasticity of demand will be -10 per cent divided by 20 per cent = -0.5. The sign (positive or negative) in this particular calculation will normally be negative. This occurs because demand decreases when the determinant increases and vice versa.

(b) *Price elasticity of supply* (PE$_s$). This shows the responsiveness of quantity supplied to a change in price. Formula:

$$\text{PE}_s = \frac{\text{Proportionate (or percentage) change in quantity supplied}}{\text{Proportionate (or percentage) change in price}}$$

For example, if a 10 per cent rise in the price of a product results in an 8 per cent rise in the quantity supplied, the price elasticity of supply will be 8 per cent divided by 10 per cent = 0.8. The sign is positive because the amount supplied increased when the determinant increased.

(c) *Cross-price elasticity of demand* (PE_{xy}). This measures the responsiveness of demand of, say, one distribution company's services to a change in price of another company's services. Formula:

$$PE_{xy} = \frac{\text{Proportionate (or percentage) change in demand for A}}{\text{Proportionate (or percentage) change in price of B}}$$

For example, if a distribution company increases its freight rate by 10 per cent which results in an increase in demand for your company's services by 20 per cent, then the cross-price elasticity of demand for your services will be 20 per cent divided by 10 per cent = 2. The sign will be positive because both the demand and the determinant increased.

(d) *Income elasticity of demand* (YE_d). This measures the responsiveness of demand to a change in consumer incomes (Y). Formula:

$$YE_d = \frac{\text{Proportionate (or percentage) change in demand}}{\text{Proportionate (or percentage) change in income}}$$

For example, if a 5 per cent rise in income causes a 10 per cent rise in a product's demand, then its income elasticity of demand will be 10 per cent divided by 5 per cent = 2. This calculation generally has a positive sign.

18. The values of elasticity
    The value of each figure, ignoring whether it is positive or negative, determines whether demand (or supply) is *elastic* or *inelastic*. This is very important because the impact on an organisation's economic viability might well depend upon the effects of any price increases, reductions or changes in income. Elasticity is said to be:

(a) *Elastic*, where E is greater than 1. This occurs where a change in the determinant causes a proportionately greater change in demand (or supply). In this situation gross revenue (or total outlay) rises for a price fall and falls for a price rise.

(b) *Inelastic,* where E is less than 1. This occurs where a change in the determinant causes a proportionately smaller change in demand (or supply). In this situation gross revenue (or total outlay) rises for a price rise and falls for a price fall.

(c) *Unity,* where demand (or supply) changes proportionately by the same amount as the determinant. This will give an elasticity equal to 1. Gross revenue (or total outlay) is unchanged.

19. Inferior and normal goods

A factor which might affect some of the calculations involving income (Y) is the concept of inferior goods and normal goods. An inferior good is one whose demand falls as income rises and a normal good is one whose demand rises as income rises. The category of each good is important at times of real wage increases as people either switch to better quality goods or increase their purchases of normal goods.

20. Complements and substitutes

A further factor affects some of these calculations, the concept of substitute and complementary goods. This simply means that an increase in the freight rate of one distribution company might well have a positive effect on the demand of a competitor's services because the competitor is a substitute. Alternatively, an increase in the price of tyres might well have an adverse effect on the demand for new vehicles because vehicles and tyres are complementary goods, i.e. they are related in some way.

Progress test 11

1. Why have large out-of-town shopping centres appeared in recent years, and what economic effect have they had on retail distribution? **(3)**

2. What effect does demand have on price and supply and how do manufacturers respond? **(6, 7)**

3. In what different ways would a large manufacturer enjoy economies of scale compared with a small business? **(13)**

4. In the maritime industry what effect does the freight rate have on the supply of ships? **(15)**

5. A manufacturer suffers from price rises of raw materials. In determining whether some or all of the price rises can be passed onto the customer, what does the manufacturer have to consider with regard to price elasticity? **(18)**

12

The finance of logistics and distribution

An introduction to finance

1. Understanding finance

Organisations concerned with one or more of the following commercial activities: procuring, manufacturing, warehousing, distributing or retailing, need to understand and implement the different facets of financial and management accounting. This chapter considers how finance relates to logistics and distribution, beginning with basic concepts and progressing through to their application.

Finance can be subdivided into three categories: financial management, cost accounting and management accounting. The distinction lies in the aim of the exercise involved. Basically, if financial figures are required for record or accounts purposes, this is considered to be financial accounting. If financial figures are required for manufacturing accounts, costing or stock valuation, this is called cost accounting; or if figures are required for budgeting, pricing, investment appraisal or financial planning, then these come under the heading of management accounting. In practice management accounting decisions often require the use of financial account records and cost accounts.

The records of accounts, including the methods used in their compilation, are similar throughout all trade and industry. The Companies Act 1985 stipulates 'minimum disclosure'. This means, for private and public limited companies, that their final accounts are published in an ascribed manner, often following a common format. This enables different company accounts to be compared. (Incidentally, sole traders and partners are not obliged by law to publish accounts. They do exist though, if only for the interest of the bank manager and for Inland Revenue tax purposes.)

2.   SSAPs (Statements of Standard Accounting Practice)

Accountants and businesses are also expected to observe Statements of Standard Accounting Practice (SSAPs). These are issued periodically by the Accounting Standards Committee (ASC) to determine methods by which certain complicated financial matters are dealt with. Again, if firms adopt these 'practices', their accounts can be compared for efficiency and performance. An example of an SSAP affecting logistics is SSAP 9, which is concerned with stocks and work-in-progress.

Although financial accounting is similar regardless of industry, this is not true with regard to cost accounting and management accounting. In logistics and distribution the nature of business is often quite different from banking, commerce and a variety of tertiary industries, and as such various techniques for determining costs, for example, have been developed. These techniques will be described in this chapter.

3.   Financial responsibility and understanding

Ratio analysis, the interpretation of accounts and the identification of costs are very important elements of successful management and every manager should become proficient in their art, regardless of his or her manager's role within a company. It is important to emphasise here that in today's modern business financial matters are not just the responsibility of financial managers. Responsibility for a cost centre, e.g. running a warehouse, or a revenue centre, e.g. selling container space, or for a profit centre, e.g. controlling a purchase and supply department within a factory, together with the accurate identification of costs, revenue and profit, is being devolved to all levels of contemporary company management and as such all managers should be acquainted with the various aspects of financial, costing and management accounting.

Therefore, this chapter of the book, no matter how interesting the reader may find the subject of finance, is as important, if not more important, than the rest of the book because business survival depends more than ever on mastering financial strategies.

Financial accounts

4. Financial accounting

The basis of financial accounting is to provide a record of income and expenditure within an organisation resulting in the measurement of profit or loss. This is recorded in a *trading, profit and loss account*. The wealth of a company is revealed on a *balance sheet* which identifies fixed and current assets, long-term and current liabilities.

The other main financial record is called the *statement of source and application of funds*, or, briefly, the *funds flow statement*. This record shows all movements of cash into and out of a business over a period of time, e.g. one year, and the net effect of these movements on working capital.

By using the figures contained in the financial statements management can ascertain the achievements of the business, or lack of them. There are various performance indicators. For example, the current ratio and the acid-test ratio determine the liquidity/solvency position of a company. In other words, whether the firm has sufficient cash or the likelihood of raising sufficient cash to pay its creditors.

Other ratios disclose important aspects of the financial performance of a business such as profitability, measured by determining the return on capital invested (ROCE). Depending on the type of firm, variations of the basic ROCE formula can be used to indicate, for example, profit on sales, asset turnover, production costs, expenses and number of sales in relation to, for example, plant, buildings, vehicles, stocks and debtors. A more detailed description of this subject can be found in the financial books within the M&E series.

Levels of inventory and inventory turnover are obviously important considerations with regard to capital being utilised and tied up in the logistics and distribution industry. Careful observation and accurate records together with sound decision making should be achieved in order to avoid the waste of capital.

5. Depreciation

Certain fixed assets are purchased by a company as an investment and are utilised in the course of business over a period of time, in some cases a number of years, in order to fulfil particular functions with the end result of contributing towards company profits. Examples of such assets are vehicles, plant, machinery and equipment. They form part of the capital expenditure rather than revenue expenditure.

Such assets have a useful or working life and through use and over time fall in value until eventually they need to be replaced because they are either worn out or have become obsolete.

Depreciation is the term given to the reduction in an asset's value. This fall in value is recorded in the profit and loss account as an expense item. Capital expenditure is long-term and the benefit is felt over a number of accounting periods. In this way an asset will be written off over its useful life and the expense transferred to reserves. In this way profits are not overstated and dividends or drawings are excluded from this reserve.

Often the fund is considered as a replacement pool of cash from which a new asset can be purchased. However, this is not strictly true because inflation will increase the price of assets and technological developments very often lead to improvements or changes in social taste, which means that a company might not want to, or is unable to, purchase an identical asset.

The other common misunderstanding concerning depreciation is the *book value* placed on assets by accountants at the end of each financial year. It is incorrectly assumed that the book value is the market value, or the true worth of the asset at a particular moment in time. The book value really only registers the reduction in value equivalent to the use and expense of the asset during the accounting period in question.

6.   Methods of depreciation

There are two methods of depreciation and also a system of revaluation which takes into account the increased value of assets as a result of inflation. The two methods of depreciation are as follows.

Straight-line method

This method assumes that the use of an asset is constant throughout its life and that any re-sale value will be proportionate to its age and condition, e.g. as with plant, machinery and equipment. The loss of value will be an equal amount each year.

Example —————————————————————————————

A machine costs £10,000 and has an estimated useful life of four years after which it can be sold for £2,000.

Calculation:

$$\frac{\text{Cost} - \text{Residual value}}{\text{Useful life}} \quad = \quad \frac{£10,000 - £2,000}{4}$$

$$= \quad \frac{£8,000}{4}$$

$$= \quad £2,000$$

This amount transfers annually to the profit and loss account. The annual depreciation and written-down value are given in Table 12.1.

Table 12.1 Straight-line method of depreciation

		Balance sheet		
Year	Charge to P & L £	Cost £	Accumulated depreciation £	Net book value £
1993	2,000	10,000	2,000	8,000
1994	2,000	10,000	4,000	6,000
1995	2,000	10,000	6,000	4,000
1996	2,000	10,000	8,000	2,000

Reducing or diminishing balance method

This method is applied to an asset which loses a greater part of its value in the early years of its life.

Example —————————————————————————————

A company purchases a new lorry for £20,000 including tyres valued at £1,250. The useful life is expected to be four years and a reducing balance depreciation method using 40 per cent per annum is adopted.

Calculation: As the tyres are considered to be revenue items their cost is deducted in all depreciation calculations. Therefore the cost of the lorry is £18,750 (less £1,250 tyres). The annual depreciation and written-down value are given in Table 12.2.

Table 12.2 Reducing balance method of depreciation

		Balance sheet		
Year	Charge to P & L £	Cost £	Accumulated depreciation £	Net book value £
1993	7,500	18,750	7,500	11,250
1994	4,500	18,750	12,000	6,750
1995	2,700	18,750	14,700	4,050
1996	1,620	18,750	16,320	2,430

Most companies adopt the straight-line method of depreciation because:

(a) it is simpler to calculate;
(b) there is less likelihood of error in the calculations;
(c) most companies buy fixed assets with the intention of utilising them throughout their useful lives rather than with the intention of selling them again.

However, the reducing balance method is considered more appropriate in many cases because:

(a) it reflects more accurately the true market value, particularly in the early years where assets tend to lose value faster;
(b) it is more appropriate where there is a high risk of obsolescence;
(c) newer assets require less maintenance and repairs than older assets, therefore the total charge for the use of an asset is more evenly balanced by utilising the reducing balance method where depreciation is high in the early years and maintenance costs low, and vice versa in later years.

Figure 12.1 illustrates this last point.

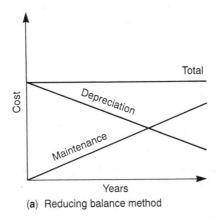

(a) Reducing balance method

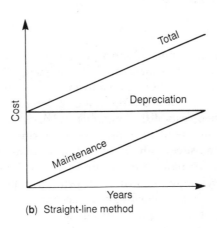

(b) Straight-line method

Fig. 12.1 *Relationship between maintenance and depreciation costs.*

Cost and management accounting

7. The relationship between cost and management accounting

In order to determine accurate costs of an organisation's various activities and functions a system called cost accounting has been devised, without which any analysis and decision making for continuity and profitability would be extremely difficult. As the figures derived in this exercise are used for decision making and planning, it is also related to management accounting.

The objectives of cost accounting centre on cost determination, planning and cost control.

8. Cost determination
Within an organisation there is a need:

(a) to know how much products cost to produce — therefore how much to sell them for;
(b) to establish departmental and functional costs;
(c) to value stock;
(d) to prepare estimates and tenders;
(e) to eliminate inefficiencies;
(f) to assess and improve profitability.

9. Planning
In the long, medium and short (budget period) term planning needs accurate cost information. A logistics, distribution or transport business will not be able to maximise earning capacity and minimise expenditure without a cost determination system. Once this has been established analysis and decision making from the information supplied must follow. Firms can often be overcome by the sheer volume of costing returns received from the various departments and functions within the organisation; however, a technique known as exception reporting can be adopted. This is simply a device introduced into a computer system whereby only those figures which fall outside the normal acceptable cost parameters are reported. In this way only the costs which need to be acted upon are referred to management.

10. Budgets and cost control
This is the regulation of costs by management action in order to contain costs within those agreed in the budget. This is not to say that a dynamic company cannot be flexible enough to react to changing circumstances; it is more the matching of expenditure to revenue at the highest possible productivity level. To achieve this aim organisations must set up effective cost control procedures which include:

(a) establishing cost centres with clearly defined responsibility and authority with cost centre managers;
(b) a method of identifying actual costs and comparing them with budget;
(c) establishing achievable cost standards;
(d) good internal lines of communication.

Costing

11. Cost classifications

Having established a costing system which can identify, accurately, all costs within an organisation the next important step is for management to use them. Several cost classifications are identified for analysis purposes but it is important to note that the costs are the same in each case, i.e. the same monetary values, the only difference being the purpose which each cost classification serves. The main cost classifications are:

(a) functional costs
(b) product costs
(c) activity level costs
(d) controllable costs
(e) relevant costs.

12. Functional costs

As their name implies these costs are classified in association with the various functions within a firm, for example:

(a) production costs — incurred in the function of production;
(b) marketing costs — related to marketing the products;
(c) distribution costs — involving warehousing and distribution costs;
(d) administrative costs — certain overhead costs which cannot be identified directly with a particular function, e.g. wages clerk;
(e) financial costs — business finance costs, e.g. interest payments;
(f) research and development costs — in developing new products.

Functional classification costs enable management to determine the effects on costs of certain sectors in the business and what percentage of total costs these functions amount to. For instance, an own-account operator might analyse the advantages and disadvantages of running its own transport when considering contract hire.

13. Product costs

A manufacturing business obviously needs accurate cost information in order to determine a pricing policy for its products, as well as to ensure efficiency and to avoid waste. In a competitive market businesses are always seeking to minimise costs and maximise profitability. In a complex organisation, even where costs are easily identified, it is important for these costs to be applied correctly and in the right proportions, particularly with regard to overheads. Only by correct allocation of costs can different products be compared for relative profitability and decision-making purposes. The terms for these costs are direct and indirect costs.

Direct costs
These are costs which can be identified directly with the product or output. They comprise:

(a) direct material costs — the materials used in the product or output;
(b) direct labour costs — wage costs of the workers directly involved in making the product;
(c) direct expenses — include items such as the hire of equipment for a particular task.

Indirect costs
This term includes overhead costs, sometimes known as production overheads:

(a) indirect material costs — include oils, lubricants and stocks universally used in the factory;
(b) indirect labour costs — salaries and wages of factory inspectors, foremen, timekeepers and labourers, e.g. cleaners;
(c) indirect expenses — include lighting, heating, power and depreciation of plant and equipment.

14. Activity level costs

The foregoing classification assumes costs will remain constant irrespective of the level of activity. However, some costs do change with different levels of activity. In order to differentiate between the changes four more classifications are applied: fixed costs, semi-fixed costs, semi-variable costs and variable costs. These categories provide management with information concerning the behaviour of costs at different activity levels. They are important when establishing output level targets. In minimising costs one method available to management is to obtain maximum output from given fixed costs.

(a) *Fixed costs* are those costs which in aggregate remain constant through different activity levels, e.g. rent, rates, depreciation, salaries of managers and supervisors, and vehicle standing costs such as insurance, vehicle excise duty and drivers' guaranteed wages.

(b) *Semi-fixed costs* are costs which are fixed over a level of output but, when this is reached, increase as a 'step', e.g. the number of supervisors and mechanics required. In the case of a workshop one mechanic might maintain seven vehicles. When an eighth vehicle is purchased an additional mechanic will be required, who incidentally could also maintain a ninth to a fourteenth vehicle.

(c) *Semi-variable costs* are those costs which have a fixed-cost element and also a variable-cost element based on the level of activity, e.g. a lorry hired under a time-based agreement might have a fixed daily charge and also a mileage charge.

(d) *Variable costs* are those costs which in aggregate vary at different activity levels, e.g. direct material costs, direct labour costs and vehicle running costs such as fuel, tyres, repairs and drivers' overtime payments and expenses.

15. Controllable costs

Financial control within an organisation is aimed at achieving planned (budgeted) targets, which themselves reflect the desired levels of efficiency and productivity. Cost control is effected in two ways, at departmental level and at product level. At departmental level, cost centre managers are given a 'total cost allowance' related to an accounting period with responsibility and authority to exercise control of costs within the cost centre. This cost allowance is stated as the budgeted costs. At product level, a 'unit cost allowance' is calculated in advance of production using standard costing for each cost unit.

Control of costs is exercised through periodic budget reports in which cost centre managers account for the budgeted costs for which they are responsible. Responsibility for costs only extends to costs over which individual managers are able to exercise control. The effectiveness of any cost control system ultimately depends upon the quality of information, lines of communication, analysis and decisions taken.

16. Relevant costs

These are costs which are relevant at a particular moment in time to be used by management for decision-making purposes. Decisions are assumed to reflect choices between at least two alternatives. In the case of decisions based on costs, management will normally select the least costly alternative, so the relevant costs are those which will differ as a result of preferring one alternative to another. Once a decision has been made the usefulness of the costs involved disappears. Costs which have already been incurred are described as sunk costs, or irrelevant costs. Tomorrow's costs are considered relevant and it is these estimated costs on which today's decisions are based.

For budgetary and decision-making purposes, the most accurate cost estimates and forecasts are required. Many logistics organisations have adopted standard costing which, through experience, enables the unknown risks to be minimised by utilising 'best method' techniques, as described in the following section.

17. Standard costing

This is a forward planning procedure which enables greater control over costs to be exercised rather than management waiting blindly to calculate actual costs after the event when it is obviously too late to prevent overspending or waste.

The standard cost of output (production or transport) is the estimated total cost of direct labour, direct material and an apportionment of overheads divided by the target unit of output. These direct costs are often referred to as standard costs, i.e. standard labour and standard material, in that a mean figure is used in any calculation. For example, a distribution company estimates its total costs to be £125,000 based on a target of 100,000 miles. The unit price would be £1.25 pence per mile (£125,000/100,000 miles) and it is this price, plus an element of profit, which the company would hope to recover when quoting for a contract on a mileage basis. Similarly, a manufacturer estimates that total costs for a particular product are £20,000 on a target output of 50,000 units. The unit cost would therefore be 40 pence each (£20,000/50,000).

A standard costing system is only useful if the costing information supplied is accurate and reliable. The difference between budgeting and standard costing is:

(a) budgets relate to the activities of the organisation as a whole;
(b) standard costs relate to individual cost units.

Standard costs are obtained in one of three ways:

(a) as a result of test runs;
(b) as a direct result of work study and other appraisals;
(c) estimates prepared by competent personnel.

18. Classification of standard costs

Three classes of standard costs exist. A company will choose one of them depending upon the tightness of control it desires to exercise:

(a) *Basic standards* — remain the same over a long period of time. They are not used as the basis of budgets but highlight trends, e.g. the effects of introducing advanced technology such as new machinery or turbo-powered lorries.

(b) *Ideal standards* — represent maximum efficiency under perfect conditions which seldom exist, e.g. a fork-lift driver could move 100 pallets in a given time provided the driver's skill was remarkable, the pallets were uniformly loaded, and the lift point, route and delivery point were ideal. In this example 100 per cent success would generally be unattainable and as each variance would produce a negative value this standard would soon discourage effort. As a result they are not often used.

(c) *Normal standards* (sometimes referred to as expected standards or currently attainable standards) — these may be achieved under normal operating conditions and include allowances for:

(*i*) wastage of materials;
(*ii*) machinery inefficiency through maintenance and breakdown;
(*iii*) labour inefficiency through time taken for training, retooling between tasks or idle periods arising from

waiting time for complementary work undertaken by
other personnel to be completed.
Normal cost standards reflect anticipation of what actual costs will
be and include price levels and rates of interest and exchange.
Targets set are designed to encourage and motivate staff, are
attainable and yet to keep tight control over costs require effort to
achieve. A balance between what is realistic and management
expectations of efficiency and productivity must be struck.

At each accounting period, actual performance costs and
standard costs are compared in the detail of:

(a) actual direct labour costs with standard labour costs;
(b) actual direct material costs with standard material costs;
(c) actual overhead apportionment with standard overheads.

19. Variance analysis

The next step is to determine the differences between actual
performance and standard performance as outlined in the budget.
This procedure is called variance analysis (or variance
accounting). The purpose of variance analysis is to assist
management to identify the reasons for the variances and to make
any decisions deemed necessary.

Some advantages of standard costing are:

(a) It is a managerial aid to budgeting and cost control.
(b) It helps monitor and control output performance costs.
(c) With the introduction of exception reporting it enables
management to take immediate action to rectify any losses or
inefficiencies.
(d) It identifies the effect on costs of rises or falls in output.
(e) It is an economical method of providing management with
accurate and reliable cost information.

20. Time costs

So far the nature of costs used has been simple and
straightforward. However, as 'time' is a dominant factor it needs
to be taken into consideration in determining a true figure in each
case. Cost is defined as that expenditure which has been incurred
in bringing a product to its present location and condition.

Organisations have to consider material costing and stock valuation, overhead apportionment and marginal costing. Each of these factors influence management decisions regarding product or output cost and therefore selling price and each is affected over time. The following sections consider each of these in turn.

21. Material costing

In a small business where materials arrive and are taken into store the cost of the materials can easily be derived from invoices, goods-received notes and posting slips. These are used to enter costs directly to a particular job account, cost account or expense account. Similarly, for materials in stock, material costs can be obtained from material requisitions and transfer notes and nothing more complicated is involved when materials are utilised.

22. Stock valuation

In a larger business this situation can become more complex with the introduction of stock valuation. This means that a large turnover of stock involving slow-moving and fast-moving items includes different priced materials being used in the same production or output process. The difficulty arises on the method adopted by management to value these stock items and materials. The value placed on stock and materials is important because it affects production costs, the selling price (which also affects profit), the value of net assets on the balance sheet and the closing end-of-year stock value (which also becomes the opening stock value for the new year).

End-of-year stock is generally the easiest to deal with. The accounting standard concerned simply states that firms should value stock at its lowest value — cost price or net realisable value (selling price less costs of completion, selling and distribution).

The difficulty arises with materials issued from stock for production during periods of rapidly changing prices. Should these materials be charged at the latest prices, earlier prices or an average price? The three most common choices are:

(a) *FIFO* — first in, first out. This method is physically applied to goods which are perishable or liable to deteriorate and the price of the oldest stock is used.

(b) *LIFO* — last in, first out. With non-perishable goods order of

use is irrelevant. In this method the price of the most recent stock is used and when any new stock arrives the new price is assumed.
(c) *AVCO*. There are two methods: simple average cost and weighted average cost. The simple average method involves adding together the prices of received items and dividing the total by the number of different prices, e.g. £47, £51, £52 and £58 = £208/4 = £52. It does not take into account the number of items at each price and is therefore not recommended. Weighted average cost, on the other hand, is identical except that the number of stock items at each price enters the calculation. AVCO is used in particular by organisations trading in goods in liquid form, e.g. petrol stations.

> NOTE: The tax authorities do not accept LIFO as a basis of evaluation as it understates profits.

Businesses also have to decide how often stock levels should be valued. The decision normally depends upon whether a business considers it desirable, and affordable, to maintain constant stock values, called 'perpetual inventory' or to value stock at intervals, called 'periodic inventory'.

23. Overhead apportionment
This is the name given to sharing indirect costs or overheads of a business over production or output costs, usually involving common costs relating to two or more cost centres. The term 'allocation' is also used, which means the allotment of whole items of cost to cost centres or cost units. Similarly, the term 'absorption' refers to the allotment of overheads to cost units by means of separately calculated rates for each cost centre.

Cost centres themselves can be divided into two categories: production centres and service centres. Production centres are directly involved in production, e.g. an assembly line. Service centres exist to facilitate production centres and also other service centres, e.g. maintenance, stores, canteens, R&D, marketing and distribution. Therefore when overheads are apportioned it becomes quite a complex matter, best illustrated in Fig. 12.2.

The overheads consist of indirect material, indirect labour and indirect expenses. These are the costs which cannot be identified directly with one product or output and therefore have to be

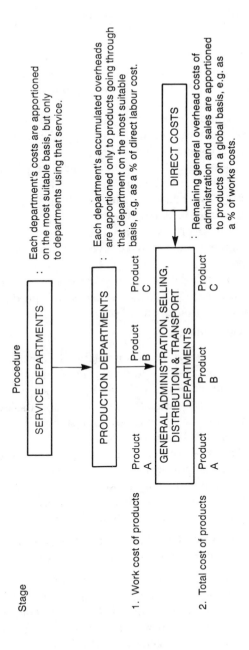

Fig. 12.2 *Overhead apportionment*

charged indirectly, or apportioned to them. Overheads can be classified as follows:

(a) Production overhead — also known as factory or works overhead and consist of factory rent, rates, light, heat, power, depreciation of plant, machinery and equipment, supervisor's and production manager's salaries.

(b) Administration overhead — includes office rent, rates, light, heat, clerical and managerial salaries, administrative and financial services, e.g. accountants and auditors.

(c) Financial overhead — includes the cost of financing the business, e.g. interest on borrowing.

(d) Marketing overhead — includes selling, i.e. sales staff and promotion, market research, advertising.

(e) Distribution overhead — includes warehouse costs, container costs, packaging, transport and delivery costs and depreciation on own transport.

(f) Research and development overhead — exists in large organisations, e.g. ICI, and consists of product research, development and improvement costs.

Types of overhead include:

(a) Fixed cost –- these remain unchanged over a long period of time and are not related to the volume of output. Examples are rent, rates, depreciation, salaries and insurance.

(b) Semi-fixed cost — are fixed costs over a specific level of output but when this is reached, increase as a 'step', e.g. the number of supervisors and mechanics required.

(c) Variable cost — these are directly related to the volume of output and include power, lubricants, salespeople's commission.

(d) Semi-variable cost — are those costs which have a fixed-cost element and also a variable cost element based on the level of activity. Examples are clerical labour, telephone and gas.

There are a number of alternative methods of apportioning indirect expenditure to production and service cost centres:

(a) Floor area — rent, rates, building expenses.

(b) Cubic capacity — heating, cleaning and decorating.

(c) Buildings and plant value — insurance and depreciation.

(d) Material volume and weight — storekeeping and handling costs are sometimes charged out on this basis.

(e) Number of employees — personnel, welfare, training, canteen and administrative costs.

(f) Metered consumption — where departmental meters exist, electricity, gas, compressed air and water charges.

24. Marginal costing

Whereas full costing of a product or service is a combination of direct costs and a share of the indirect costs, marginal costing relates to the variable cost element concerning output. Fixed costs are unavoidable costs. This means that they have to be paid for regardless of the amount of output. On the other hand, variable costs are also called avoidable costs because their costs are dependent on the unit price of output. Simply stated — no output, no variable costs. However, the nature of any business is to produce an output or service rather than to avoid it, therefore the significance of marginal costing is to determine how much more it will cost to produce one extra unit, or how much is saved by producing one less unit.

Economists are interested in average costs and marginal costs to determine 'economies of scale' referred to in 11:**13**. This is also relevant to the finance accountant in so far as establishing the most cost-effective and efficient production centre. However, this is where the economist and accountant part company from each other's theory. The economist determines that as all costs are variable the marginal cost per unit will vary with each extra or less unit produced. The accountant accepts the fact that in the short term, normally within a year, there are both fixed and variable costs. The variable costs associated with output are going to remain the same regardless of the number of units of output.

Rents and rates of a factory, depot or warehouse are good examples of fixed costs which are not avoidable. Direct material cost is an example of a variable cost. Total cost = Fixed costs + Variable costs.

25. The relationship of costs to output

An example of a simple graph which expresses the relationship of costs to output is shown in Fig. 12.3. Two vehicle hire firms charge for their vehicles on both a daily rate and a mileage rate. Firm A charges £20 per day and 50 pence per mile. Firm B charges

£10 per day and 70 pence per mile. On what basis would choice of firm be made?

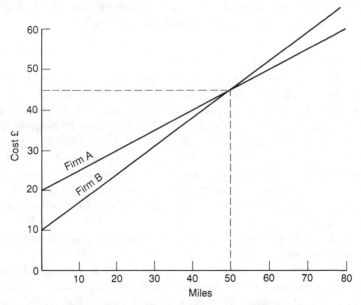

Fig. 12.3 *Relationship between costs and output.*

This graph illustrates the simple relationship between fixed and variable costs. The criterion for selecting either Firm A or Firm B is determined by the proposed mileage. Total cost is equal at the intersection of the total cost lines at the 50-mile point when each firm would charge £45. Therefore if the proposed journey exceeds 50 miles Firm A would be chosen and if less than 50 miles Firm B would be selected.

26. Breakeven analysis

The idea expressed in Fig. 12.3 is used by firms to depict costs, sales revenue and output when the breakeven point is that level of output where sales revenue just equals total cost.

Example

A manufacturer produces a product which sells at the wholesale price of £10. Its fixed distribution costs are £50,000 per annum and variable costs, using standard costing, are £5 per unit. The firm needs to know the answers to two questions. First, how many units does it need to sell to reach its breakeven point, and secondly, if the firm has capacity to produce 20,000 units, what is its margin of safety assuming it is presently at 75 per cent? Figure 12.4 illustrates the answers.

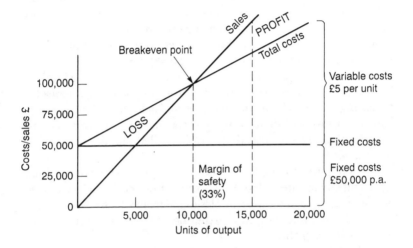

Fig. 12.4 *Breakeven point and margin of safety.*

Breakeven is reached at 10,000 units when sales just equals total costs of £100,000. Output of less than this amount would result in a loss with the possible necessity of reducing distribution costs. Greater sales would produce a profit, the size of which could be read off the graph at a glance, being the vertical distance between the total cost line and the sales line.

Also shown in the graph is the margin of safety which represents the proportionate fall in output which could take place before a loss is incurred. In this example, the present level of output of 15,000 units could fall to 10,000 units before a loss commences. Therefore the margin of safety is 33.3 per cent.

The construction of Fig. 12.4 entailed drawing the fixed-cost line first with the variable cost on top which formed the total cost line. It is possible to draw a breakeven chart in a slightly different manner which produces the same result but with additional useful information.

27. Variable cost analysis and 'contribution' to fixed costs

If the variable cost line is drawn first and then the fixed cost on top, the resultant total cost line is the same as the original diagram above. However, the reason for the change in construction is to illustrate what is known as 'contribution'. This term denotes the difference between sales value and variable cost only. Profit can be said to have been gained if contribution is larger than the variable costs, although obviously this is only at an intermediate level before fixed costs have been charged.

This can be equated as Sales − Variable costs = Contribution. In marginal costing terms a distribution company might consider accepting a 'one-off' contract if it is established that all the variable costs (in transport called 'running costs') have been covered and a contribution to fixed costs (in transport called 'standing costs') has been made.

In a manufacturing firm making a range of different products which all contribute to fixed costs this is understood to mean that a contribution to a common pool is made from which costs are paid and profit remains. This can further be equated as Contribution − Fixed costs = Profit.

The breakeven chart in Fig. 12.5 uses the same data as Fig. 12.4 but with the variable-cost line drawn first. The 'contribution' area is clearly indicated, together with the areas of profit and loss. The

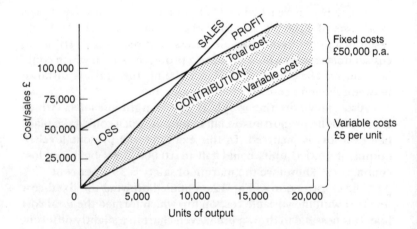

Fig. 12.5 *Contribution.*

amount of contribution towards fixed costs can be obtained by measuring the vertical distance between the variable-cost line and the sales line and transposing this to the vertical scale on the left-hand side.

A strict definition of marginal cost is 'the change in cost which occurs when the volume of output is increased or decreased by one unit'. Marginal costing is therefore dependent upon being able to identify and separate fixed and variable costs.

Transport costs

28. The nature of transport costs

As described earlier transport costs consist of fixed- and variable-cost elements. The logistics and distribution industry consists of transport organisations which are not part of a manufacturing or retailing organisation and those which are. In the case of pure transport companies their overheads are simpler to apportion than for firms which predominantly manufacture or retail products or services where the transport element is only a small percentage, albeit an important part, of turnover. The allocation of overheads in these cases is similar to Fig. 12.2 in **23**. However, when considering the nature of costs in a transport company or the transport department of a large organisation, they are the same.

29. Standing costs

These are the fixed costs which will be incurred whether the vehicle operates or not. They do not vary with output and they are neither avoidable nor escapable in the short term. Standing costs are normally calculated on a time basis, i.e. per year, per month, per week or per day. Examples are operator's licence, driver's licence, vehicle excise licence, vehicle insurance, vehicle depreciation and driver's guaranteed wages and administrative costs.

In the same way that manufacturing costs were identified as direct costs and indirect costs so can transport costs. If the vehicle is considered to be the cost centre the direct costs are the driver's wages, licences, insurance and depreciation. The indirect costs are the administration costs and other depot overheads which will have to be arbitrarily apportioned in some way. Three examples of indirect overhead apportionment to vehicles are:

(a) Dividing the overheads by the number of vehicles.
(b) Dividing the overheads by the total weight carrying capacity of the vehicles.
(c) By a combination of the two, i.e. half on the number of vehicles and half by carrying capacity.

30. Running costs

These are incurred only when the vehicle operates. The major components of this category include fuel and lubricants — based on cost per litre or kilometres per litre; tyres — based on expected life in kilometres; repairs and maintenance.

31. Profit margin

A reasonable profit has to be determined for continuity of the business, but how much is considered reasonable is open to speculation. The economic climate, interest rates and inflation are obviously important factors to be taken into consideration.

The four steps in achieving the profit margin are as follows:

(a) Determine the capital employed in the business.
(b) Express the required profit and return on capital employed.
(c) Calculate profit required to produce the chosen return on capital employed.
(d) Express the profit as a percentage of total costs of operation to determine how much to add to those costs.

32. Vehicle utilisation factor

Vehicles obviously will not run 365 days a year therefore before a rate is calculated, the number of days of expected vehicle utilisation has to be estimated. Generally this will be in the region of 240–250 days a year. If 365 was used in error the overhead and profit rate would be understated.

33. Calculating a rate

The four factors required to enable a rate to be calculated are: vehicle standing costs, vehicle running costs, profit factor and vehicle utilisation rate. The rate can be calculated on a mileage basis, a time basis or a combination of the two.

Logistics costing

34. The nature of logistics costs

Transport costing related to the operational costs concerning the movement of goods may be termed logistics costing and as such is concerned with the goods themselves either in the form of unit loads, products or consignments, whether single or multiple in magnitude. Various financial aspects need to be determined and these include warehousing costs, distribution costs, trunking costs, delivery costs, and product and customer profitability.

As mentioned at the outset of this chapter, the term logistics is concerned with efficiency and effectiveness. A manufacturing company requires raw materials to be delivered safely, in the right quantities, at predetermined times in order to produce its products. Any transhipment of semi-finished goods, inter-factory/firm movements of goods and products and final storage and delivery to wholesalers, retailers and customers must also be achieved to the same standards.

For all the firms involved in this logistical exercise to make a profit the additional costs, thus far not mentioned, must be identified and accurately assessed. Many planning and strategic decisions are based on these particular costs and very often these decisions can make or break a company.

35. Warehousing costs

These are derived from the obvious, i.e. the price of land, the cost of buildings, maintenance, equipment (e.g. fork-lift and stacker trucks), insurance, power, heating, lighting and staffing. However, other financial considerations include the type, volume, size, weight and throughput of the goods themselves. The handling and storage requirements are also significant factors too, for example refrigeration, security and perishability, all of which involve additional costs. Finally, the number and location of depots will also affect total costs.

36. Distribution costs

The cost of distribution often includes 'trade-offs'. This is the term used to describe an extra expense in one activity for a larger cost saving in another. Distribution concerns the delivery of products, either directly to a customer or via a distribution depot or depots. The financial implications concern the costs of owning, maintaining and operating warehouses and transport or utilising third-party contractors. Even the difference between outright purchase, hire-purchase or leasing vehicles and equipment will affect cash flows, opportunity costs, (using available cash for other purposes) and profitability. Distribution cost analysis is the term used in deciding the best 'trade-offs' for a given set of circumstances, which will vary from company to company and from time to time.

37. Trunking costs

Determining transport costs can be simplified if one large vehicle delivers an entire consignment to one destination, whether this is to a distribution centre or direct to a customer. In logistics terms this is referred to as a 'single drop load' and the number of products in the consignment divided by the transport cost will produce a unit cost which must be recovered, for instance, by being included in the product selling price.

When the distribution is an own-account operation the transport costs will include direct costs (vehicle costs, maintenance, driver's wages and running costs, e.g. fuel, tyres and lubricants) and indirect costs for overhead apportionment (depot costs, administration, and an element of the service departments, as described earlier in the chapter). In the case of contract hire the agreed price includes the contractor's costs plus an element of profit. However, the situation is compounded with a 'multi-drop delivery'. The difficulty is not the identification of the volume of each 'drop' but the costs attached to each consignment if delivery is being made for different customers on the same vehicle to various destinations.

38. Delivery costs

Having determined the trunking costs the delivery costs added to this figure will produce a total distribution cost. Sometimes there is only the one journey from origin to customer, in which case the need to break down the cost into trunk and delivery components is unnecessary. The problem concerns multi-drop delivery and in particular the route. In this case a distribution network is constructed which includes all the known variables, for example:

(a) distance from origin to delivery zone (the 'stem' distance)
(b) number of 'drops'
(c) distance between 'drops'
(d) vehicle capacity
(e) average volume of each 'drop'
(f) frequency of 'drops'
(g) loading and unloading times
(h) drivers' hours considerations.

Having itemised all the variable factors the number of journeys can be determined from which the normal transport costs can be calculated using time and mileage figures as described earlier. Individual customer consignment costs will also be a beneficial by-product of such a distribution analysis.

39. Product and customer profitability

These two factors are interrelated. A manufacturing company aims to maximise product profitability whereas a customer aims to minimise cash tied up in stock. The 'just-in-time' (JIT) principle might aid the customer but in many cases can increase costs for the manufacturer. This is simply explained by stating that maximum product profits can be earned by supplying bulk consignments infrequently. However, minimising stock is achieved by the customer ordering small quantities frequently.

It can be seen that in this scenario distribution costs would turn a profit into a loss. Suppliers therefore undertake distribution cost analysis (DCA) into which of their products and customers are the most profitable to them. This involves an analysis of unit costs including all variable factors such as the cost of marketing the product, costs of servicing the customer and the transport and distribution costs. Any customers who are shown to be unprofitable would have some revision to their deliveries, such as the imposition of a minimum sized order, a change in delivery frequency, or indirect deliveries, e.g. the customer changing to a wholesaler rather than receiving direct delivery from a manufacturer.

Inventory costs

40. The importance of inventory management

Inventory management is an important aspect of the logistics function and the financial implications regarding carrying stock, storage and transport need to be analysed and resolved.

41. Stock

Within the manufacturing industry stock comprises of raw materials, work in progress and finished goods, A value is attached to each, and during the process of transformation to the final state value is added. However, if the products are never sold their true value is zero. In other words, until they are sold they represent an increasing cost burden.

This dilemma has led in recent years to the widespread introduction of JIT (just-in-time) management and, through the greater use of information technology, trade-offs with regard to levels of stock held, the type and amount of storage capacity, the size of orders and the relevant transport costs.

A chocolate factory obviously needs the various ingredients to make chocolates in stock. This is called working stock and equates to the predetermined amounts required for each working day. As the quantity and type of chocolates manufactured varies seasonally, and not forgetting the two peaks at Christmas and Easter where disproportionate amounts of particular chocolates are purchased, the stock levels will vary in accordance with demand.

As certain ingredients may sometimes be difficult to obtain, especially from less accessible parts of the world, safety stock (also referred to as buffer or fluctuation stock) will be held as a contingency.

Sometimes what is called speculative stock will also be held. This is stock which may be used in the event of tastes changing to manufacture a new product or extend the production run of an existing brand in the hope that the market for it will pick up. The chocolate industry is also known for buying in additional raw materials speculatively to counteract shortages or price increases.

The cost of this inventory has to be carefully calculated. Trade-offs, as far as the risk of running short of certain commodities is concerned, has to be balanced against the cost of tying up too much capital.

42. Storage
Warehouses and distribution centres are extremely expensive assets. The following are the main costs of stockholding (storage):

(a) Storage space, i.e. the building, including the price of land.
(b) Specialist storage facilities e.g. refrigerated plant and secure premises.
(c) Materials handling equipment including fork-lift trucks, stacker and overhead cranes.
(d) Labour costs.
(e) Racking, pallets, bins, etc.
(f) Power, heat and lighting.
(g) Insurance, rent and rates.
(h) Maintenance of plant and equipment.

Many of the above also have depreciation costs as an operating expense.

43. Trade-off – frequent deliveries vs. bulk storage
The costs referred to this time are the total costs of more frequent deliveries of stock against the cost of less frequent bulk deliveries plus the cost of inventory and storage. This is one of the more complex trade-off decisions.

Budgeting

44. The need for budgeting
Every business organisation agrees policy objectives. These are decided upon through discussions and decisions at board and senior management levels and a strategy for the organisation to follow is normally expressed in the form of a long- or medium-term plan, sometimes called a business or corporate plan. The contents of the plan would consist in general terms of details concerning trends, changes and the direction in which the organisation desires to move.

In the case of a distribution company this strategy might include:

(a) a review of previous performance;
(b) the present and future economic situation;
(c) action of competitors;
(d) future investment opportunities;
(e) abandoning some existing markets;
(f) moving into new markets;
(g) appraisal of present performance;
(h) the disposal, continuing use and purchase of new assets, i.e. how many vehicles need replacing, are the warehouses fully utilised and are they situated in strategic locations for future anticipated business.

This is not a complete list but a representative sample of items senior management might consider at the planning stage.

The first year, or possibly two, of the business or corporate plan is translated into monetary terms and the document produced in this exercise is called the budget. This document can run to many pages depending upon the size of the organisation and contains not only financial tables but explanations and descriptions which justify the budget figures. Figures produced in a budget should be based on sound, realistic judgments about what is likely to occur in the future, not what is hoped will occur.

45. A budget definition

A budget is a document which expresses in financial terms a physical situation over a specified period of time and, assuming the policy objectives of the organisation are adhered to, provides guidelines as to performance achievements at specific intervals.

Budgets vary in size from the complete organisation budget called the master budget to function budgets such as a human resources budget (manpower plan) which determines the establishment requirements in terms of how many drivers, engineers, storemen, procurers, administrators and supervisors an organisation requires including their costs, i.e. wages, employer's national insurance contributions, pension funds, holiday and overtime pay.

It is important at this stage to differentiate between a budget and a forecast, which are often confused. A budget is a plan expressed in financial terms; a forecast is a competent judgment or prediction. A forecast is part of the initial planning process when senior management discusses the possible scenarios of future trading. The budget is much more of a financial directive, a set of instructions written in financial language to fulfil these forecasts.

46. Producing the budget

Once an organisation's future objectives have been set and the policies for achieving them agreed the next step is communicating them to the line management responsible either for profit centres, revenue centres or cost centres (further divided into production centres which are directly involved with production costs, and service centres which facilitate production).

The managers, supervisors, foremen and chargehands, to name only a few, must have an input in the budget preparation stage if during trading they are expected to conform to it. Low morale and poor performance from responsible staff members can result if their specialised knowledge is ignored at this stage. Communication is achieved through meetings and memoranda which convey the objectives and policies to follow. Each function and unit of the business will provide financial information together with justifications and assumptions on which these figures are based. These are then merged and aggregated to produce section and then departmental budgets.

Finally these are consolidated to form the master budget. The cycle is completed when the board or senior management consider this budget, amend and adjust it and finally agree it.

47. Budgetary constraints

The process of preparing a budget can be a complex business as the staff involved are constrained by what are called *limiting factors*. This means that a budget must begin with a realistic 'physical base'. It is unhelpful to consider changing an entire sector of a business and trading in a different market if the company would need to dispose of its present assets, invest in a whole range of new assets, retrain its staff and then compete for new business.

An organisation must start any new budget from its existing physical base, i.e. its present assets and staff. In anticipating volumes of business the limiting factors will also include storage capacity, carrying capacity, whether the right type and quantity of vehicles are available, particularly those required for specialist tasks, e.g. refrigeration vehicles and tankers.

New developments and investments are obviously not ruled out but they must be planned and phased in as a direct response to market forces and not just introduced to satisfy the whims of an uninformed management. The marketing memory aid 'SWOT' is useful: identification of Strengths and Weaknesses (internal), Opportunities and Threats (external).

48. Types of budgets

This topic can be divided in two. First, there is the length and characteristics of a budget, and secondly the nature of a budget. Length and characteristics of budgets are:

(a) The most common is the 'one-year self-contained budget'. The preparation of this type consists of using figures from the previous year's trading results as a basis and retaining the majority of account headings. As its name implies this budget is for one year, It is set in concrete in the sense that it is not usually adjusted part way through the year in the light of either internal or external variations, e.g. unplanned wage increases or rising interest rates.

(b) The 'rolling budget'. This type of budget was introduced in order to overcome the problem of external changes which affected the trading periods towards the end of a budget. High rates of inflation in particular have been responsible for invalidating the basis on which forecasts are based. Rolling budgets are constructed by adding a new trading period to the end of a budget each time a trading period has been completed and deleting the earliest month. In the case of a six month rolling budget the next six months' trading results are based on the previous six months. In this manner trends and changes can be incorporated into the budget in a much more flexible way.

(c) The 'two-year budget'. This type of budget is very similar to the one-year budget except that the second year would not be prepared in as much detail. Obviously it would be extremely difficult to give precise financial details for every situation 23 months hence, e.g. the need to expand storage capacity or the number of new vehicles required. However, the second year becomes the basis of the new first year next time round and in itself this reduces the amount of preparation time required and also brings about greater continuity in running the business.

(d) 'Standard costing budgets'. As described in the costing section some organisations adopt a standard costing system. This is reflected in how the budget is produced. A target output figure is agreed, e.g. annual production or annual miles to be operated. The actual results when compared are considered in the light of either exceeding the target or not achieving it.

The fixed cost element is apportioned per unit based on the target figure. If the target is exceeded then the actual fixed costs apportioned will be less than the budgeted figure as a greater number of units will have been produced. If the target is not reached then the fixed costs per unit will be greater than budget because fewer units will have been produced over which the fixed costs can be shared. Variable costs per unit are normally assumed to remain the same regardless of output.

(e) 'Zero-based budgets'. This type of budget is still considered to be a recent innovation. It involves, as its name suggests, beginning a new budget each time from a zero base. This means a fresh start with no preconceived costs or previous years' trading results as an overruling guide. All revenue and expenditure items to be included in the budget have to be justified independently from present performance, which is quite a difficult task. However, the advantage of this method is that poor performance, waste and inefficiencies can be eliminated. Therefore a true picture can be compiled and with tighter control possibly better results based on the new figures will emerge during the forthcoming trading period.

49. Nature of budgets

This section concerns the various departmental budgets which are compiled and when merged together form the main or master budget. There are a number of key budgets:

(a) *Sales or revenue budget.* This concerns anticipated revenue from operations during the budget period. It is the central budget on which all the other company budgets are based. It is also the most difficult budget to prepare because of the various external factors which can affect it including:

    (*i*) market demand

    (*ii*) economic trends

     (*iii*) competition
     (*iv*) prices
together with internal constraints including:
     (*i*) pricing policy
     (*ii*) marketing and advertising strategy
     (*iii*) human resources
     (*iv*) state of fixed and current assets.

(b) *Operating budget.* This is also referred to as the expenditure, production or distribution budget depending upon the type of organisation. This budget is an agglomeration of various departmental and functional budgets produced in order to quantify the costs involved in supplying the output itemised in the revenue/sales budget. If for instance the traffic department of a distribution company requires a certain contract to be fulfilled conveying consignments between various locations over a specified time period, these budgets would detail the operating costs involved. They might include functional activities, e.g. vehicle running costs, driver costs, handling and storage costs, to name but a few.

(c) *Capital expenditure budget.* This budget is prepared in order to highlight the anticipated changes in the value of fixed assets as revealed on the balance sheet. The changes arise through the purchase and sale of fixed assets either for replacement or expansion purposes. This budget also takes into account the impact of depreciation charges on the profit and loss position of the company.

(d) *The financial budget or cash budget.* This budget is prepared in order to trace the organisation's cash flow position throughout the trading period. It incorporates all revenue and expenditure transactions and enables decisions regarding, for example, the right time to purchase new vehicles, when a borrowing requirement could arise or when surplus funds might be available possibly for short-term interest bearing investment.

In addition to the above, other key budgets are also prepared including a human resources, manpower or personnel budget. This is obviously needed in order to determine the numbers and types of personnel required, including any recruiting, training, retraining or redundancy situations, in order to fulfil all the requirements of the revenue/sales budget.

50. Budgetary control

For any planning and budgetary procedure to be totally effective a control system must be devised, otherwise all the preparation will have been wasted. Budgetary control is a technique introduced to compare actual results with budgeted forecasts. The first essential is for the financial returns to be produced using exactly the same account headings as framed in the budget otherwise it would be extremely difficult to make comparisons.

Returns are also produced at the same intervals of time as the periods within the budget, normally every month, four weeks or whatever interval adopted within individual organisations.

For example, a haulage company at the end of a month's trading period might compare actual results with forecast, not just for the present month but normally with the previous month, the cumulative totals to date and with the same periods of time during the previous year. In this way the company will be able to determine trends and identify if it has exceeded revenue expectations, by what percentage and by how much. It will also see the expenditure results and be able to determine whether in relation to budget they are higher or lower. The technical term for this is *variance analysis* which simply means identifying the differences between actual results with budget and ascertaining the reasons why.

If budget control stopped at the variance analysis stage, again the whole exercise will have been wasted. From this analysis comes appraisal and decision making. Once the reasons for the variances have been identified the company must, in order to maintain profitability, act upon them. Sometimes the variances will be favourable and the company could possibly capitalise on the situation. Others will be unfavourable, in which case the company must take steps, wherever possible, to correct, adjust and eliminate the poor performance.

Financial planning and investment appraisal

51. Financial planning

The practical application of financial planning in the logistics and distribution industry is of vital significance for the success of any company. The section on budgeting actually incorporates elements of this topic in so far as the budget is the first part of a corporate plan compiled in monetary terms. An important element of a long-term plan is the anticipated financial situation. In this respect two factors are considered:

(a) *External factors*. These relate to how outside forces will influence the company, the majority of which the company has little or no control over. These include the economic climate, both nationally and internationally, whether the economy is expanding or contracting, the level of inflation and interest rates, what the competition is doing, changes in social tastes which might influence the manufacture and movement of products, the cost and availability of labour, and others.

(b) *Internal factors*. This is the 'physical base', meaning the type, number and condition of company assets with which to undertake activity and so earn money to survive and succeed, the availability of relevant trained labour and the necessary capital to expand or move into new markets.

Forward planning and anticipation are valuable attributes of good managers but financial planning is the key to implementing sound decisions rather than dreaming dreams. It begins with good housekeeping, i.e. investing at the beginning of periods of high income rather than in the middle of a slack period. In a transport company a new vehicle would be purchased at the start of a new contract, not at the end, a building company would order roofing tiles when the walls are nearly complete and delivered on site 'just in time'. Many companies fall down by purchasing too much inventory which takes up space, ties up capital and risks becoming obsolete, all for the sake of a bulk purchase discount. Each financial decision needs to be thought through using the economist's phrase 'opportunity cost' as a guideline, meaning which decision produces the best financial return for the company, either in the short or long term, whichever is expedient.

52. Investment appraisal

This topic really concerns capital investment over relatively long periods of time and requires comparisons to be made concerning various projects, their return on investment and, most importantly, their profitability. The projects could include a choice of investing in new buildings, new machinery or new vehicles, either to expand or replace obsolete and expensive assets. The decision on which project to choose is critical because it often involves large sums of money, the effects on the company last for years, in particular on profitability, and once embarked upon the decision is usually irreversible.

A number of techniques are used by senior management to evaluate which projects to undertake, as described in the following sections.

53. Payback method

This technique simply ranks projects in order of how much time it takes to pay back the initial capital outlay. For example, a company is considering investing £2 million on one of two projects, either building a new distribution and storage warehouse or installing new, high-technology machines on a production line replacing time-expired costly machines. The cash outflow and anticipated net cash inflows from each project are as follows:

	Project A *£000*	*Project B* *£000*
Initial outlay	2,000	2,000
Anticipated cash inflows		
Year 1	900	400
2	1,100	1,000
3	500	1,200
4	300	600

If the cost of capital is the same and the residual value for both projects after four years is zero then Project A payback period is 2 years and Project B $2\frac{1}{2}$ years. On this basis Project A would be selected as returns after the payback period are ignored, which is often a disadvantage with this method as long-term profitability is disregarded. Rejected Project B actually earns £3.2 million compared with Project A of £2.8 million.

These disadvantages are overcome in the second method described in **54**.

54. Average rate of return (ARR)

This method considers profitability rather than the payback

period. The ARR is calculated by dividing the average net cash inflow by the average investment, expressed as a profit.

Using the previous example the calculation is as follows:

Project A (in 000s):

$$\frac{900 + 1,100 + 500 + 300}{4 \text{ years}} = \frac{2,800}{4} = \text{£}700$$

Project B (in 000s):

$$\frac{400 + 1,000 + 1,200 + 600}{4 \text{ years}} = \frac{3,200}{4} = \text{£}800$$

The average investment is the same for both projects, i.e. the mid-point of the project's life or £2m/2 = £1m.

If depreciation is also considered, then using the straight-line method over four years the initial investment would reduce in value by £500,000 per year (£2m/4). This amount of depreciation is deducted from the average profit for each project, i.e. Project A £700,000 – £500,000 = £200,000, and Project B £800,000 – £500,000 = £300,000.

The final part of the calculation involves dividing the average annual net profit by the average investment:

$$\text{Project } A: \quad \text{ARR} = \frac{\text{£}200,000}{\text{£}500,000} \times 100 = 20\%$$

$$\text{Project } B: \quad \text{ARR} = \frac{\text{£}300,000}{\text{£}500,000} \times 100 = 30\%$$

On the basis of ARR project B would be selected.

The ARR method is definitely more comprehensive than the payback method but its major disadvantage is the fact that the cash inflows do not represent a true present value of money. In other words the value of money in normal circumstances reduces over time by the rate of inflation. In the case of foreign investments the value would be subject to fluctuating exchange rates.

55. Discounted cash flow (DCF)

Assuming that £500 in a year's time will be worth less than £500 today, a method has to be employed whereby future amounts can be assessed at today's value. The method must reduce the value of future earnings by an estimated amount equivalent to the loss in its buying power. Interest rates and the rate of inflation are the indicators used and the method employed is called 'discounting'.

Over short periods of time and for small amounts interest rates and inflation can be ignored as their effects will be insignificant. However, investments over long periods involving large sums of money need to be carefully appraised concerning the changes in monetary values.

Discounting is the opposite of compound interest. For example, if £1 is invested at 10 per cent compound interest it will be worth £1.10 (£1 + £0.10) in one year's time, and after two year's it will be worth £1.21 (£1.10 + £0.11).

The formula for compound interest is $A = P(1 + i)n$, where A is the amount of capital plus interest gained, P is the principal or original sum invested, i is the rate of interest, and n the number of years. The formula for discounting is:

$$P = \frac{A}{(1 + i)n}$$

Using a 10 per cent discount factor, £1 received in a year's time would be worth today:

$$\frac{£1}{£1.10} = £0.9091$$

£1 received in two years' time would be worth today:

$$\frac{£1}{£1.21} = £0.8264$$

There are two DCF methods employed by companies which are described in the following sections.

56. Net present value

The future cash inflows are discounted at a minimum rate of return acceptable to the company, in this example at 10 per cent. Evaluating each project, the results are as in Table 12.3.

Table 12.3   Project evaluation using net present value

	Project A			Project B		
Year	Cash flow £000	Discount factor at 10%	Present value £	Cash flow £000	Discount factor at 10%	Present value £
0	(2,000)	1.0000	(2,000,000)	(2,000)	1.0000	(2,000,000)
1	900	0.9091	818,190	400	0.9091	363,640
2	1,100	0.8264	909,040	1,000	0.8264	826,400
3	500	0.7513	375,650	1,200	0.7513	901,560
4	300	0.6830	204,900	600	0.6830	409,800
			NPV +307,780			NPV +501,400

The company would compare the NPVs of competing projects and normally choose the one with the largest NPV — in this case project B.

57. Internal rate of return (IRR)

This method attempts to identify the true interest rate earned by a project. It is calculated by determining, almost by trial and error, which interest rate when applied to future cash flows will reduce the NPV of the project to zero.

For Project B the interest yield is calculated as in Table 12.4.

Table 12.4   Calculating internal rate of return for Project B

Year	Cash flow £000	Discount factor at 20%	Present value £	Discount factor at 21%	Present value £
0	(2,000)	1.0000	(2,000,000)	1.0000	(2,000,000)
1	400	0.8333	333,320	0.8264	330,560
2	1,000	0.6944	694,400	0.6830	683,000
3	1,200	0.5787	694,440	0.5645	677,400
4	600	0.4822	289,320	0.4665	279,900
		NPV	+11,480	NPV	(29,140)

The internal rate of return is between 20 per cent and 21 per cent. This return is compared with the minimum acceptable return, which normally equates to the maximum a company is willing to pay for finance. The project with the largest IRR will be selected.

58. Payback vs. IRR

The payback method is the most commonly used method in practice as the quickest return on an investment is particularly attractive, and often has fewer risks attached. The biggest drawback to all methods of investment appraisal is the fact that net cash inflows are normally based on best estimates, which in time can prove to be erroneous, especially from factors outside the control of a company. Another factor is the estimates and assumptions of what future inflation and interest rates will be. The longer the time period involved the more difficult it is to make sound judgments.

Progress test 12

1. What is the purpose of financial accounting? **(4)**

2. A vehicle costs £40,000 and has a useful life of five years. Assuming a residual value of £5,000, how much depreciation is charged as an expense using the straight-line method, and to which record of accounts is it charged, the profit and loss account or the balance sheet? **(5)**

3. In stock evaluation, what do the initials FIFO, LIFO and AVCO mean? **(22)**

4. What is the difference between functional costs and activity costs? **(12, 14)**

5. Why is it important to understand the term 'contribution' as it applies to marginal costing? **(27)**

6. State a definition of a 'budget'. **(45)**

7.   In the subject of transport costs, describe the difference between standing costs and running costs.   **(29, 30)**

8.   For investment appraisal purposes organisations use DCF. What do these initials stand for and describe the two methods employed.   **(55, 56, 57)**

Logistics in a European context: developments and the future

Internationalisation of distribution

1. Introduction

Apart from further developments in technology, in logistics management as a business science and continually evolving principles of best practice in commercial management, one of the major sources of change faced by logistics and distribution managers is the trend in international trade.

2. Logistics and distribution in Europe

Over time, logistics management has developed as a fully fledged business discipline. In tandem with such a relatively recent development have come planned changes on the international commercial scene which will pose even further challenges to managers in this area of corporate responsibility. The concept of 1992 and the Single European Market (SEM) should open completely the gates of intra-Community trade, and mean not only freer movement of goods and commodities, but the adoption of a pan-European logistics and distribution strategy by the majority of companies. Running concurrent with progress toward this ideal is the continuing excavation of the Channel Tunnel — due for completion in 1993. Such a unique communications link would, alone, offer considerable opportunities for developments in methods of European transport and distribution. Coupled with the abolition of all Community trade barriers, the possibilities for change and innovation in the logistics industry are numerous.

The main vehicle for potential change can thus be seen as the 'Europeanisation' of industry as a whole. If first the Community as an economic federation, and secondly continental Europe as a geographic area, are to be considered as a single market, then logistics strategies of both UK and international companies must be the subject of a substantial reappraisal.

No logistics or distribution system can be planned in a vacuum. As the means of bridging the time and space gap, it cannot effectively fulfil its role until these factors are quantified. Similarly, in logistics management, it would be difficult to develop efficient transport networks or optimise modal benefits in the absence of a strategic operating framework. In such a process, corporate management attention will most likely be focused on four major facets of this development:

(a) Re-configuration of market areas
(b) Facilities location
(c) Modal selection and transport networks
(d) Intermodal transport and the Channel Tunnel
(e) Information systems and communications links.

3. **Re-configuration of market areas**

The extent to which UK companies' markets may need to be geographically redefined will depend on the extent to which each organisation has already become commercially integrated in Europe. As over 40 per cent of UK international trade is now with our EC partners, the assumption that our business contacts and infrastructure are well-established on the Continent is perhaps excusable. But much still remains to be done if our geographic separation from the European mainland is to be overcome, and British companies genuinely believe their markets to be increasingly located — and expanding — in a south-easterly direction across the Channel.

Taking the European Community alone, it has a core area — represented principally by the geographic centre of developed Western Europe and the Community's founder countries — and a peripheral area, the slightly less-developed newcomers to the EC farther from the geographic and commercial centre, namely Portugal, Spain and Greece. Differentiating between these two groups within the Community may well mean identifying different markets to which individual logistics strategies may apply. Nevertheless, the perception of Europe in this context as a unified, comparatively homogeneous market is a relatively short-term view.

The opening up of Eastern Europe as a potential market for EC industry must be borne in mind. It may well be some years before tangible results are achieved in this direction, but the possibilities of Europe as a single market expanding substantially eastward are very real. Any corporate European business plan must therefore provide for this eventuality, and ensure that further modification and expansion of business activity can be accomplished with minimum cost and reorganisation.

4. Facilities location

One of the main decisions to be taken by any business in this context is location of its facilities and operational infrastructure. The approach of 1992 has already generated widespread reappraisal of many companies' networks — factories and plants, storage and warehousing facilities, distribution centres, and in some cases product outlets. With Britain effectively appended to the Continental mainland by means of the Channel Tunnel, the fulcrum of UK distribution into Europe has already shifted. Potential distribution locations — mostly in northern France and Belgium — are being advertised in the British commercial press, and being acquired or considered by UK companies. The problem for firms is whether to rely on current or developing transport links to enable them to provide the appropriate level of service to European customers, or whether to invest in distribution facilities across the Channel to underpin customer service levels on the new open market.

For many companies familiar with state-of-the-art logistics management techniques, the solution will lie in modification of long-term plans to include expansion of their distribution infrastructure into certain carefully selected Continental locations. Major decision criteria will be location of suppliers and possible transport options — in addition to location of main markets and demand centres. However, not all companies will be in a position, or perhaps have the commercial confidence, to branch out into such relatively unknown business territory alone.

Dependent on circumstances, mutual cooperation with foreign operators or agents may be the best initial move, until they can consolidate their financial and business base sufficient to warrant a more committed approach to the concept of total European distribution. A further possible means of entry to the new market might be acquisition of an existing European operator, possessing both network and local expertise, available for servicing the needs of a new parent company. With free movement of not only goods and services, but also finance under the SEM banner, such transactions might become commonplace — either UK firms buying into Europe or vice versa.

Any changes in facilities location as a result of identifying new markets or expansion of existing ones will create new or different materials and commodity flows which, in turn, may require a review of transportation.

5.   Modal selection and transport networks

The operating pattern since the late 1960s has been largely characterised by a growing two-way flow of road freight vehicles across the Channel between the UK and Europe, lightened by a certain amount of rail freight. British road hauliers and distribution contractors accustomed to our relatively short island distances have extended their operations to such a degree that throughout-by-road international deliveries are seen as the norm. Likewise, the appearance of foreign vehicles on our roads has, for some years now, been quite commonplace. Unitised traffic, in the form of road trailers and containers, but including rail wagons also, accounts for approximately 75 per cent of this cross-channel flow.

With the definite prospect of even greater cross-Channel traffic, and the coincidental opening of a direct connecting link, the way is open for a searching review of distribution methods and networks in Europe. Opportunities for long-haul through transit of freight by rail — particularly containers and swap-bodies — to Continental and Mediterranean destinations are considerable. With intermodal road/rail transit systems already well-established in both France and Germany, and provision for such traffic to be operated in most other member countries by existing agreements, there must surely be a very strong case for increased rail freight transport as part of the new European logistics infrastructure. Railfreight Distribution's strategy for Europe, for example, has targeted the development of main traffic flows in block train form. Continental rail systems' capability to carry road freight vehicles, particularly following the Channel Tunnel's opening, also brings road transport operators the benefits of shorter journey times, as well as reducing the impact of drivers' hours restrictions.

Despite increased use of rail as a means of freight transport and distribution in some member countries, capital investment must be increased in order to maximise potential benefits of the Channel Tunnel and a much more integrated Community rail network. There is a need for more purpose-built rail/road terminals at strategic locations as part of the consolidation of intermodal logistics transport across the Single Market area. Although much attention is concentrated on the more prominent, larger member countries in north-west Europe, others such as Italy and Greece with their Mediterranean locations still feature prominently on the total Community transport scene. A great deal of through transport reaches Italy by road, and connecting long-distance road/rail services from countries such as Germany into Greece and Turkey.

This potential rail bias could, however, be countered by the abolition of permit restrictions and legalisation of cabotage, thereby encouraging further expansion of road-based transport and distribution operations. Legalised cross-trading — transport between two countries by a third-party contractor not resident in either — could also swing the balance in favour of road.

Other variables on the modal selection scene include the future role of sea and inland waterway transport, the impact of a much larger Germany on Community economics and dynamics, and increasing environmental awareness in many member countries, particularly in view of the hold road-based transport still has on logistics operations in Europe as a whole. These issues could raise questions such as whether the total environmental lobby will press for greater use of rail and water-borne transport.

It is impossible to predict the course of these developments, but a stage has been reached where Community industry and state governments alike have a unique opportunity to create an efficient Europe-wide logistics transport network with a strong intermodal bias. Moreover, the Common Transport Policy, unlike its agricultural counterpart, has so far been reasonably successful. In order to achieve the optimum result, member countries need to agree a broad-brush, Community-wide policy regarding means of both primary and secondary distribution. Should they fail to take the initiative, the commercial companies and operators will find and implement their own solutions; these, whilst being at first glance cost-effective, may not prove so in the longer term and when viewed from a broader perspective.

Intermodal transport and the Channel Tunnel

6. General

The continuing trend of unitisation and containerisation has been synonymous with increased use of intermodal systems in the field of international logistics and distribution. In the field of ISO container operations alone, the balance of Freightliner's carryings is now in the region of 80 per cent maritime and 20 per cent domestic.

Three major factors have been instrumental in underpinning this development:

(a) increased benefits of using intermodal systems;
(b) the Channel Tunnel;
(c) the environment.

7. System benefits

The increased benefits of intermodal systems have accrued to UK industry over the last 26 years. Since the inception of Freightliner operations in 1965, companies have realised and experienced the advantages of containerised transport methods in the form of faster transit and transhipment times, greater security and consignment integrity, and fewer claims and damages.

With the disappearance of Speedlink as a separate unit, Railfreight Distribution plans to undertake door-to-door deliveries using new generation intermodal equipment as part of its involvement in Charterail — a joint initiative with GKN.

Groupage operations remain a large sector of containerised transport, with use of both air and maritime containers by specialist companies in this field, including a number of freight forwarders and some international courier services. This allows smaller firms — or firms with smaller consignments — to have joint use of a container with consignors of other similar part-loads, with the result that each of them enjoys the benefit of containerised movement at a fair freight rate.

8. The Channel Tunnel

The Channel Tunnel provides a unique opportunity to rationalise and improve international transport and distribution systems. It is, however, only one development — albeit a major one — in the industrial and commercial Europeanisation or even globalisation process. Part of the significance of this for intermodal transport is that such systems have already been *in situ* in both France and Germany for many years.

Both the French 'Kangourou' and German 'Kombiverkehr' systems are capable of carrying loaded vehicles and demountable bodies over long distances. These networks have been developed to service not only most main centres in Western Europe, but also many peripheral eastern European and Mediterranean destinations such as Greece, Yugoslavia and Turkey. Journey distances average in excess of 1,000 kilometres — notably longer than average UK trunking distances — and services are operated by fast, scheduled train services, dedicated to intermodal traffic.

The Channel Tunnel will provide the opportunity of linking the UK directly into this growing network, therefore making intermodal operation a much more viable option for many companies whose distribution is currently road-based.

According to SNCF, the French rail service, such a move will create 'an EC-wide rail network for swap-body traffic, operating direct trains over long distances at high speeds, and linking the UK with continental Europe. The joint traffic potential will be in the region of 6.5 million tonnes per annum through the tunnel, 4 million tonnes of which will be intermodal traffic — containers and swap-bodies.' BR's forecast, however, is for 6 million tonnes upwards.

Examples of likely transit times via the Channel Tunnel might be:

Manchester to Dijon	–	26 hours
Glasgow to Paris	–	28 hours
Ipswich to Milan	–	40 hours

9.   The environment
The environment remains an area of concern for both government and people. Industry and commerce have for some time been feeling the pressure for change in their operating methods, not least the transport and distribution sector. If not the operators themselves, certainly the large client companies many logistics companies serve, have felt the need to develop a 'green' policy. This, needless to say, has impacted on many major players in the distribution and logistics management industry.

A CBI estimate of the cost of UK road congestion alone reaches a phenomenal £15 million per annum in delays, fuel consumption, vehicle wear and tear, and wages paid for work which is essentially non-productive. Current forecasts place the increase in road traffic by the second decade of the twenty-first century at between 50 and 100 per cent of today's figures.

Use of rail services for primary distribution — whether in the form of unitised or vehicular traffic — would be a means of lessening environmental impact, whilst retaining levels of service acceptable to transport and distribution operators, companies and consumers.

Using intermodal methods of transport in whatever combination — road/rail/sea, road/air/road, etc. can often utilise the best features of each to the benefit of both consignor and consignee. On an environmental note, it may not be long before the completely road-based logistics operation is a thing of the past. To ensure survival, forward-looking organisations must examine their options in order to avoid unnecessary costs, comply with likely future environmental legislation, and remain competitive not only in terms of service to their customers, but also *vis-à-vis* their corporate image.

Notwithstanding these issues, movement of goods and materials is always initiated by transmission of instructions and information. Pan-European logistics management cannot therefore be planned and developed without an appraisal of information technology's crucial role.

The role of information technology

10.   Information systems and communications links
Even before the advent of the Single European Act, the

significance of modern technology in business has been all but universally acknowledged. The importance of communications as part of information technology's role, both within an organisation and externally, must be realised for firms to achieve and maintain the required sharpness of competitive edge. Fast, accurate information flow is vital to the success of any business, for planning, decision making, operational control and ensuring both the smooth and timely flow of goods and materials.

11. Networking and EDI

State-of-the-art information and communications systems can be instrumental in companies achieving and maintaining a more competitive position in their field. One of the most important among such developments in information technology is that of networking. Electronic data interchange (EDI) becomes possible when two computer systems are linked to provide a total information exchange facility. This could take the form of orders for distribution the following day, or operational data for analysis and reporting procedures. The basic principle is that speed of information transmission is used as an operating management tool, and as an aid to more timely decision making.

Similar methods have, for some time now, been the basis of many UK logistics and distribution information systems. Now, with the ability to utilise wide-area networks — international links using telephone lines, satellites and microwaves — the potential for the fast, free flow of information throughout a Europe-wide logistics and distribution infrastructure is an element no would-be major player in the Single European Market can afford to ignore.

Information is the life-blood of any business and, as mentioned above, often the key to success. The importance of its accuracy, and often instantaneous availability, cannot be over-stressed. Most large, international companies already have networks spanning Europe through scores, perhaps hundreds of locations, supporting manufacturing, distribution, accounting and other business functions. Many smaller firms are also connected to networks which provide some of these facilities.

Such means of communication are rapidly becoming essential both to effective logistics and distribution operations and to wider business success. They are among the tools which will enable a company's management to take advantage of the opportunities which are likely to present themselves when the Single European Market opens for business.

12. Implications of developments in communications technology

Future trends suggest the introduction of telephones with screens whereby communicants can see as well as talk to each other. Electronic gadgetry already enables certain transactions to be undertaken by telephone, e.g. home banking. Progress in this area tends to suggest that home shopping for all our needs, not just catalogue shopping, and certain people working at home rather than in an office will become the norm. If so, these changes will undoubtedly have a major impact on present-day logistics, and in particular, distribution methods.

The economic balance of network trading will be affected. Trunking operations might well decline with a vast increase in small delivery vehicle firms, capable of home delivery. If instead of going to the supermarket for shopping all selections are made at home then this again will have a major impact on the retail trade. Demographic changes already suggest an increase in corner shops; home shopping might well be the death knell to hypermarkets and out-of-town shopping centres. In their place there will be regional distribution centres.

Greater world-wide communications lends itself to a much more efficient use of finite resources. If information technology has a beneficial use it must be to act as a database for raw materials, commodities and demand. By matching up supply and demand, storage facilities could be reduced or no longer required. Advanced orders from consumer durables and semi-finished parts to raw materials should reduce waste and inefficiency.

The EC Common Transport Policy — implications for logistics management

13. General background

The European Community was created by the Treaty of Rome as early as 1957, but the UK's accession to the Community did not occur until 1972. Articles 74 to 84 of the Treaty place a duty on the Council of Ministers to prepare and implement a Common

Transport Policy which will remove obstacles to the free circulation of goods by inland, sea and air transport.

Some important definitions are as follows.

The Council of Ministers, and not the European Parliament, is the supreme legislative body of the EC. Regulations and Directives are drafted by the Commission for ratification by the Council. *The Commission*, or 'Eurocrats' as they have been dubbed, is the 'civil service' of the Community. *Regulations* (for example, Regulation 3820/85 on Drivers' Hours) are binding on member states, but *Directives* merely require each member state to achieve a particular result through their own legislation. (Thus in the UK the Goods Vehicle (Operator's Licences, Qualifications and Fees) Regulation 1984 implements EC Directive 561/74 on Admission to the Occupation of Road Haulier.)

14. Liberalisation of transport

The underlying principle of the Common Transport Policy is that the advantages of *competition* should be more fully utilised to the mutual benefit of transport users. Although this policy was decided upon by the Council in 1961, by 1985 so little progress had been made towards its realisation that the European Commission was compelled to go to the European Court and obtain a judgment. The Court found the Council at fault. In the same year the Single European Act was passed committing the UK and the other member states to implementing the Single European Market in 1992.

Since then progress has been more rapid as the SEM approaches. This is partly because of a change in the way in which the Council of Ministers now decide on the Regulations and Directives presented to them by the Commission. Instead of requiring an unanimous majority vote, these can now be passed by 'qualified majority', thus removing member states' *de facto* powers of veto.

15. Deregulation and free competition

As well as providing for free competition (the so-called level playing field), liberalisation implies the deregulation of transport.

As long as member states such as Germany pursue quantity controls of road haulage and road passenger transport to protect their nationalised railway undertakings and waterways, or European air transport capacity and fares continue to be controlled by member states through bilateral agreements and strict quantity licensing, there will continue to be distortions in the transport market. The ultimate aim of the Common Transport Policy is to eliminate such distortions.

The Treaty of Rome prohibits member states discriminating against carriers from other member states, although there is an exceptional provision permitting Germany to adopt special measures to compensate certain areas which suffer a disadvantage due to the former division of Germany. For example, freight rates from the Ruhr to Hamburg by West Germany's railways (the Deutschbahn) are kept artificially low to protect the port against competition from Rhine shipping and the Dutch port of Rotterdam. Such exemptions are likely to be removed now that Germany is re-unified.

Whilst competition and deregulation are clearly prerequisites of liberalisation, this will only be fully completed by *restructuring* the transport industry so as to decouple, as far as is possible, transport providers and state subsidies. This does not necessarily mean ending all state ownership of transport, as the UK government attempted with the 'privatisation' of the National Freight Corporation and the National Bus Company. The British Railways Board and London Regional Transport, for example, are still state-owned.

16. Normalisation of accounts

However, the clear intention of Brussels is that the accounts of state-owned transport undertakings should be 'normalised', in other words drawn up in such a way that subsidies are 'transparent' and are for purposes allowed by the Common Transport Policy, such as the provision of unremunerative but socially desirable services. They should not be applied in such a way as to unlawfully distort free competition. Any 'acquired' or historic costs, such as the provision of pensions to ex-employees or the servicing of commencing capital debts (inherited upon nationalisation) are required to be separated out from the main accounts.

With the completion of the Channel Tunnel, the normalisation of the accounts of the member states national railways, (whether or not BRB is by then 'privatised') will assume greater urgency. An EC Directive already requires the separation of 'commercial' and 'state funded' activities in railways' accounts, and the Commission have suggested that, in order to ensure fair competition between the users of different states' railways, the actual operation of freight and passenger services should be carried out by separate commercial railway operating companies trading 'at arm's length' from their owners. A difficulty in this approach is that different EC states have different interpretations as to what are or are not 'social' railway services.

This model would allow for, amongst other options, complete privatisation, a shared ownership (as in the French SNCF rail operation), or a separate state-owned 'track authority' to 'franchise' the railway operating companies. Such systems were common on the continent in the last century, particularly on branch lines in France.

17. Implications for logistics managers

The important factor from the viewpoint of the logistics manager is that the EC Common Transport Policy aims to prevent discrimination by carriers on grounds of country of origin or destination.

In the UK, road haulage was of course deregulated over two decades ago by the Transport Act 1968 which swept away the then existing quantity controls and substituted a system of quality licensing. From the advent of the SEM after December 1992 the Community system of road haulage licensing will also be governed solely by qualitative criteria, and, some EC member states will no doubt find great difficulty in switching from their existing protectionist quantity licensing systems. Nevertheless, the regulations on the new criteria have been adopted, and UK logistics and distribution managers who are familiar with the workings of a deregulated road haulage market in their own country should therefore be well-placed to take advantage of the SEM.

European distribution

18. Differences from UK distribution

Fundamental differences exist between UK logistics management practices and those of our European partners. In the

UK approximately 50 per cent of distribution is now 'retail-led', with retailers' own vehicles or the vehicles of bespoke distribution service providers delivering from consolidation depots to retail outlets. The continental preference is for 'manufacturer-led' distribution, a costlier alternative. Manufacturers' own vehicles or 'bought-in' haulage deliver direct to stores or retailers' own warehouses. This creates a multi-user as opposed to the UK dedicated operation. UK expertise in retail-led distribution is certain to become increasingly in demand in Europe post 1992.

19. Combined transport

Although the EC is working towards a system of abolishing quantitative controls on international road freight (the quota permit system described in 23 below), a problem which such liberalisation would do nothing to address, and in some cases would actually worsen, is the amount of transit traffic which passes through some member states without either originating or terminating there.

In France or Germany, road/rail permits are freely available and issued over and above an operator's quota entitlement where a movement takes place by means of such combined transport methods as the German Deutschbahn Kombi trains or the French SNCF Kangourou trains. These enable road vehicles, or their trailers, to travel by rail between rail heads at ports like Dunkirk or rail centres such as Cologne.

The EC Transport Commissioner Karl van Miert has said that 'combined transport and the development of the European network to service it are a priority, especially for the "transit" countries' (*Transport*, May 1990). He also highlighted the same problem with non-EC transit countries such as Austria, Switzerland and Yugoslavia.

Obviously the completion of the Channel Tunnel will give an enormous boost to the development of combined transport operations between the UK and the rest of Europe. Provided the necessary rail infrastructure can be put in place in the UK to match equivalent rail investment by our European partners, the Channel Tunnel will provide new competitive opportunities for rail freight right through to the heart of the European market, with significant benefits for the logistics and distribution industry. In addition it will offer a frequent all-weather shuttle for road freight, and will give, together with air transport and sea ferries, four modes of cross-channel freight movement.

A further boost to combined transport will inevitably come because of growing environmental pressures. All EC governments now recognise an urgent need to relieve road congestion caused by heavy lorry movements. An obvious way to do this is to carry 'platoons' of HGVs on rail waggons.

The opening up of Eastern Europe could boost the fortunes of combined transport even more. Even longer transit hauls will need to be made across both EC and non-EC countries, many of whom, so-called 'transit states' like Austria, perceive their road systems as being exploited by hauliers merely passing through. The viability of combined transport is to some extent a function of distance, and this, together with its obvious environmental benefits, could well lead to changes in legislation which will favour it.

20. International conventions

The UK and the EC are signatories to a number of international conventions on matters affecting distribution. Some of these derive from the United Nations in Geneva, others from the European Council of Ministers of Transport (ECMT). The following is a by no means exhaustive list:

(a) *1975 TIR Customs Convention on the International Transport of Goods.* This permits the movement of goods across frontiers provided that the vehicle or container in which they are carried is sealed by customs at the consignors. Within the EC the Community Transport procedure, for which the relatively new Single Administrative Document (SAD) can now act as the Community Transit Document, negates the need to apply full TIR procedures. This is one way in which the EC attempts to satisfy one of the aims of the Common Transport Policy which is to eliminate as far as possible border delays within the SEM.

(b) *The 1956 CMR Convention on the Carriage of Merchandise by Road,* which sets out the rights and liabilities of consignors, consignees and carriers on international carriage by road. Similar conventions cover other modes, for example the Warsaw Convention on Air Transport 1961, the CIM Convention on Rail Transport, the 1971 Hague-Wisby Rules on Maritime Transport and, more recently, the yet to be ratified (by the UK) TCM convention on combined transport.

(c) *The 1968 ADR Convention on the Carriage of Dangerous Goods by Road*. Many UK operators are concerned that the standards of labelling of hazardous goods which are set out in the convention are in fact less comprehensive that the standards embodied in the UK 'Hazchem' warning panels!

(d) *The 1985 ATP Convention on the Carriage of Perishable Foodstuffs.*

(e) *The AETR (European Agreement on Drivers' Hours of Work and Records)* applies to all goods vehicle international movements outside the EC. The EC Drivers' Hours Regulation 3280/85 replaces this on international journeys within the EC.

(f) *The 1957 Convention on the International Taxation of Road Vehicles*. In broad terms this UN Convention provides for the temporary import of vehicles into a signatory state without that vehicle becoming liable to pay the equivalent of vehicle excise duty.

21. Differences in road and fuel taxes

Harmonisation of fiscal duties is a central prop of the Common Transport Policy. Hauliers of one state may be competitively disadvantaged *vis-à-vis* those of another state simply because both operate under different tax regimes. In 1990 the Commission recommended a system of vehicle taxation aimed at recovering the infrastructure costs associated with different classes of vehicles. This they say should be based on gross vehicle weights and axle configurations, as is done in the UK.

However, there is still considerable distortion in this area. Some countries outside the EC impose additional taxes in the form of time, mileage and/or tonnage taxes, and there are many toll roads within EC member states. (The UK too is considering the provision of privately funded toll roads to ease congestion — *New Roads by New Means*, HMSO, 1990.) The issue is further complicated by disagreements as to the calculation of the true 'infrastructure costs' of heavy commercial vehicles, which ultimately road taxes must reflect.

22. The problem of 'transit countries'

More serious is the disproportionate use of the road infrastructure by 'foreign' vehicles in 'transit countries'. Austria, for example, imposes a tonne/kilometre transit tax on vehicles passing through to Middle East destinations. Even the UK can claim to be a transit country in respect of the large number of vehicles from the Republic of Ireland running between Stranraer or Holyhead and from the Channel ports (and eventually the Tunnel). The Eire government, with an eye on future combined transport, is pressing the UK government to electrify the Holyhead to Crewe rail link.

Germany's decision to impose a transit tax on lorries over 18 tonnes, requiring them to display a 'vignette' or German tax disc indicating payment of their road tax for the duration of their visit, is being challenged by the Commission in the European Courts. Such a system, known as 'territoriality', if imposed EC-wide, would, despite its superficial 'fairness', undoubtedly be very complex to administer without a sophisticated system of computer-aided vehicle tracking and road pricing. In the long term of course, this may well come.

23. Permits and controls

Although some countries allow free access for foreign hauliers (and most do so for manufacturers' and retailers' 'own-account' vehicles) others still require vehicle operators to obtain permits entitling them to deliver to or collect from the country issuing the permit.

The issue of permits, and in particular the 'quota' of permits for specified numbers of *journeys* or specified *periods* of validity, is either negotiated between the member states concerned, reaching agreement on a number of *bilateral permits* or, increasingly, is negotiated on a European-wide basis within the EC or ECMT. These latter *multilateral* permits allow hauliers to 'tramp' by delivering to one member state, and then take a further load from there to a third member state.

Clearly the issue of such quotas is against the spirit of the Common Transport Policy, which is to promote the free movement of people and goods. As a first step towards complete liberalisation within the SEM the Commission has for some time been reducing the number of bilateral permits by substituting the equivalent capacity in multilateral permits.

Nevertheless the situation has not yet been reached where permit supplies meet natural demand, and the International Road Freight Office (IRFO) of the Department of Transport is still forced to ration the UK's quota of permits to operators. From January 1993, of course, the Community system will be governed solely by qualitative criteria.

At the same time the Commission intend to dismantle haulage tariff controls which have, in the deregulated UK haulage market, increasingly been seen as irrelevant and largely ignored!

24. Cabotage

Whilst the total abolition of the quota permit system should remove many of the barriers to competition for international transport services, it does nothing to open up the internal transport markets of member states to competition by foreign carriers.

At present, even with a multinational permit, a UK haulier delivering to Paris could not pick up a load for Lyons, although he would be free to take a load to Turin! In the same way, a French haulier delivering to Birmingham, could not 'backload' to London. Such movements, technically described as 'cabotage', make economic sense in so far as they can reduce the wasteful cost of empty running.

The Council of Ministers in December 1989 agreed a transitional phase of cabotage, to operate until the full SEM and the adoption of a definitive cabotage regime in January 1993. This involves a cabotage quota for each state. Of course, in the current transitional phase, it will still be a prerequisite of cabotage that the haulier has the relative international permit in the first place to reach the state within which he intends to use his cabotage permit!

There are also obvious environmental benefits from a relaxed cabotage regime since if vehicles which would normally return empty can do so loaded this will reduce both the total number of vehicles used and the distance they travel.

Statutory control of distribution

25. General

The distribution industry, like any other industry, must operate within a legislative framework. Those who do otherwise, by ignoring legislation, obviously incur lower operating costs and are able to compete unfairly. This is why enforcement is coming to be seen by the EC Commission as a vital part of the harmonisation of market conditions, and Directives increasingly stipulate enforcement standards. For example, minimum levels of fleet inspections and roadside checks are now prescribed, together with systems of cooperation between member states over cross-border offences.

Chapter 8 sketched the comprehensive array of UK legislation relevant to goods vehicle operation (*see* 8:9–22). Much of this is intended to implement EC Directives. For example, the operator licensing requirement as to the professional competence of transport managers contained in the Goods Vehicle (Operator Licensing, Qualifications and Fees) Regulations 1984 implements EC Directive 561/74 on Access to the Occupation of Road Haulier.

26. Harmonisation of UK and EC law

EC regulations, such as Regulation 3820/85 on Drivers' Hours of Work, are enforceable in the UK as the law of the land, and, increasingly as the SEM approaches, UK legislation will reflect that of the EC.

Ideally, if free competition is to be a reality, no national legislation should exist which could interfere with this. The Commission therefore has a programme of harmonising fiscal, technical and social legislation for this purpose. Each of these is considered below, with relevant examples.

27. Harmonisation of fiscal legislation

Mention has been made of the discrepancies in vehicle excise duties between member states, the attempts by the Commission to introduce a harmonised infrastructure tax, and the German preference for a system of 'territoriality' whereby visiting vehicles in effect pay member states' taxes on a daily basis.

Even a resolution of this problem would not necessarily remove all barriers to fair competition since fuel tax is also different in each member state. There are also significant differences in vehicle prices which cannot entirely be explained by reference to different VAT rates.

The UK government is pressing the Commission to take

action to minimise the extent to which UK transport operators and exporters are put at a competitive disadvantage by tax regimes.

28. Harmonisation of technical legislation

This is one of the most contentious areas of harmonisation. A steady flow of Directives from Brussels requires implementation by member states. Underpinning many of these is the system of European Type Approval, which is conditional on compliance with prescribed Directives on matters such as vehicle lights, braking standards and construction. Vehicles imported from outside the EC are subject in the UK to Type Approval by the Department of Transport. Any vehicle which is EC Type Approved can be used legally in any EC member state, and any national legislation (such as recent UK lighting regulations which required new vehicles to be fitted with 'dim dip' headlights) can be, and in this case was, interpreted by the European Courts as a barrier to competition, the legislation being described as 'protectionist' to the UK vehicle manufacturers.

More seriously, a further example is the EC adaptation of a two-line braking system between vehicles and trailers in preference to the three-line braking system originally required in the UK, and which many transport managers considered superior. In addition, the standardisation by the EC of the ADR Convention on the Carriage of Dangerous Goods by Road (*see* **20**) could cause the replacement of the UK hazard warning panel by the far less informative ADR markings.

Undoubtedly, however, the weights and dimensions of goods vehicles are the areas of greatest contention. Table 13.1 shows the weight limits agreed by the Council of Ministers for 1992. However, the UK has obtained 'derogations' (also shown in the table) enabling it to implement these limits at a later date. In the highly emotive case of the 40-tonne maximum and 11.5-tonne drive axle, the derogation was obtained to run until 1999 at the time when decisions were taken in the Council by unanimous vote, and the UK could in theory therefore veto any move to 40 tonnes until that time.

In practice there is bound to be some 'horse trading' on vehicle weights before then, as foreign hauliers do not wish to be limited to 38 tonnes on journeys to the UK, but also because the other derogations, having been obtained much later, can be ended by the other member states' 'qualified majority .

Table 13.1   EC weights and dimensions of goods vehicles for 1992

Vehicle type	Max. weight (tonnes)	UK derogation (tonnes)
2-axle rigid	18	17
3-axle rigid	25	24
with air suspension	26	24
4-axle rigid		
with 5t/m axle space	32	30
4-axle artic	38	32
5-axle artic	40	38
Drive axle	11.5	10.5

There is also support by a majority of EC member states, including the UK, where the change has been implemented, for a maximum dimension of 18.35 metres for draw-bar combinations (as opposed to the present 18-metre limit). This, coupled with a maximum load carrying length of 15.65 metres and a ban on the dubious practice, rife in the UK, of using extending couplings to enable draw-bars to be close-coupled and yet turn sharp corners (when they are then in any case effectively extended beyond 18 metres). However, this harmonisation of technical legislation disguises a piece of social legislation in that the dimensions proposed (*see* Fig. 13.1) effectively give a minimum cab length space of 2.35 metres, thus obviating the need for cramped roof pod sleeper cabs and indirectly improving the driver's working conditions.

29. Harmonisation of social legislation

Transport is a labour-intensive industry, and labour costs obviously affect competitiveness.

Common rules on the hours of work of road transport drivers go a long way to eliminating unfair competition by operators exploiting their drivers. The Commission, advised by the

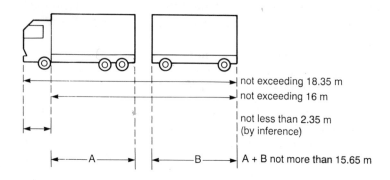

Fig. 13.1 *Proposed maximum dimensions of road transport.*

Economic and Social Committee (ECONOSOC — representing trade unions and trade associations) is on record as being of the view that the revision of the Drivers' Hours rules in 1985 (Regulation 3820) was flawed in that the limits on work or duty were only stated by inference, i.e. any time not spent driving or required for statutory rest could count as duty time. A proposal for a maximum 90 hours' work per fortnight is being considered.

Of course, differences in labour markets in each member state, creating wage differentials and pools of 'cheap labour' in peripheral areas of the Community (for example Eire, Southern Italy, Greece and the Iberian Peninsula), can also distort transport rates. The EC Social Contract — which the UK government is at present unwilling to ratify — with its provisions such as minimum wage levels is intended to remove these discrepancies.

A further issue having a significant bearing on distribution costs is the introduction in 1991 of a new unified European driving licence. The effect of this in the UK is that the present dual system of vocational (HGV) licences (issued by the Traffic Commissioners) and ordinary licences (issued by the Vehicle and Driver Licensing Centre, Swansea) will be replaced by a single unified (ordinary/vocational) licence from DVLC. Traffic Commissioners will, however, retain their disciplinary powers over HGV drivers.

Three classes of commercial vehicle licence are envisaged in order to comply with EC Directive 80/1263:

(a) Class D1 will cover goods vehicles subject to operator licensing (i.e. over 3.5 tonnes GVW) but not more than 7.5 tonnes GVW.
(b) Class D will cover all existing HGV licences for rigid goods vehicles, replacing the present Class 2 (three or more axles) and Class 3 (two axles).
(c) Class D+E will cover all non-rigid goods vehicles, i.e. the present articulated vehicle (Class 1) licence, and be required by drivers of all draw-bar trailer outfits.

Because of the importance of draw-bar trailer operation in the distribution industry this particular attempt to harmonise social legislation is bound to have profound repercussions on the industrial relations and training strategies of major distributors.

Environmental issues

30. Logistics and the environment

Environmental issues are now very much in people's minds. Media attention and a greater personal awareness of environmental problems quite rightly make technological progress and economic growth still desirable but only if the cost to the environment is also considered and a reversal of present methods, where harmful, undertaken.

The logistics and distribution industry, like many others, has its part to play. It would be nice to see more goods moved by rail and fewer heavy lorries on the roads but the practicalities of this are limited. However, the lorries on the roads are becoming more friendly to the environment. New technology is being introduced, including electronic monitoring devices which determine optimum maintenance periods thereby preventing harmful exhaust emissions. Weight is now spread over a greater number of axles resulting in less road damage. Wind deflectors are fitted to improve fuel consumption. New types of exhaust systems which remove harmful gases from emissions are being designed and fitted. Spray suppressors are now standard as are side lights fitted at regular intervals along vehicle bodies and trailers, which means safer driving for everyone.

The location of new factories, warehouses and distribution centres all have an impact on the environment. Access and personal mobility are featured at the planning stage. Deliveries to town and city centres have a much lower profile than in the past. This has arisen because of recent developments including the construction of urban clearways and motorways, overnight deliveries, pedestrianisation and the changing nature of urban centres (*see* Chapter 11 on the economics of logistics for a greater explanation).

31. Global issues

With regard to the greater environmental problems, i.e. acid rain (caused by sulphur and nitrogen emissions), the greenhouse effect (caused by carbon dioxide), depletion of the ozone layer (caused by CFC gases in aerosols, refrigerators and the manufacture of polystyrene foam), nuclear radiation, land and river pollution, the logistics and distribution industry has an indirect but not insignificant role to play. Raw materials, semi-finished parts and manufactured goods are procured, stored and delivered by the industry. The processes involved in between these stages are often the greater offenders but three points do affect logistics and distribution personnel:

(a) *Ignorance*. It is often not for many years that the nature and causes of environmental damage are realised.

(b) *Cost*. It is often said that the polluters do not pay. One solution is payment and compensation for all environmental damage caused by each particular industry.

(c) *Present gains for future costs*. Present-day methods of operation which have long-term costs for future generations will have to cease, even if it costs more today.

Progress test 13

1. Outline the significance of market configuration and facilities location to logistics operations in the Single Market. **(4)**

2. What will be the role of information technology in European logistics? **(10)**

3. When did the UK's accession to the Community occur?   **(14)**

4. List the three prerequisites of liberalisation.   **(14, 15)**

5. List the three prerequisites of harmonisation.   **(27, 28, 29)**

6. Distinguish between an EC Directive and an EC Regulation. **(15)**

7. What do you understand by the 'normalisation' of accounts? **(16)**

8. What are the main differences between UK logistics practices and those in other EC member states?   **(18)**

9. Give an example of a combined transit system.   **(19)**

10. Harmonisation of fiscal duties is a central prop of the Common Transport Policy. Why is this so?   **(21)**

11. What is a 'transit country'? Is the UK a transit country?   **(22)**

12. What will be the main effects of the SEM on international transport operation in the EC?   **(4, 11, 19)**

13. Define cabotage. Give an example.   **(24)**

14. Distinguish between unanimous voting and qualified majority in the EC Council of Ministers. What effects is the latter system having on the harmonisation of technical standards?   **(28)**

15. Outline two major benefits to logistics operations of the Channel fixed link.   **(8)**

Examination technique

1. Introduction

The examination is when the 'chickens come home to roost' for students. If they have organised their studying and applied themselves diligently and often, they should have nothing to fear from their terminal examinations. And yet, inevitably, all students are apprehensive as exam day approaches.

There is such a thing as an exam technique which anyone can develop, indeed should develop, if they are to do themselves justice and not waste all their previous efforts.

However, before students ever sit in the exam room there are things they can do to ensure that they not only know the subject on which they are to be examined, but that they know as much as possible about the exam.

2. Learn the material

Students may have a visual memory and find reading and copying effective, or they may have an aural memory and find it useful to make a tape of key points and play this back to themselves. Or they may prefer to devise mnemonics, rhymes and word associations. But students should invent their own system, if it works, then it's right.

Two final pieces of advice: do not overdo it and do not leave it all to the last minute.

3. Examine your exam

Long before taking the exam it is essential to know as much as possible about it. Find out what kind of questions it contains — essay type, short answers, problems, or multiple choice. Also find out if there is a choice of questions or if some or all of the questions are compulsory. Only if there is a wide choice of questions is it safe, (and not always even then) to omit one or two topics when revising. It may be possible to spot a pattern of questions re-appearing every year or less frequently.

4. Read the paper carefully

At the start of each paper there is usually a 'rubric' such as 'Answer all questions' or 'Answer two questions from Part A and three questions from

Part B'. The examiner cannot give students any extra marks for answering a third question in Part A, however well they may do this. They are only penalising themselves by using up valuable time.

Similarly, read the questions carefully. If the examiner is asking candidates to:

compare	look for similarities and differences
define	give a precise meaning
discuss	examine the statement and give reasons for and against it
illustrate	give a concrete example to explain a theory
criticise	give your opinion on the merits and demerits of a case
review	summarise and examine the subject critically.

Above all, give the examiner what he asks you for, not what you believe he is asking for!

5. Have a strategy

Take time to read the paper and decide which questions to answer. This is time well spent, even though you may feel that you are wasting time when, as inevitably happens, other (less prudent) candidates are already writing furiously. Divide your available time between the questions, if possible leaving a small margin at the end of the exam for checking over what you have written. Try and keep to your timetable, but do not follow it slavishly, and do not fret if you are five or ten minutes out at 'half time' — you will probably find that you have a bit less to write on the last question if you have ranked them in the order in which you can best answer them. However, you should guard against 'over answering'. If an answer is taking longer than the time allowed for it, re-read the question in case you have misunderstood it.

If you find yourself running out of time in the last question then resort to short notes. These show the examiner that you have a grasp of the main points of the answer, even if you do not have time to give a polished performance.

6. Do a final check

Do leave time to read over your answers and correct any silly mistakes. Even the best candidates make these, exams, after all are stressful, despite all you can do to relieve the stress. In particular make sure that your candidate number is on your paper and on any supplementary papers which you might be attaching to your script.

Index